*Real Knowing*

# REAL KNOWING

## New Versions of
## the Coherence Theory

LINDA MARTÍN ALCOFF

*Cornell University Press*

ITHACA AND LONDON

An earlier, shorter version of chapters 4 and 5 appeared under the title "Foucault as Epistemologist" in *Philosophical Forum* 25, no. 2 (Winter 1993): 95–124.

First published 1996 by Cornell University Press.


Printed in the United States of America

⊖ The paper in this book meets the minimum requirements
of the American National Standard for Information Sciences—
Permanence of Paper for Printed Library Materials, ANSI Z39.48–1984.


*Library of Congress Cataloging-in-Publication Data*

Alcoff, Linda.
   Real knowing : new versions of the coherence theory / Linda Martín Alcoff.
     p.   cm.
   Includes bibliographical references and index.
   ISBN 0–8014–3047–X (alk. paper)
    1. Knowledge, Theory of.   2. Truth-Coherence theory.   I. Title.
BD161.A43   1996
121—dc20                                      95–53329

*For my mother, Laura,*
*who had children instead,*

*and for Larry,*
*who helped me have children anyway*

I think Mordecai Rich has about as much heart as a dirt-eating toad. Even when he makes me laugh I know that nobody ought to look on other people's confusion with that cold an eye.

"But that's what I am," he says, flipping through his scribble pad. "A cold eye. An eye looking for Beauty. An eye looking for Truth."

"Why don't you look for other things?" I want to know. "Like neither Truth nor Beauty, but places in people's lives where things have just slipped a good bit off the track."

"That's too vague," said Mordecai, frowning.

"So is Truth," I said. "Not to mention Beauty."

—Alice Walker, *In Love and Trouble*

# *Contents*

# Acknowledgments

I have been moved by the kind help and encouragement I have received over the years in the course of writing this book. Most important has been my family. My sons' pride and support have been great sources of strength, and I in turn have been proud of their ability to empathize with their mother's extra-motherly pursuits. My brother, Rafael Martín, generously provided the artwork for the cover, and also several much-needed vacations from the brutal winters of central New York. My "real" father, Ted Woodward, has been a consistent champion of my intellectual abilities, and his care and unflagging confidence have nurtured me more than he knows. My husband, Larry Alcoff, cooked, cleaned, parented, listened carefully, stayed out of the way when I needed him to, and used his genial humor to bolster my self-confidence whenever it faltered. My mother, Laura Woodward, shared and nurtured my penchant for pondering the universe, and told me in confidence when I was very young that girls could do anything. Her strength has made possible my own.

I am also very grateful for the substantive comments and suggestions, as well as encouragement, that I have received from Richard Schmitt, Ernest Sosa, Martha Nussbaum, William Alston, Michael Kelly, Joseph Rouse, Lynn Hankinson Nelson, Georgia Warnke, and Roger Haydon. I have learned a great deal from numerous conversations on these topics with Elizabeth Potter, Vrinda Dalmiya, Susan Bordo, Elizabeth Grosz, Hilary Putnam, Mario Saenz, Thomas Thorp, Sandra Harding, and Martin Bernal. Several of my students provided helpful comments on drafts of chapters, especially Marianne Janack, Anita Canizares, Raul Vargas, Joel Garver, and Michael Lynch. My colleagues at Syracuse University, especially Sue McDougal, William Alston, Stewart Thau, José Benardete, Phil Peterson, Jonathan Bennett, and Peter van Inwagen, have been helpful in numerous ways. I received crucial financial support from both the American Council of Learned Societies and the College of Arts and Sciences at Syracuse University. Roger Haydon at Cornell University Press was also helpful in several ways, not the least of which was in being so patient!

I also acknowledge here the senior women in philosophy (senior not necessarily in age, but in experience), besides those already listed, who have offered their advice over the years and from whom I have learned so much, both from their writings and from our conversations about philosophy and that peculiar institution we call the academy: Sandra Bartky, Linda Bell, Marilyn Frye, Catherine Lord, María Lugones, Elizabeth Spelman, Nancy Fraser, Alison Jaggar, Margaret Simons, Seyla Benhabib, Naomi Scheman, Lenore Langsdorf, Linda Nicholson, Iris Young, and Judy Butler. These women have truly paved the way for my generation of women philosophers, facing down enormous obstacles with persistent resolve and demonstrating the intellectual capacity of women even under often horrendous conditions (even worse than we now have!). Moreover, they have been willing to use some of their newly found clout to help more junior women both to improve our work and to gain a larger audience. I have come to believe that, because of their efforts, the future will finally be different from the past.

L. M. A.

*Syracuse, New York*

*Real Knowing*

# Why Coherence?
# Why Epistemology?

Epistemology has too often operated as a private conversation presuming to sit in judgment on the whole expanse of human knowledge yet separating itself from actually existing knowers. Epistemologists pare down the complex variety of real knowing practices to a few supposedly paradigmatic cases ("Jones owns a Ford") whose simplicity is purported to allow a close examination of epistemic justification. As a result, philosophers continue to struggle over finely tuned analyses of simple inferences, observational beliefs, and memory while other fields have moved light years ahead in developing more complex and realistic accounts of socially and historically situated belief-formation. In an era that has seen knowledge increasingly produced through international networks in virtual space-time, too many epistemologists seem content to spend their lives analyzing the belief "The cat is on the mat." Sometimes it seems as if the information age has passed philosophy by.

This book arises out of a concern that epistemologists must begin to reflect on and address recent developments in the analysis of how knowledge and meaning are actually produced, how science truly proceeds, and how certain bodies of theory get to count as knowledge. No longer can we envision an individual knower grappling with nature's secrets, or a text as having a single, decisive interpretation. No longer can we assume that power and desire are eliminable elements for either justification or belief-formation. Nor can we romanticize science or the university as politically neutral meritocracies unsullied by racist and sexist hierarchies of class, nor plausibly maintain that such facts have no significant bearing on the theoretical products of these institutions.

Of course, I am romanticizing "our" agreement on these issues. On the basis of the statements I have just made, many analytic philosophers will close this book right now. Even Richard Rorty, the enfant terrible of the American Philosophical Association, tends to dismiss much of current continental philosophy, which invokes concepts such as "power" and "desire," as faddish, anarchist nonsense. In a similarly dismissive move, many continental philosophers seem to believe that epistemology and perhaps philosophy itself have outlived their paradigms and must face the revolutionary firing squad. Michel Foucault himself, despite his concern with knowledge, evidently believed that epistemology was obsolescent. I have little sympathy for either of these dismissals. As I shall argue in the following pages, there is an ongoing need for theorizing knowledge in a fashion that is epistemic and not just sociological, that is, which understands that the line of demarcation between truth and falsehood is not in every case completely determined by and reducible to ideology, mob rule, or unconscious desires. The dawning recognition that such elements as desire and power are *always* involved in the determination of validity conditions for knowledge does not entail the claim that they are *all* that is involved. At the same time, there is a pressing need to produce epistemologies that will acknowledge the ubiquity of these elements in all processes of knowing. The task of epistemologists is therefore not outdated; it just has become more difficult.

### Why Epistemology?

This book is located within what is, I hope, an emerging paradigm shift in epistemology that might broadly call itself "social epistemology" (although the work that currently uses that name is still too narrow, in my estimation).[1] This new paradigm is identifiable by its project to address both of the following concerns: the need for a normative theory of knowledge that can offer an epistemic account of how evaluative distinctions between competing claims should (and can) be made, and the need for an account of knowledge that is self-conscious about the interconnections between knowledge, power, and desire. Such a project would try to answer the following questions: Given a richer and more politically attuned analysis of the production of knowledge, how should we *epistemically* characterize a validity claim? Which criteria should be given priority in demarcating bet-

---

1. See, e.g., Steve Fuller, *Social Epistemology* (Bloomington: Indiana University Press, 1991) in which the "social turn" is described without mentioning or citing a single feminist theorist working in this area and without raising any issues in regard to gender or race. "Social" here evidently refers to the society of white men.

ter and worse theoretical claims? How, given our new (forced) self-consciousness, are we to conceptualize the precise nature of the relationship between politics and knowledge?

These questions suggest and, I will argue, require a dialogue between analytic and continental philosophy. Analytically trained epistemologists have made significant contributions to our understanding of knowledge, justification, and belief, but they have generally been unwilling to explore the implications that follow from recent work in the sociology of knowledge, feminist epistemologies, continental theories of meaning and interpretation, and the whole press of forces which are demanding that we begin to take a close look at the politics of knowledge. Epistemologists should not continue to act like ostriches in the face of these new developments and pretend that they are either wholly and completely false or entirely irrelevant to contemporary epistemological theory. The corresponding mistake, made by many continental philosophers and those influenced by them, is to pretend that we need only expose the faulty presumptions of reference and the fictional binaries in traditional accounts of knowledge. But this critical focus conveniently overlooks the continental philosophers' own claims to epistemic authority, claims that need not rest on referential ontologies to be authoritative. By refusing to offer new validity conditions for justified belief, these theorists only protect their own implicit epistemological commitments from scrutiny. Part of the task of this book is to reveal these commitments, in the work of Hans-Georg Gadamer and Foucault, so as to assess and learn from them.

I shall argue that no account of knowledge, *pace* the wishes of many analytic and continental philosophers (surprisingly in agreement on this point), can be separated ultimately from an account of truth and ontology. Any claim to validity, authorization, or legitimation implies a position on how the world is to be conceptualized and understood in its relation to the sphere of the social and the knowledge under dispute. Claims to know are claims *about something*, and the way in which this "aboutness" is understood, as well as the way the "something" is conceptualized, needs to be explored. Traditional realist notions of reference and representation do not exhaust all the possibilities. I believe that Jacques Derrida no less than Roderick Chisholm has a metaphysics implicit in his discourse on *différance* and the (inevitable) deferral of meaning. (This statement sounds counterintuitive because we have come to define truth monolithically as correspondence, as I will discuss shortly.) In analytic terms, my claim is simply that justification requires truth-conduciveness, and that truth is nonreducible to language; in other words, the validity conditions for any serious speech act will involve a presupposed commitment to specific metaphysical views. Analytic philosophy cannot skirt the question of the ontology of truth or hide its ontological commitments behind its semantics, as I shall try to show: Alfred Tarski's equivalency schema ("P" is true iff *p*) does not say everything there is to say about truth, and the correspondence theory can no longer be taken as self-evident. Similarly, continental philosophy cannot repudiate dominant notions of truth without implying an alternative conception of reality as well as an alternative criterion of validity. The point is not so much to shift the research agenda of continental philosophy to epistemological reconstruction as it is to suggest that such reconstruction has already implicitly begun in writings that offer metacritiques of philosophy. But the question of truth must be brought out into the open.

It will be obvious by now that my usage of terms such as epistemology, metaphysics, and ontology swims upstream from current philosophical fashions. In these pages *metaphysics* will not refer only to the working out of first principles; *epistemology* will not refer to a foundationalist, anti-skeptical project; nor will *ontology* refer to the carving up of essential categories. These traditional definitions represent specific problematics or research programs, not the whole or defining criteria of the enterprises. I want to promote a usage of these terms which will be more general and therefore more inclusive, and so in these pages *epistemology* will refer to the theorizing of knowledge, and *metaphysics* and *ontology* will refer to the theorizing of reality, full stop.

Besides, what is most original about contemporary postmodernist (for want of a better word) theory is not that epistemology and metaphysics have finally been abandoned, although it is true that how knowledge and reality are conceptualized and understood has been radically transformed. Postmodernism is still engaged in the work of conceptualizing knowledge and reality in some way recognizably continuous with the philosophical work that has gone before. Its originality lies, rather, in its large-scale attack on the borders and boundaries between philosophy and other enterprises of theoretical thinking. The autonomy and integrity of epistemology, for example—considered to be unique and separable from sociology, political theory, and psychology, among other disciplines—can no longer hold firm. The new theory understands that questions about the justification of belief require cross-disciplinary exploration, and that such forays cannot be restricted to the biological sciences or to artificial intelligence studies, as analytic philosophers seem to think. I realize many philosophers hold that sociology and related disciplines may tell us how beliefs *actually* attain justification, but that epistemology alone pursues the question how they *should* attain justification. But this border between the normative and the sociological is perhaps the most important border that needs to be crossed, as this study will try to show. Let those of us working in the United States never forget that border control has no intrinsic value.

## Why Coherence?

It is precisely the breakup of the old borders between disciplines, and of the dichotomies and dualisms marking those borders, that brings us to coherence epistemologies. If Rorty is correct (which he is, occasionally), Donald Davidson's conversion to coherentism was motivated by the project to think past a subject/object dualism or mediation which posits the two as separable poles with language in between.[2] Rorty also associates this coherentist project with Harold Bloom's claim that the meaning of a poem can be found only in its relations to other poems, a view that (in its numerous and varied incarnations) has become de rigueur among contemporary literary critics. A further movement toward coherence can be found among the historicist philosophers of science, including Imre Lakatos, Larry Laudan, and even Karl Popper, for whom both the meaning and the validation of scientific theories is to be found ultimately in their relationships to other theories.[3]

Throughout these disparate fields of inquiry, coherentism signifies the view that would seek to explain meaning, knowledge, and even truth by reference to the interrelationships between assorted epistemically salient elements. A typical formulation of coherentism goes as follows: "A belief is justified to the extent to which the belief-set of which it is a member is coherent."[4] What it means for a set of beliefs to be coherent is more variously defined. Some minimalist formulations of coherence require only simple consistency, while other, stronger versions require mutual entailment. The problem with the latter requirement is that it renders most actual belief sets incoherent and therefore unjustified, whereas the problem with the former is that it would force us into the position of accepting a huge number of questionable or even fictional systems as justified beliefs if only they have internal consistency. A middle position which avoids these problems requires that the elements in a belief set be mutually explanatory. This involves symmetrical relations of support rather than the relations of logical dependence implied in the concept of mutual entailment. Explanatory support can be offered by inference, correlation, analogy, or even similarity.

If a coherence theory of truth is adopted along with a coherence theory of justification, then it is held that "a proposition is true iff it is a member

2. Richard Rorty, *Contingency, Irony, Solidarity* (Cambridge: Cambridge University Press, 1989), p. 10.
3. See Robert D'Amico, *Historicism and Knowledge*, chapter 2, for a compelling argument that Popper is a historicist (New York: Routledge, 1989).
4. Jonathan Dancy, *Introduction to Contemporary Epistemology* (Oxford: Basil Blackwell, 1985), p. 116.

of a coherent set."[5] This more robust form of coherentism is the one I shall be principally interested in, since it alone offers the possibility for reconceptualizing the ontology of truth. Ontologically, robust coherentism has the neo-Hegelian aspiration to locate knowledge in such a way that the binary between nature and human construction is transcended. Knowledge has most often been defined as a kind of affinity between two essentially dissimilar entities: a linguistic item and a bit of nature or a phenomenological experience, a mental entity and a corporeal one, a systematized set of propositions and a Ding an sich. Truth has been located at the intersection, as a bridge spanning the chasm between two "worlds" or as piercing an obstructive "veil."

Coherentist epistemology, at least in its more robust manifestations and certainly as I shall treat it here, is an attempt to reconfigure and transform—not merely rearrange—the basic building blocks of truth: knowledge, reality, social practice. If this project is a viable one, it holds out the promise of avoiding the problems of both foundationalist philosophies and epistemologically nihilist ones.

Foundationalist epistemologies that identify knowledge in terms of its relationship to a mind-independent reality have become increasingly difficult to maintain. One of the principal reasons for this is the changing conception of the sciences since the nineteenth century. Science, and particularly natural science, has served as the paradigm of justified belief in the West since Bacon (although the cause of its valued status arguably has had more to do with the role science could play in the societies of burgeoning commodity capitalism and colonialism than with Bacon's formulation of the scientific method—on this view, his contribution was to provide an ideological articulation for the latest form of epistemological authoritarianism). Nonetheless, scientific beliefs had seemed to instantiate a level of objectivity elusive for other fields of inquiry. Bacon's formulation ensured this identification between science and objectivity by claiming that it is nature herself (this is Bacon's gendering, not mine) that determines which theories will be confirmed, which knowledge claims accepted and which rejected, rather than the desire of some experimental scientist or the consensus of judgment among communities of scientists.

But as science has become more and more removed from commonsense beliefs and observable experience, or, to use W. V. O. Quine's terminology, as the recognized disparity between our meager input and our torrential output has expanded, this assumption of the determining role of nature has become increasingly implausible. The past hundred years have witnessed a growing amount of evidence against and suspicion about this belief. Since

5. Ibid., p. 112.

Popper, it has become widely accepted, for example, that it is impossible actually to *confirm* theoretical claims in science. This is not to say that there is no reason to continue to accept science's claims, but to suggest that we must reconsider what their acceptability *means*. There is no available method by which we can isolate singular scientific claims for epistemic evaluation. Nor have we been able to rid science of its reliance on and use of irreducible metaphysical assumptions. The project of finding a justification for our dependence on induction has failed, at least thus far. We have not been able to explicate methodically the rules for induction or the most reliable processes for the discovery of hypotheses. For the most widely used and confirmed theory of the twentieth century—quantum mechanics—we have failed to translate its implications into a coherent ontology. And ironically, despite obvious advances in technological production, many philosophers concur that we have no way to prove that, at least in traditional realist terms, the knowledge we have about nature has actually progressed.

For many of us, the implication to be drawn from these failures, and from the growing sense that we cannot completely erase the effects of the knower on the known, is that we need to redefine and rethink what claims "to know," in science as well as elsewhere, actually mean. Analytic philosophers are overly fond of using such examples as whether "it is raining" to support correspondence theories of truth, but relatively few truth-claims (and certainly none of the interesting and complicated ones) permit such easy characterizations. When any of the sciences are used in place of immediate sensory experience as the paradigm of knowledge, it quickly becomes apparent that our assumptions about truth as correspondence to the intrinsic features of a mind-independent reality and our notion of reason as a transhistorical and rule-governed methodology are dubitable and inadequate, if not laughably simplistic.

Quine and Chisholm represent two of the most important responses to this predicament that analytic epistemologists have developed. Quine has opted for a radically redefined empiricism in which coherence is the primary criterion for truth, since it is the coherence requirement that defines what can count as evidentiary support. For Quine this criterion operates outside of history, culture, or political influence. Chisholm has attempted to create a new foundation, this time not based on Descartes's skimpy enthymeme or Kant's synthetic a priori truths or Moritz Schlick's thin, unstatable observation reports but on self-presenting, incorrigible phenomenological states. The problem here is how to move from such subjective, internal states to the torrential output of claimed knowledge. A third major response has been to reduce epistemology to semantics and deny the necessity for an ontology of truth at all (paradoxically, both Tarski and Rorty would fit here). Interestingly, all three responses involve a kind of avoidance of the problem of truth that highlights justification as the central concern of epistemology and relegates the issue of truth and its ontology to a minor if not nonparticipatory status.

I find it fascinating that, though they arise out of a significantly different historical problematic, continental treatments of knowledge have largely turned away from the ontology of truth as well. The reasons given for this turn include the new skepticism toward a naive scientific realism discussed above, but are also based on the ultimately undecidable status of meaning. If meaning is based not on identity (as it would be if it were determined by reference, for example) but rather on difference, then meaning can have no intrinsic content that remains stable outside the constantly shifting terms within multiple contexts which determine it. Unlike sameness or identity, which could offer a determinate meaning, difference always involves an open relation ("difference from $x$," where $x$ is an undefined variable) and therefore it is never fixed or finally decided. In Derrida's early writings he claimed that truth talk in the West has denied this instability of meaning and has pursued identity through a metaphysics of presence, a transcendentalized ontology which would stabilize meaning. But this pursuit, according to Derrida, is grounded in a philosophical error with violent political effects. Claims to truth are inevitably grounded on elements which would undermine the claims if they were made perspicuous, and thus they inherently require exclusion and avoidance. It is the business of deconstruction to reveal this unpleasant underside of truth-claims, the constitutive exclusions by which truth-claims maintain their illusion of full presence or identity. While Derrida has never contested either the value of truth or its existence, his belief in the infinite deferral of meaning contests truth's claim to stability and thus (so Derrida thinks) to any ontological status. The only recourse is to be anti-ontological. "Discourse, therefore, if it is originally violent, can only *do itself violence*, can only negate itself in order to affirm itself, make war upon the war which institutes it without ever *being able* to reappropriate this negativity, to the extent that it is discourse. . . .This secondary war, as the avowal of violence, is the least possible violence."[6] Derrida realizes that this anti-ontological project can never be fully carried out, but he has consistently held that the inherent violence of presence cannot be reduced by an affirmation of another presence. Thus, truth must exist without ontology.

The poststructuralist turn away from ontology has also been motivated by an acknowledgment of the constitutive influence of what is called the "other" of reason: most notably, desire and power. As already indicated,

6. Jacques Derrida, "Violence and Metaphysics: An Essay on the Thought of Emmanuel Levinas," trans. Alan Bass, in *Writing and Difference* (Chicago: University of Chicago Press, 1978), p. 130.

deconstruction is motivated not just by the paradoxical nature of validity claims, with their erroneous understanding of how meaning operates, but by the political absolutism that is produced by a metaphysics of presence. Truth talk serves to close down discussion and debate by claiming a relationship to a realm that is constant and fixed and therefore beyond challenge or debate. For Jean-François Lyotard, claims to truth, which by definition would presume to structure the field of possible moves within a language game, are "terrorist." If truth exists, it exists in the realm of the ineffable; within language, there is only heteroglossia. Therefore, "consensus has become an outmoded and suspect value."[7] According to Lyotard, we should not strive for consensus or for coherence or for any stable system, but for an open system like science, in which the only constant value is the ability to generate new and different rules.[8] Thus, many poststructuralists conclude that the problems with foundationalism point not so much toward the need for a radical rethinking of knowledge or a reconstruction of epistemology as toward a repudiation of the possibility and desirability of offering any determinate account of knowledge, or any normative epistemology at all. What I am calling epistemological nihilism is this rejection of normativity, which is based on a cynicism about the possibility of improving on the *epistemic* status of what passes for knowledge.

The dilemma between rearticulated foundationalisms and epistemologies of pure negativity is not only unsatisfactory: the thought of it can make one queasy. On the one side we have epistemologies which continue to be rooted in ahistorical pretensions, and on the other we have an apparently unresolvable nihilism. Both orientations divert us from the work at hand: reconstructing epistemology and reconceptualizing the ontology of truth with a newly awakened recognition of the complexities involved.

My working hypothesis in this book will be that, beyond or alongside the theoretical tendencies just described, there is a discernible move toward coherentism on both sides of the analytic/continental divide in philosophy. This move is motivated by a desire for a newly reconstructed epistemology, by which I mean not merely developing a new, specific theory of knowledge but reorienting epistemology's understanding of its own program of inquiry, including its goals, methods, and disciplinary location. Through an exploration of the work of Davidson, Gadamer, Foucault, and Hilary Putnam I will develop the main contours of this reconstruction and attempt to demonstrate that it can help resolve some of the impasses that are now inhibiting discussions of coherence. I will not try to develop an account of coherentist epistemology that synthesizes all the works discussed. That

7. Jean-François Lyotard, *The Postmodern Condition*, trans. Geoff Bennington and Brian Massumi (Minneapolis: University of Minnesota Press, 1984), p. 66.
8. Ibid., p. 64.

would be too ambitious, and the disparity between such thinkers as David-son and Foucault is too great to produce a single epistemology, or a coherent one! Nor is my aim in this study to put forward a new and better, fully developed theory of knowledge. Rather, I intend to explore developments and themes in the new coherentist accounts of knowledge that can address long-standing objections to coherence and thus shift the debate over coherentism to new ground. I will also try to show how, through these newly articulated coherentisms, epistemology can survive the emerging self-consciousness of its own political, historical, and social embeddedness.

But why coherence in particular? A coherentist account of knowledge has the potential to clear important hurdles that previous epistemologies—primarily foundationalist ones—are inherently incapable of overcoming. There are at least three such hurdles that will be discussed throughout this book.

First, coherentism can provide a more realistic and feasible account of the way in which beliefs are justified than accounts that would require an uninterpreted, pretheoretical, self-presenting experiential state or mode of cognition. Coherentism traditionally holds that beliefs are justified by other beliefs, which means that a correspondence relation between beliefs and an extradiscursive, transparent reality is not required for knowledge. The experience and empirical evidence that play a determining role in the confirmation of many beliefs can be acknowledged as themselves the product (at least in part) of interpretation and theoretical commitments. This follows because on a coherentist view experience and evidence are recognized as beliefs, not self-presenting phenomenological states whose meaning is transparent. Coherentism also takes account of the actual mechanisms most often used to judge new contenders for belief: their plausibility in light of the beliefs one already holds and the tendency we all have to conserve beliefs. Coherentism thus posits a picture of belief-formation that does not require the knower to be able to suspend all of her or his beliefs, and that does not present a pristine mind confronting a transparent reality, what John Dewey called the "spectator theory of knowledge" and Theodor Adorno named "peephole metaphysics." In contrast to such metaphysics, coherentism starts with a knower who always already has a great many beliefs, and thus is always already "in the world." Coherentism further recognizes that these prior beliefs interpret and inform every experience the knower has. This makes it easier for coherentism to shift from an individualist account of knowing to a collectivist account—a shift long overdue in Western epistemologies—because coherentism posits the knower as always already committed to a variety of beliefs based on the testimony of others. And this suggests that for coherentism the interpersonal and cooperative nature of belief-justification will more readily be included as part of the central issues for an epistemology to address, rather than being thought of as side issues or even irrelevant considerations. (Of course, it is true that Anglo-American coherentisms have by and large failed to address this issue. But I am arguing here for the *potential* of coherentist epistemologies, a potential that is developed by the theorists I shall be discussing.

A second advantage is that coherentism can provide a way to show how and why apparently disparate elements are and even should be involved in theory-choice and belief-justification. Political considerations, moral commitments, even metaphysical beliefs, have not been considered germane to the justification of beliefs that claim referentiality or truth, and desire and power—the "other" of reason—are regarded as even less relevant. To admit the ineliminable influence of such elements would seem to spell the demise of any hope for knowledge. But this is only because traditionally dominant accounts of justification have presented, as Peirce said long ago, a linear, single-line, inferential model of knowledge in which politics, values, and desire could only be seen as obstacles at worst, irrelevant at best.[9] Coherentist models, in which the process of justification involves not a single linear chain of inference but a complicated, heterogeneous web of belief, make it much easier to see how different kinds of elements can be involved not only in justification but in justification-conferring. On a linear model, the claim that authoritarianism is involved in the justification of master-molecule theories will seem highly implausible; the two ideas may appear metaphorically similar but it will be difficult to show how a biological theory could reasonably follow from a political premise which operates in a different plane of discourse. On a coherentist model, however, the metaphorical similarity between political authoritarianism and master-molecule theories can be seen to offer mutual support, and thus the relevance of various political assumptions to theory-choice in the sciences can be more easily explained, and explained in a way that does not attribute intentional bias to most scientists (or, for that matter, philosophers). Where coherence is taken to be the principal criterion for knowledge, and where the entire web is involved in the process (though different parts of the web are involved to different degrees), it becomes much easier to account for the inclusion of politics in science, ethics in epistemology, and desire in philosophy.[10]

9. Charles Sanders Peirce, *Collected Papers* (Cambridge: Harvard University Press), 5:265, quoted in Richard J. Bernstein, *The New Constellation* (Cambridge: MIT Press, 1992), p. 327.
10. Linda Alcoff, "Justifying Feminist Social Science," *Hypatia* 2 (Fall 1987): 107–27; Lynn Hankinson Nelson, *Who Knows: From Quine to a Feminist Empiricism* (Philadelphia: Temple University Press, 1990).

The third advantage that coherentist accounts can claim accrues only to what I have called more robust accounts, when coherence is taken to involve in some manner the definition of truth rather than (as Laurence Bonjour argues, for example) simply the means by which one can achieve truth in the sense of correspondence. Less prejudicially, I will refer to the latter as coherentist accounts of justification, whereas when a coherentist account theorizes both justification and truth via coherence I will refer to it as a coherentist epistemology. I will argue that an advantage of the latter is that it can offer what might be called an immanent account of knowledge.

Coherence epistemology is frequently cited as the principal contender against and ultimate contrast with a foundationalist view.[11] I believe that this opposition is based primarily on the fact that coherentism offers an immanent account of knowledge against foundationalism's transcendental account. For coherentism, knowledge is ultimately a product of phenomena that are immanent to human belief systems and practices, social organizations, and lived reality, whereas for foundationalism, if a belief is to count as knowledge it must ultimately be able to establish some link to transcendent phenomenon or to something that is entirely extrinsic to human existence (that is, the way the world would be if we had never existed). Whereas foundationalism ties justification to an external realm beyond beliefs and belief sets and understands truth as a relationship of a certain sort with this external realm, coherentism holds to an understanding of knowledge as immanent. Justification is an immanent feature of beliefs in that it refers to their interrelationships, and if truth is defined as what coheres, truth is also emergent from immanent relationships rather than from relationships with an external or transcendental realm.

This immanent account is advantageous principally because it does not require us to first posit and then find access to a realm defined as beyond all human interpretation and knowledge. Nor does it necessitate establishing a God's-eye view so that we can step outside of language, all belief systems, and interpretive modes to check on the correspondence between human claims and an extrahuman reality. This is not because coherentism posits a Berkeleyan idealism in which reality is conceived to be causally determined by "mind" or simply to consist in mental properties, but because, at least as I shall tell the story, coherentism starts from a Hegelian phenomenological ontology that sets up no absolute separation between human beings and the world but sees us as always already in the world, engaged in practical activities, encumbered with myriad beliefs and commit-

11. An intriguing exception to this is Michael Williams, who has recently argued that coherentism is a form of foundationalism. See his *Unnatural Doubts: Epistemological Realism and the Basis of Scepticism* (Cambridge, Mass.: Basil Blackwell, 1991). I discuss this analysis in Chapter 7.

ments, and constitutively linked in various complex ways to that about which we are seeking to know. This is a more metaphysically adequate descriptive starting point from which to think about knowledge, and it has the added bonus of making the problem of skepticism vanish from the frame. It also allows us, as I shall argue in later chapters, to account for the historical and social embeddedness of all truth-claims without lapsing into epistemological nihilism.

For all these reasons, which shall be developed in more detail in the pages that follow, coherentism has at least the potential to provide a more realistic account of the way in which we make our epistemic commitments. Like Marx, I will hold that no absolute separation should exist between the way in which we actually justify our beliefs and the way in which we *should* justify them: all prescriptive proposals must be grounded firmly in current, actual practices since these alone can circumscribe the possible. This is not to say that the realm of the actual will dictate the epistemic good, but that there is a normative relevance to having realistic accounts of the production of knowledge.

The above three points serve to justify this excursion into coherentist epistemology by arguing that coherence can overcome some of the current impasses in the theorizing of knowledge. But what about the theoretical impasses within coherence accounts themselves? There are certainly many of these. Coherentism has been charged with irreducible vagueness, with justifying coherent fictions, with being unable to privilege experience or empirical sources of evidence, with placing overly stringent requirements on justification, and with entailing an absolute relativism between coherent systems. These traditional objections have recently been given adequate answers by Ralph C. S. Walker, BonJour, Davidson, Jonathan Dancy, and others, and thus should not continue to debilitate the development of coherentist accounts.[12] There are still more objections, however, which have not been answered adequately as yet, and thus continue to deserve serious attention. I will use the authors discussed herein to suggest new refutations to these objections. Both the objections and the answers to them that I shall develop are briefly outlined below.

(1) The criterion of coherence itself as the test of knowledge would seem to have no necessary connection to truth; the fact that a claim coheres to a body of beliefs does not establish it as true or likely to be true unless that

12. Ralph C. S. Walker, *The Coherence Theory of Truth* (London: Routledge, 1989), pp. 1–40; Laurence BonJour, *The Structure of Empirical Knowledge* (Cambridge: Harvard University Press, 1985), pp. 94–153; Donald Davidson, "A Coherence Theory of Truth and Knowledge" and "Empirical Content," in *Truth and Interpretation: Perspectives on the Philosophy of Donald Davidson*, ed. Ernest LePore (Oxford: Basil Blackwell, 1986), pp. 307–32; and Dancy, *Introduction*, pp. 110–40.

body of beliefs can be shown to be true. The puzzle then becomes, if one wants what is sometimes called a pure coherence theory, how to establish that a body of beliefs is true on the basis of coherence alone, since it is certainly the case that a body of beliefs may attain a high level of coherence without being truthful. This has been perhaps the most serious objection to coherence accounts of knowledge since their inception, and no fully adequate answer has been developed that does not simply define knowledge as coherence or base its claim on making an appeal to noncoherentist elements. I will argue that the new versions of coherentism discussed here, and most importantly the work of Gadamer, suggest a new answer to this old objection, principally through devising a new ontology of truth or an account of the relationship between true beliefs and reality. This new ontology is not merely an ad hoc, opportunist maneuver tacked on in order to establish the truth-conduciveness of coherence as a criterion of knowledge, but a different ontology with independent arguments in its favor.

(2) The second objection I will address does not originate among analytic philosophers. In fact, what I am calling an objection here does not even address itself to coherence epistemology, and yet it presents in my view one of the most serious obstacles coherentism must face. Joseph Rouse has recently offered a critique of accounts that present science as a "field of practices rather than a network of statements."[13] He suggests that the work of Thomas Kuhn, among others, constitutes a significant trend in philosophy of science away from "representationalist, theory-dominant" accounts in favor of ones that highlight science's practical and experimental everyday character. To distill science into the set of truth-claims in statement form collected in journal articles and textbooks, or to equate its documentary aspects with the entirety of "science," is phenomenologically incorrect and has led to many egregious mistakes in the epistemologies of science, since such distillations present distorted images of the actual processes by which theories are chosen.

I would make a broader claim about knowledge as a whole, similar to Rouse's claim about philosophies of science. To distill the amalgam of knowing practices into a string of propositions to which I can give or from which I may withhold mental assent, is a mistake begun by Descartes and mystifyingly persistent in contemporary epistemology. Aristotle knew that propositional knowledge was not the only kind of knowledge, as did Gilbert Ryle, Wittgenstein, and the American pragmatists. I suggest that feminist epistemologies and recent continental accounts of knowledge are also more open to the idea that knowledge is, as Rouse describes science, a

13. Joseph Rouse, *Knowledge and Power: Toward a Political Philosophy of Science* (Ithaca: Cornell University Press, 1987), p. 26.

field of practices only some of which can be translated into propositional form and represented in a logical schema.

Coherentist accounts of knowledge have repeated this erroneous focus on propositions. Coherence accounts, remember, tie everything to beliefs: webs of belief, systems of statements, networks of propositions.[14] Coherence describes justification as a process whereby a grouping of beliefs is brought to bear on a contending belief. Thus it is clear that coherence epistemologies are very much predisposed to view knowledge as consisting entirely in statements and sets of statements.

Foucault's work can be usefully applied to this problem, since he suggests a form of coherentism that does not focus mostly or exclusively on statements but includes a larger constellation of elements. Foucault, continuing the tradition of Aristotle, Ryle, Wittgenstein, and the pragmatists, conceives of knowledge not only as beliefs but also as networks of practices and forms of life. For Foucault, the coherence necessary for knowledge must link a wide range of disparate elements—modes of perception, experimental methods, skills, experiential interiority, and institutions—all interwoven with power effects and various pleasures. Foucault's understanding of knowledge thus makes it possible to avoid the statement-dominant problem and suggests an expanded conception of coherence whose many advantages I will strive to retrieve from their obscurity.

(3) A final objection I will take seriously is one that will be found not in analytic circles but among poststructuralists. This objection would hold that coherence itself is a misguided goal, because it is doomed to failure and based on totalitarian impulses. This would surely be Lyotard's and Gilles Deleuze's claim, if they were to address themselves directly to coherence epistemologies. The attribution of coherence requires similarity, sameness, and thus the denial or de-emphasis of difference. Such denials of difference are well known to have played an important role in many forms of oppression, in their attempts to force nonidenticals together by erasing specificities and in their assumption that likeness has a higher value than its converse. For these reasons, the preferred aim among poststructuralists is never coherence or even consistency but heteroglossia, heterotropy, paradox, fragmentation, and paralogy. The desire for coherence is seen as a desire for control and domination, an obsession with identity, which thus produces an epistemology well-suited not only for Western imperialism but for the anal-retentive.

Fragmentation and contradiction are indeed inevitable, and the achieved balance of coherence is partial and momentary, both fallible and unstable.

---

14. Walker is one of the few coherence theorists to discuss the problem of coherentism's exclusive focus on beliefs and propositions (*Coherence Theory*, pp. 84, 94).

The view that difference is a priori problematic is both pernicious and unnecessary. But coherence does not require identity or the elimination of difference, only a way to eliminate debilitating contradictions. The pursuit of coherence and the criterion of coherence as the test of epistemic adequacy remains defensible. As Richard Bernstein and Nancy Fraser have pointed out, the problem with poststructuralism is its one-sided valorization of negativity and rupture and its inability to produce the reconstructive analyses called for by its own critiques.[15] The productive contributions of negativity and difference and the inevitability of rupture and instability do not entail that coherent systems of thought and practices cannot be developed, though they should scale down our expectations of how much can be realistically achieved, and for how long.

Furthermore, the desire for coherence can come from a variety of sources, not all of which are pernicious or pathological; it is ironically a universalist error for poststructuralists to hold that coherentist aspirations are always grounded in something politically retrograde. Consider the desire to appease one's conflicting moral commitments as far as possible, which Martha Nussbaum discusses in rich concreteness within an argument that overall seeks to establish the very impossibility of perfect coherence.[16] Or consider the desire for coherence that Simone de Beauvoir describes in her analysis of the forced contradictions between constructed femininities and the achievement of personhood.[17] While ruptures may be inevitable, the desire for coherence is inevitable as well and can often be productive. Fragmentation and conflict can be painful to live through, and while I too share the current sensibilities toward finding positive elements in irreconcilable differences rather than uselessly pining for a lost sense of oneness, it remains the case that harmony is at least some of the time an understandable as well as realistic goal.

The cautious attitude toward coherence that poststructuralism displays is also shared by some critical theorists who work in the tradition of the Frankfurt School. Adorno argued that for those of us interested in social criticism and social change within the context of "affirmative culture" (commodity capitalism), it is of paramount necessity to find and produce negation and contradiction. But the productive effects of determinate negation (a goal shared by all self-respecting neo-Hegelians) only work within

15. See Bernstein, *New Constellation*; Nancy Fraser, *Unruly Practices* (Minneapolis: University of Minnesota Press, 1989).
16. Martha Nussbaum, *The Fragility of Goodness: Luck and Ethics in Greek Tragedy and Philosophy* (Cambridge: Cambridge University Press, 1986).
17. Simone de Beauvoir, *The Second Sex*, trans. H. M. Parshley (New York: Random House, 1952).

a context where the contradiction produced by the negation pushes forward a new and higher synthesis, motivated precisely by the discomfort caused by conflict and the absence of coherence. Rupture thus produces social change *because* of the desire for coherence, and the subsequent determination of those who recognize the current contradictions to rebuild new, more coherent structures.

It is also important to note that coherence can be variously defined. It need not, and in fact usually is not, equated with strict sameness or logical entailment, but with compatibility and a consistency alongside—a kind of epistemic peaceful coexistence. The dangers of authoritarianism can be offset by such milder formulations and may in fact be overstated.

I have tried to establish in this Introduction why the project of epistemology must continue, and why coherentist accounts are worth pursuing. The question that remains is, why explore the work of Gadamer, Davidson, Foucault, and Putnam within this context? An answer can only unfold in the chapters that follow.

# CHAPTER ONE

# "*Allowing what is to be . . .*": *Gadamer's Philosophical Hermeneutics*

> It is the task of philosophy to discover what is common even in what is different.
>
> —Hans-Georg Gadamer, *The Relevance of the Beautiful*

Hermeneutics has been historically defined as "the classical discipline concerned with the art of understanding texts."[1] Early hermeneuts developed theories of interpretation and understanding from their work of biblical exegesis and their attempt to translate texts written in ancient languages. Determining the meaning of such texts presented uniquely difficult issues since their languages, historical and cultural context, and intertextual references varied so much from those of the translators. The attempt by translators to overcome these complicated obstacles spawned the development of metatheories of interpretation and a new discipline that came to be named hermeneutics.

It was not until the twentieth century, however, that the lessons of hermeneutics would be used to develop a more general account of the nature of all understanding. This has been the task of what Hans-Georg Gadamer has called his philosophical hermeneutics: to illuminate the interpretive and linguistic context in which all understanding occurs. His project has actually been threefold: to refute the Enlightenment and positivist orientations toward knowledge which counterpose reason and tradition and which promote an ahistorical, decontextualized methodology; to critique earlier versions of hermeneutic theory which lapsed into a positivist fetishism of method and the belief in rule-governed processes of inquiry; and to develop a philosophical account of understanding which can acknowledge its irreducible historical dimension, its linguisticality, and its human context.

---

1. Hans-Georg Gadamer, *Truth and Method*, 2d rev. ed., trans. Joel Weinsheimer and Donald G. Marshall (New York: Crossroad Press, 1991), p. 164. Hereafter quotations from this text will be cited in parentheses after the quotation.

Despite the broad scope of this last project, Gadamer's account will seem at odds with the tradition of epistemology. He has criticized epistemology's entire project since Descartes as the fundamentally mistaken pursuit of a method of inquiry. Nor is Gadamer clear whether his analysis of understanding can be applied to all types of knowledge or whether it should be restricted to knowledge in textual interpretation and the *Geisteswissenschaften*. For these reasons, many if not most of his readers have taken him to present an alternative to epistemology, as Richard Rorty famously did in *Philosophy and the Mirror of Nature* when he called one of his chapters "From Epistemology to Hermeneutics."

Against these readings which contrast hermeneutics and epistemology, and which to some extent include Gadamer's own, I will argue that Gadamer's work should not be relegated to the internal phenomenological and hermeneutical debates in European philosophy or to general discussions focused on questions of interpretation, and that in fact his analysis is quite relevant to epistemological concerns about the nature of justification and truth. I will argue that Gadamer's philosophical hermeneutics is actually a theory of knowledge, that his epistemology is coherentist on both justification and truth, and that he offers original and interesting alternative conceptions and arguments concerning the ontology of truth which can enlighten Anglo-American debates.

The point here is to establish not simply that Gadamer belongs within a coherentist tradition in theorizing knowledge but that the version of coherentism which develops out of the conjunction with Gadamer's philosophical hermeneutics is highly attractive and distinct from traditional accounts. For one thing, the movement of coherence in understanding, as Gadamer tells it, is not at all about closure but about a repetitive play of to-and-fro motion antithetical to a goal-oriented, teleological form of endeavor. This marks Gadamer's difference from and advantage over Hegel, whose formulation of a coherence theory of truth is based on absolute identity and wholeness: for Gadamer (building on Heidegger here) the essence of truth is not the absolute but an openness precisely to the new, the other, and the changing motion of history.

Moreover, Gadamer argues for this dedication to openness on both epistemic and ethical grounds. He explicitly contrasts his view of knowledge with one that would promote the domination or appropriation of its object; instead, he valorizes a passive and receptive orientation. This provides us with a theory of understanding thoroughly embedded within a morality of social relations, thus exemplifying Gadamer's repeated repudiation of contrasts and separations between the normative and the cognitive. Because he also intriguingly suggests an orientation to knowledge that incorporates traditional feminine as opposed to masculine forms of behavior, Gadamer could be seen as nascently feminist, insofar as he asserts the cognitive validity of historically derided "feminine" ways of being and knowing.

Thus, my reading of Gadamer explores and highlights elements that will problematize his label as a conservative who is completely at odds with poststructuralist tendencies. Paradoxically, Gadamer has been judged a conservative because he would have us reclaim the value of tradition against the Enlightenment's repudiation of it in favor of an ahistorical reason. This is a paradox because in this move Gadamer proves to be a more thoroughgoing critic of the Enlightenment than many other anti-Enlightenment postmoderns, for whom tradition has no reality, much less value. Still, it is of course correct that there are many senses in which the conservative label is apt: in Gadamer's valorization of the authority of tradition, in his anti-Marxism, and in his orthodox Christianity. Nonetheless, a careful reading of his sense of tradition will reveal that a defense of past ways is not sustained on this account. We will return to this issue in the next chapter.

I will defend the analysis I offer of Gadamer here as a careful reading, but it is also admittedly one that emphasizes some elements over others and transposes some of his ideas into new contexts. As will be seen, this is entirely consistent with Gadamer's own theory of interpretation and meaning as based on a "fusion" between past and present, text and reader. For Gadamer, understanding can only be achieved through an interactive process that brings together what are always diverse historical and interpretive perspectives. The interpretation I will present enacts just such a fusion of Gadamer's texts with my particular antifoundationalist, poststructuralist, radical "prejudgments." Although such a project of fusion is certainly legitimate from his own perspective, it is not the case that Gadamer's account would justify any interpretation at all or an infinite plurality of interpretations. Some interpretations must be ruled out, and given the specific dangers involved in the sort of reading I engage in here, it may seem that just this sort of interpretive project *should* be ruled out.

The principal danger may follow from presenting Gadamer's hermeneutics as an epistemology. Many of the terms and concepts I will bring to this discussion are from the discourse of Anglo-American analytic epistemology. Gadamer avoids terms like epistemology and justification, employing instead terms like understanding, hermeneutic, interpretation, and dialectic. In some cases he uses the same terms but with radically different meanings, as with the term truth. Furthermore, the dialogue or debate within which Gadamer is engaged and toward which he directs his arguments involves figures such as Hegel and Dilthey, Heidegger and Schleiermacher, and not W. V. O. Quine or Hilary Putnam. It is against the views of the former philosophers he polemicizes, but it is always their assumptions he shares and with them that he seeks a common ground.

How, then, can my enterprise proceed? Is there some language that is neutral between epistemological traditions into which I can translate Gadamer? He would not think so, and neither do I. Given this, my project of translating Gadamer into the language of Anglo-American epistemology may seem an inevitable distortion of his real views. Throughout this book, however, I will contend that the agendas, approaches, and theories of philosophers who ask questions about knowledge from the continental perspective are not incommensurable with the project of the Anglo-American philosophers; in fact, they overlap and can be viewed as belonging to a single debate. Such a contention can best be defended by a demonstration. If I can show that Gadamer's views are sufficiently similar to the views of the other philosophers I will discuss so as to be comprehensible and relevant to their concerns, and yet sufficiently different so as to offer an original contribution, then my contention will be vindicated. It is of course possible that such a demonstration will (apparently) succeed only because the reinterpretation of Gadamer renders his real views invisible. This possibility, however, is akin to the possibility that the skeptics are right, and all our apparent knowledge is false. Such a possibility can only be addressed by taking care to avoid distortion and to avoid privileging either Anglo-American or continental terms or perspectives; it should not be addressed by giving up the project altogether before it is begun.

In this chapter I will provide an exposition of the main tenets of Gadamer's philosophical hermeneutics in order to highlight the framework within which his conceptions of justification and truth emerge. The next chapter will focus on these latter issues in more detail, as well as on the major problems his work must address, such as relativism, subjectivism, and the need to distinguish epistemically between better and worse pre-judgments and traditions. Readers familiar with Gadamer may want to skip on to the next chapter at this point.

## An Overview of Philosophical Hermeneutics

For Gadamer, hermeneutics is not a methodology of inquiry nor a useful tool in procuring knowledge. Neither is it merely a position of self-reflection setting itself above or apart from an engagement with the outside world.[2] Rather, hermeneutics sets out the conditions necessary for under-

---

2. For this latter reason, I disagree with the claim that Gadamer is simply a conservative. See John D. Caputo, *Radical Hermeneutics* (Bloomington: Indiana University Press, 1987), esp.

standing to occur: "The question I have asked seeks to discover and bring into consciousness something which methodological dispute serves only to conceal and neglect, something that does not so much confine or limit modern science as precede it and make it possible" (*TM* xxix). The task of hermeneutics is "not to develop a procedure of understanding, but to clarify the conditions in which understanding takes place" (*TM* 295). Gadamer thus takes some pains to distinguish a hermeneutics that focuses on understanding in the human sciences from the attempt to develop a methodology or to explicate a procedure of inquiry. (See, for example, *TM* 295–96, xxiii, xxviii–xxix.) He characterizes his project as more in line with Kant's question, "How is knowledge possible?" than with Descartes's search for a critical method as a means to epistemic certainty (*TM* 239). Partly this is because Gadamer eschews any agenda that would "make prescriptions for the sciences or the conduct of life" (*TM* xxiii). He wishes to separate his inquiry as far as possible from the positivists who see themselves as philosophical assistants to the sciences. It is also, however, because Gadamer rejects the ontological picture of inquiry upon which such pursuits of method depend, as exemplified most importantly in Descartes and in the Enlightenment. Descartes' belief that a method can be found which will lead us to the truth only obscures from view the real nature of inquiry.

Gadamer considers his picture of inquiry distinguishable from the picture that Descartes and the Enlightenment gave us in several important ways. We can look at how he sets up this distinction apart from the issue of whether it is an accurate portrayal of the Cartesian tradition. According to Gadamer, for Descartes and the Enlightenment knowledge is produced when reason is combined with observation. Reason is conceived primarily as a method, or set of universal rules, and is contrasted with an approach which would privilege arguments based on tradition or authority. All traditions must be subjected to the light of reason; they have no intrinsic worth, at least no intrinsic epistemic worth. The subject who practices this method of reasoning is postulated as fairly self-contained, and opposed to or separated from the object of inquiry, which is passive in the process of inquiry and autonomous, a thing-in-itself. Truth is thought to be discovered on this view when one discovers the intrinsic characteristics of the thing-in-itself, and the debates over rationalism and empiricism are arguments over the best means of determining these intrinsic characteristics and gaining access to this thing-in-itself. Such debates are made ur-

---

chap. 4. Though Gadamer is heavily influenced by Heidegger's account of *Dasein*'s fore-understanding and the essence of truth as a kind of *aletheia*, Gadamer's highest aim is not a contemplative, meditative mode of comportment toward Being.

gent by the ever-present skeptic who contends that we cannot justifiably believe in any such access at all.

Gadamer charges the Cartesian paradigm with an erroneous account of the *ontology* of understanding, or the basic description of the conditions in which all understanding takes place. Gadamer (following in a well-trod Hegelian path) challenges the separation of (knowing) subject and (known) object, the idea of a thing-in-itself which is the object of inquiry, the glorification of method as a means to ensure access to reality, and in fact the whole preoccupation with access itself endemic to the Cartesian epistemological tradition. That preoccupation with a route of access is derivative upon the prior ontological configuration of knowing, which involves a separated subject and object; it is that very separation which then calls out to be spanned.

Gadamer further challenges the Cartesian presupposition that we can distance ourselves from our assumptions, prejudgments, and the subjectivity of our historical perspective or tradition. For Gadamer, Cartesian epistemology's fundamental error is its ahistoricality. This is an error that hermeneutics corrects through a renewed focus on the fact that all understanding occurs within a specific historical location. Although he wishes to highlight the historical dimension of understanding, however, throughout *Truth and Method* Gadamer repudiates historicism, or the view that one should attempt to discern meaning at a past historical moment just as it existed then (see, for example, *TM* 373). Such a historicism would itself seem to be based on a type of Cartesian epistemology, to the extent that it defines the past historical moment as a thing-in-itself separable from but knowable by the knower who uses the correct methodology. Thus Gadamer's account rejects a Cartesian ontology of understanding, and both ahistorical and historicist versions of knowing.

It is easier to understand what Gadamer rejects than to comprehend his alternative. Before we try, however, we must note that throughout his works Gadamer uses the reading of texts as the model for the inquiry he wishes to describe. In this he is simply continuing the preoccupation of previous hermeneuticists with the explication of ancient texts. This constant focus on reading should not be taken to indicate that the relevance of Gadamer's theory of inquiry is limited to mere textual interpretation. The issue of the relevant scope of Gadamer's account of understanding will be addressed in the next chapter.

Gadamer uses the term "understanding" (*Verstehen*) rather than "knowing" in describing inquiry. Why does he choose this term? Joel Weinsheimer and Donald G. Marshall, the translators for the second edition of *Truth and Method*, suggest that it is because Gadamer stresses the close connection between *Verstehen* and *Verstandigung*, the latter meaning "coming to an agreement with someone" (*TM* xvi). Thus for Gadamer the term "understanding" connotes more easily the dialogic character of knowing that he wants to emphasize. It is also true that in both German and English there are similar differences in the way we use the terms "understanding" and "knowing," or *Verstehen* and *Wissen*. "Knowing" and *Wissen* are more easily associated with the knowledge of information and facts, or science, whereas a synonym that could be used for "understanding" or *Verstehen* is "to realize."

It is interesting to note the difference caused for English speakers by the use of the word "understanding" in discussing epistemic concerns in place of the more common word "knowledge." The term "understanding" incorporates a broader conception of cognition than the term "knowledge." For example, it is a common way of speaking to say that I may *know* predicate logic after having memorized the rules, but that I only come to *understand* predicate logic from an exploration of the philosophy and historical development of logic. Here the term "understanding" indicates an appreciation for something beyond mere factual (and objective) information and implies a deeper, richer, and more comprehensive epistemic state that subsumes the category of knowing within it.

Gadamer's central thesis about understanding makes sense of these different connotations: understanding, he insists, is not a method but an event. It is not something one can appropriate and utilize within a specified time period, as one might pick up and use a broom, but is rather an event over which one has only partial control. "*Understanding is to be thought of less as a subjective act than as participating in an event of tradition,* a process of transmission in which past and present are constantly mediated. This is what must be validated by hermeneutic theory, which is far too dominated by the idea of a procedure, a method" (*TM* 290). As we read a text, understanding occurs when we place ourselves within the tradition of which the text is a part, thus opening ourselves up to what the text has to say. The key to clarifying Gadamer's account of understanding will be exploring his concept of tradition.

### Tradition

The concept of tradition is used in two ways by Gadamer. First, it refers to the entire set of practices and assumptions which make us who we are. Our individual identity is not constructed ex nihilo, but represents a continuation that is only partially affected by the processes of reflection in which we formulate our own individual founding histories. Thus our identity is best thought of as a *historical* entity, that is, a tradition.[3] Second, Gadamer uses tradition to refer to the broadly historical legacy of which we as individuals are only a part, and in relation to which we can articulate specific aspects, for example, a philosophical problematic, a particular constellation of meanings, or a set of beliefs about knowledge. It is tradition in this latter sense that is most important for Gadamer's epistemology.

Gadamer's overriding aim, for which he has been labeled a conservative, is to convince us to open ourselves up to tradition. The Cartesian focus on an extrahistorical method of validation to which all traditions must be subject and the Enlightenment rejection of the intrinsic authority of tradition have together created an entrenched presumption, a veritable tradition of suspicion against tradition itself. But for Gadamer it is both undesirable and ultimately a delusion to believe that we can set tradition aside.

By the tradition of a text, Gadamer means to refer to the guiding assumptions and framework within which the text makes sense and to the question the text answers. These elements extend beyond the author's intentions or the text's explicit, surface content. To be open to the tradition of a text is to share at least some of the assumptions and perspective of that tradition, and Gadamer holds that having something in common with the tradition of a text is unavoidable as well as necessary if we are to understand the text at all (*TM* 294). This claim should be familiar to analytic philosophers from the influential post-Kuhnian arguments of Donald Davidson and Alasdair MacIntyre that all interpretation and translation require some common ground, some commensurability.[4] It is only against the backdrop of shared agreement that differences can become apparent, and only when we assume the overarching validity of the other's claims that we can identify error and falsehood. A condition of absolute incommensurability precludes the communication of both shared and different views; a condition of complete falsehood precludes the possibility of understanding.

Gadamer develops this point in a different way from either MacIntyre or Davidson. For Gadamer, the necessity of assuming the truth of the tradi-

3. For an excellent discussion of Gadamer's concept of the self in relation to tradition see Brice C. Wachterhauser, "Must We Be What We Say? Gadamer on Truth in the Human Sciences," in *Hermeneutics and Modern Philosophy*, ed. Brice C. Wachterhauser (Albany: State University of New York Press, 1986), pp. 219–40.
4. See Donald Davidson, "On the Very Idea of a Conceptual Scheme," in *Inquiries into Truth and Interpretation* (Oxford: Clarendon Press, 1984), pp. 183–98; Alasdair MacIntyre, "Epistemological Crises, Dramatic Narratives, and the Philosophy of Science," in *Paradigms and Revolutions: Applications and Appraisals of Thomas Kuhn's Philosophy of Science*, ed. Gary Gutting (Notre Dame: University of Notre Dame Press, 1980), pp. 54–74. Their arguments build on Kuhn's that the identification of both anomalous and confirming observational data requires a stable background body of theoretical commitment, although MacIntyre uses precisely this point to criticize Kuhn's claim about the incommensurability of paradigms.

tion of a text has an ethical dimension as well as an epistemological one, for it involves an attitude of openness and receptivity to what the "other"—in the sense of a partner in dialogue, a text, or a contrasting tradition—has to say. Richard Palmer characterizes this as a particular form of the experience of relationship between self and other, or I and thou. "This is the relationship that does not project the meaning from the I but has an authentic openness which 'lets something be said.' . . . It is the kind of openness that wills to hear rather than to master, is willing to be modified by the Other. . . .This consciousness consists of a relationship to history in which the text can never be fully and objectively 'other,' for understanding is not the passive 'recognition' of the otherness of the past but rather a placing oneself so as to be laid claim to by the other."[5] Thus for Gadamer understanding necessitates an openness that implies and is built on common ground. It is on this basis that Gadamer can claim that the hermeneutic account of knowledge is not founded on domination and does not enact a kind of appropriating gesture, and thus is distanced once again from the Enlightenment orientation (*TM* 311).

Gadamer also goes further than Davidson or MacIntyre, in their own renewed appreciation for the context of knowing, by his attack on the Enlightenment presupposition that tradition and authority are opposed to reason (*TM* 281–82). He argues that, since understanding requires that we share assumptions with that which we are seeking to understand, we cannot fulfill the Enlightenment mandate to put all prejudices to the test of reason. Gadamer's concept of prejudice builds on Heidegger's conception of the fore-structure of understanding, but he develops Heidegger's account into a constructive project which seeks to develop a better account of human rationality.[6] On Gadamer's view, the maintenance of prejudice, which is simply a form of prejudgment or judgment prior to the process of inquiry that informs that process, is an act consistent with reason. This is because understanding, which is a cognitive faculty, can operate only within a situation of active prejudgments. Therefore, the picture of the modern scientist eschewing all tradition and putting every assumption to the test of reason, where the latter is conceived as a presuppositionless method, is a naive and wrongheaded illusion. Sounding like Thomas Kuhn here, Gadamer points out that only within a situation where we preserve a body of assumptions (or a paradigm) can we *use* reason, that is, engage in the act (or participate in the event) of understanding. One implication of this contention is that the standards and procedures we use in justification are themselves seen as historicized, evolving through the process of inquiry

5. Richard Palmer, *Hermeneutics: Interpretation Theory in Schleiermacher, Dilthey, Heidegger, and Gadamer* (Evanston: Northwestern University Press, 1969), p. 193.
6. See Caputo, *Radical Hermeneutics*, p. 111.

rather than intact before it is begun. A Cartesian might formulate the elements of inquiry as including a presuppositionless knower, a method of reasoning, and an object about which the knower seeks knowledge. On Gadamer's view such distinctions are meaningless. Each element involved in understanding is constituted within the process.

Are our prejudices irreproachable, then, either too deep to uncover and analyze or impossible to discard given their involvement in understanding? Gadamer asserts that the preservation of tradition is a "freely chosen action" and that traditions need to be "affirmed, embraced, cultivated" (*TM* 281–82). Much of the motivation for his work, as has been stated, is to promote our active preservation of tradition, and it is our very prejudices that are the medium of continuity through which tradition survives. There is a tension in Gadamer's work, however, between his claim that "we always stand within tradition" and thus that the maintenance of tradition is inevitable, and his claim that we must actively affirm and preserve traditions. Let us look more closely at this claim that prejudices must be actively preserved.

If such active preservation is to be possible, then prejudices and the traditions of which they are a part must be observable and isolatable. We must be able to identify them if their preservation requires a freely chosen action and is not simply an implicit or unconscious part of our cognitive processes. If we can identify prejudices and choose to affirm them then it must be possible to choose to reject them. This is, in fact, Gadamer's position. He argues that the adherence to tradition is not blind obedience: "Acknowledging authority is always connected with the idea that what the authority says is not irrational and arbitrary but can, in principle, be discovered to be true. This is the essence of the authority claimed by the teacher, the superior, the expert. The prejudices that they implant are legitimized by the person who presents them" (*TM* 280). Such a view of authority sounds closer to the Enlightenment than it does, for example, to Kierkegaard's account, which defines authority precisely as criterionless or immune to critical judgment by those who would respect it. Kierkegaard argued that if we subject authority to such criticism as the very condition of our acceptance, then we are not truly accepting *its* authority but simply our own, since we are relying on our own powers of judgment to determine whether what it says to us is in fact valid.

For Gadamer, on the contrary, reason and the authority of tradition are not in opposition because reason is used in deciding whether or not to accept a tradition. Acceptance of a tradition is therefore nonarbitrary and not without criteria (*TM* 268). Gadamer's difference with the Enlightenment consists in his account of how one chooses to preserve a tradition. One does not choose to accept a tradition by subjecting each of the tradition's beliefs to a method of analysis, as the Enlightenment proposed. That would not be accepting the authority of the tradition at all, but simply subjecting its beliefs along with all others, without presumption in their favor, to one's procedures of inquiry. To accept a tradition is to use one's reason to decide whether or not to accept the authority of the tradition itself rather than subjecting each one of its beliefs to scrutiny. This is akin to accepting the authority of a teacher based on her or his wider experience and longer period of study rather than testing each of the teacher's beliefs. The acceptance of such authority does not entail committing oneself to agree with each and every claim the teacher makes; rather, the commitment involves giving presumption in favor of the teacher's claims. To accept the authority of a tradition, and thus actively to preserve it, requires a similar presumption, or presupposition, that the tradition holds truth. Against Kierkegaard, therefore, Gadamer describes a relationship to tradition that is neither a blind leap of faith nor a repudiation of its epistemic authority.

In light of our active preservation of tradition and its authority, Gadamer argues that our relation to tradition is not merely a reproductive one but a productive one as well. Traditions must be interpreted and applied, not merely reproduced. "Tradition is not simply a permanent precondition; rather, we produce it ourselves inasmuch as we understand, participate in the evolution of tradition, and hence further determine it ourselves" (*TM* 293). This passage brings us to two further critical aspects of Gadamer's account of tradition, his claims that tradition is a fusion of historical horizons, and that our relationship to tradition is a dialectical one. We need to look at these in more detail.

For Gadamer, tradition does not exist simply or primarily in the past. It is a continuous movement from the past through the present toward the future, a movement along a continuum in which we exist and a movement with a direction we can affect. It is not determinately directed from the past, but exists in relation to the present and is constantly open to reinterpretation based on our present vantage point. In fact, tradition only exists at all to the extent that it is connected to the present and is interpreted and mediated in light of present conditions. Gadamer thus defines tradition as a fusion of horizons which are "the range of vision that includes everything that can be seen from a particular vantage point" (*TM* 302). Tradition fuses the vantage points or horizons of past and present.

It is important to understand where Gadamer locates this fusion. For a positivist, the fusion of reader and text might be said to occur when the reader discovers the intrinsic truth of a text, and thus the fusion takes place within the text, where the reader, using the correct interpretive methodology, arrives at the real meaning of the text. For Gadamer, however, the fusion involves a reciprocating movement of both text and reader. The historical horizon of the text comes together with the historical horizon of the reader, carrying tradition forward and making understanding possible. Understanding occurs at a point of interaction between text and reader, and not at the point of the text itself.

The sense in which Gadamer means to say that our relationship to tradition is dialectial is harder to elucidate, but it will return us to the apparent contradiction I mentioned earlier between Gadamer's claim that standing in a tradition is inevitable and his claim that tradition must be actively preserved. Gadamer argues that we become aware of the prejudices we hold when they yield unexpected meanings, which cause a disruption and sense of confusion in the normal flow of reading. When such a disruption occurs, which Gadamer describes as the experience of "being pulled up short by the text," we are suddenly made aware of the previously hidden assumptions we were making (*TM* 268). Given his assertions that we can become aware of prejudices and that we must actively preserve tradition, this leads us to believe that tradition is something we can identify and toward which we can adopt various possible attitudes. Gadamer also claims, however, that "our usual relationship to the past is not characterized by distancing and freeing ourselves from tradition. Rather, we are always situated within traditions, and this is no objectifying process—i.e. we do not conceive of what tradition says as something other, something alien. It is always part of us" (*TM* 282). We cannot, therefore, stand completely outside of all traditions and freely choose what will be preserved and what will be relinquished. This double-edged relationship to tradition Gadamer calls "dialectical." But does simply calling it "dialectical" explain how we can be unable to distance ourselves from tradition and yet have the ability to actively preserve it?

In Gadamer's view, we can be partially successful in becoming aware of the prejudices we carry and in reflecting upon them but we will never be totally aware of all our prejudices. We can never achieve complete self-awareness or self-knowledge: "The illumination of this situation . . . can never be completely achieved; yet the fact that it cannot be completed is due not to a deficiency in reflection but to the essence of the historical being that we are. *To be historically means that knowledge of oneself is never complete*" (*TM* 302). Gadamer says further that "the overcoming of all prejudices, this global demand of the Enlightenment, will itself prove to be a prejudice, and removing it opens the way to an appropriate understanding of the finitude which dominates not only our humanity but also our historical consciousness" (*TM* 276). Human finitude is bounded by the historical dimension of our capacities, that is, it consists in our historical horizon. This vantage point or horizon is both a limit on what we can see and that which allows us to see anything at all, and it is in this sense that the relationship between tradition and our capacity to achieve understanding is a dialectical one. A historical horizon has a dialectical relationship to our understanding in that it both allows for and limits understanding.

Gadamer's description of the historical dimension of understanding raises a number of epistemological questions. When we are disrupted in the process of inquiry and come to be aware of our previously hidden assumptions, what criteria can we then use to judge, justify, or reject these assumptions? If prejudice plays a significant role in our judgments of meaning, then prejudices must play a role in our judgments of prejudices themselves.

On Gadamer's view, we cannot reflect upon or subject to scrutiny all the criteria of judgment that are operative in our epistemic determinations. This introduces the possibility that our judgments are seriously misguided and without any means for correction or even apprehension. Through this door a skeptical argument could enter, but it is clear that refuting the possibility of skepticism is not one of Gadamer's concerns. Why is Gadamer so unconcerned with skepticism, given that it arises from his very account of the historical horizon of knowledge? His claim that we are always embedded within an ongoing tradition and that we must remain open to the truth of that tradition militates against the viability of entertaining skeptical doubts. This is because our embeddedness entails that we are always already in a position of knowing truth, that the positing of such a position is the only way of rendering our situation at all intelligible, and therefore that a radical skepticism which would question whether we know any truths at all is actually unintelligible. Moreover, skepticism is itself an issue embedded within a particular horizon (or more than one), involving presuppositions about the nature of doubt and of inquiry. And these are among the presuppositions Gadamer believes we can now reflect upon and should in fact reject.

A further question arises in connection with the possibility of claiming or identifying cognitive progress. If there are no criteria external to a horizon by which we can judge it, then it seems we have no way of asserting historical progress in the development or accumulation of knowledge. We have no way to justify our intuition that the set of assumptions Aristotle was working with was any less cognitively reliable than the set of assumptions we are working with today, if there are no external or cross-horizon criteria for judgment. This contradicts the common intuition that we can provide transhistorical or cross-horizon evidence of the increased reliability of our epistemic framework as against Aristotle's. On Gadamer's view, we can only provide such evidence from within our horizon, and thus any claim about progress will be contextualized and relative. Philosophical hermeneutics cannot then validate the belief in progress as it is usually formulated.

Like the problem of skepticism, however, this objection carries with it its own horizon of presuppositions which we may well want to reject.[7] For example, why is it the case that a belief in progress requires one to be able to step outside of one's own immanent theoretical and historical context? Why is it not the case that accounts of progress are made on the basis of criteria embedded within such contexts? Though the belief in progress has been persistent in modern Anglo-European societies, the criteria by which that progress has been identified have changed. For example, conceptions of political progress have shifted from ones that ignored the daily material conditions of the majority of people or of women to ones that take those conditions as precisely the main point. These shifts rely on changes at the level of historical prejudgment or theoretical background assumptions (which can in most cases be made explicit). Yet this reliance does not in any way reduce the viability of the various claims for progress. Thus it would seem that an ability to produce a transhistorical (or apolitical) criterion of progress is not in fact a necessary requirement for validating the belief in progress.[8]

A third problem arises from within Gadamer's own framework. If complete self-knowledge is unattainable, if horizons are both perceptively enabling and limiting, and if any assessment of a horizon besides our own will be mediated *through* our own, it is not at all clear that horizons can be usefully delineated. This endangers Gadamer's concept of tradition, since tradition is defined as the fusion of horizons, and Gadamer's whole theory of understanding depends heavily on his inclusion of tradition in the process of cognition. Before this problem can be adequately explored, however, we need to look at Gadamer's views on interpretation, application, and the transcendence of the subject/object separation in hermeneutical inquiry.

## Understanding as Interpretation and Application

Schleiermacher's hermeneutics was based on the idea that the goal in explicating ancient texts is to provide an exact reproduction of the histori-

---

7. For example, if we assume the definition of progress given by Larry Laudan or by Imre Lakatos, Gadamer's position does not create obstacles for the belief in progress. See Larry Laudan, *Progress and Its Problems* (London: Routledge and Kegan Paul, 1977); Imre Lakatos, *The Methodology of Scientific Research Programmes* (Cambridge: Cambridge University Press, 1978).
8. This issue obviously raises the spectre of realism, and the question whether a commitment to the historical embeddedness of all knowledge can be made consistent with a realist interpretation of the meaning of knowledge claims. I will discuss this issue throughout the book, and Gadamer's position in particular in Chapter 2.

cal context and historical meaning of the work (*TM* 166–67). Gadamer
holds such a project to be futile: understanding is not a simple process of
discerning the meaning that lies there on the page but of actively interpreting and applying the text in relation to one's own horizon. Understanding,
interpretation, and application are Gadamer's holy trinity. He argues that
they comprise "one unified process" (*TM* 308), but the best approach for
us will be to look at the connection between understanding and interpretation and then at the connection of understanding with application. "Interpretation is not an occasional, post facto supplement to understanding;
rather, understanding is always interpretation, and hence interpretation is
the explicit form of understanding" (*TM* 307). When we seek understanding as we read a text, a kind of translation occurs, the translation of the
text into something that we can understand given our own horizon of
background assumptions and knowledge. Gadamer argues that the act of
translation is "fundamentally the same" as the act of interpretation (*TM*
387). A translator must "bridge the gulf between languages" to recreate a
"new" text which is intelligible within a linguistic context different from
that of the original. Similarly, an interpretation requires the development of
an agreement between disparate points of reference, embedded in reader
and text, out of which will emerge something new. The historical horizons
of text and reader are fused in the act of interpretation, and it is out of just
such fusions that traditions are created (*TM* 328).

Obviously, then, to understand a text does not mean, for Gadamer, to
appropriate the singular, uniquely true interpretation that captures the
"real" or essential meaning intrinsic to the text. As he puts it, "The meaning of a text is not to be compared with an immovably and obstinately
fixed point of view that suggests only one question to the person trying to
understand it" (*TM* 388). Given this, a certain degree of relativism must inevitably enter in, to the extent that there will be different interpretations of
the text which represent the fusion of different horizons; that is, there will
be a number of different "correct" interpretations. Not all interpretations
will be considered correct or epistemically equal, but there cannot be simply one correct interpretation of a text for all time because the reader's
horizon is a "decisive" constitutive component of any interpretation (*TM*
388). Thus, the concept of an intrinsic meaning, or of a textual or authorial privilege over meaning, or of a meaning which is simply discovered,
must be discarded. As Gadamer explains:

> Every age has to understand a transmitted text in its own way, for the text be-
> longs to the whole tradition whose content interests the age and in which it
> seeks to understand itself. The real meaning of the text, as it speaks to the in-
> terpreter, does not depend on the contingencies of the author and his original

audience. It certainly is not identical with them, for it is always co-determined by the historical situation of the interpreter. . . . Not just occasionally but always, the meaning of a text goes beyond its author. That is why understanding is not merely a reproductive but always a productive activity as well. (*TM* 296)

Just as when I interpret my four-year-old's sometimes confusing stories into something that *I* can understand, through a process of translating his grammar and terminology into my own, so my prejudices about language and reality are presupposed in any interpretation that I make. Understanding my son's speech requires an interpretation that includes the use of my prejudices, and improving his ability to communicate consists largely in teaching him to share my prejudices.

Gadamer's insistence that understanding also inherently involves application is a very closely related point. He begins this argument by introducing the model of legal and theological hermeneutics. The work of the U.S. Supreme Court can be taken as a paradigm of legal hermeneutics—the translation of codified law into case law, or the application of the constitutional text to particular cases requiring adjudication. Understanding the Constitution in this context just means being able to apply it to a given case. Theological hermeneutics operates similarly with sacred texts such as the Bible or Talmud, in which the stories and parables of the text must be applied to questions of current concern. Gadamer's argument is, then, that all understanding works in a way analogous to legal and theological hermeneutics (*TM* 312).

Gadamer claims that in order to understand a text we must apply the text to a given situation—that is, the context of the reader, which includes the reader's historical horizon, prejudgments, and the question that motivates the reader to read. Understanding is a fusion of present and past, and legal hermeneutics which involves the application of a text to a present situation is the "model for the relationship between past and present that we are seeking"(*TM* 327–28). Thus, the purpose of equating understanding with interpretation and application is to assert and emphasize the *interactive* nature of understanding. Gadamer replaces the notion of understanding as a discovery of intrinsic meaning through the utilization of a universal method with a concept of understanding that is both reproductive and productive, and includes both the text and the reader's horizon. On his account, meaning must therefore be to some extent creative and unique to a particular interpretive event, though it is not arbitrary. Neither the reader nor the text has hegemony over meaning.

The meaning of a text and tradition itself are open-ended and constantly changing or evolving, just as the text of the U.S. Constitution has been used to justify slavery, to condemn slavery, and then to support civil rights. "The historical movement of human life consists in the fact that it is never absolutely bound to any one standpoint, and hence can never have a truly closed horizon. The horizon is, rather, something into which we move and that moves with us" (*TM* 304). Impermanence and open-endedness are thus essential to Gadamer's philosophical hermeneutics because the historical horizon through which the past is interpreted is never fixed or conceivable in its entirety but always developing. Moreover, Gadamer insists that the very basis of the concept of knowledge is, in fact, not the statement or proposition but the question. He suggests that for the Greeks it is the dialectic of the *question* which motivates knowledge, rather than the pursuit of certainty, as in Descartes. Knowledge's "superiority over preconceived opinion" consists precisely in the fact that it considers "opposites," that it can "conceive of possibilities as possibilities" (*TM* 365). "Only a person who has questions can have knowledge" (*TM* 365).

How can we articulate a concept of truth that accords with Gadamer's emphasis on both the openness and the finitude of understanding? If understanding is a fusion of moving horizons and must therefore itself be constantly moving, can there be no final and absolute understanding of a text? Does the finality invoked by the term "true" conflict with philosophical hermeneutics' account of understanding? Gadamer sometimes takes the position that "the discovery of the true meaning of a text or a work of art is never finished: it is in fact an infinite process" (*TM* 298). Thus, at times he speaks as if the designation "true" should only be applied to the infinite process of understanding, interpreting, and applying a text, so as to avoid a representation of truth that would render it stable and closed rather than open and ongoing.

If "true" can only refer to the infinite process of understanding, then Gadamer's concept of truth sounds decidedly Hegelian, to the extent that truth is defined as the absolute whole or the entire process of knowing (in Hegel's case, this would be self-knowing) which incorporates the whole of history. But there is a significant distinction between Hegel's concept of truth and Gadamer's (see, for example, *TM* 355–57, 341–46, 371–72). The distinction is based on the fact that for Hegel there exists the existential possibility for a kind of perfect fusion between consciousness and object. This perfect fusion is only perceivable from the perspective of the whole, but it remains nonetheless as the principal signifier of truth or criterion by which epistemic progress should be judged. Gadamer denies the possibility that there ever existed any such absolute wholeness and closure from any perspective. The very essence of knowledge is openness, finitude, and impermanence. Thus, his project is opposed to Hegel's insofar as it is motivated not to overcome our limitations but to acknowledge them. The dialectic of understanding is not moving toward closure, nor is such closure necessary to establish its epistemic validity. These points will be further explored in the next chapter.

The infinite process of discovering the true meaning of a work is then truly an *infinite* one, without any final end that encapsulates the whole. But which process should be designated by the term "true": the infinite series of fusions or each particular (justified) fusion? It would seem that either option is plausible, or both. Without Hegel's *Zeitgeist*, Gadamer need not privilege only the infinite process of understanding as "true," since it will have no apparent epistemic superiority over particular understandings except in its comprehensiveness. But this raises the question what the designation "true" can mean within philosophical hermeneutics; that is, it raises the question on what basis a claim for epistemic superiority can be made at all.

Gadamer's concept of truth is predicated on his rejection of the separation traditionally made between subjects and objects, involving the notion of the privileged position of the knowing subject and the objective remoteness and independence of the object of inquiry. Gadamer identifies the human sciences in particular as a discipline in which the object of inquiry is not separate or opposed to or set against oneself. Thus in history "the so-called subject of knowledge has the same mode of being as the object, so that object and subject belong to the same historical movement" (*TM* 528). The idea here is that the historian, for example, is, as Hegel said, "a part of the process he is studying" (*TM* 515), and therefore no antithesis can be drawn between subject and object. According to the accepted model of this antithesis in the natural sciences, the objects of scientific inquiry will behave as they will and obey causal laws whether or not the scientist is around, except perhaps in the case of biology. The scientist or subject is wholly peripheral to the spectacle of natural (objective) facts in the universe. These facts may affect the scientist, but there is no reciprocity of impact. Hence the world studied by the scientist is conceived as a world-in-itself, radically cut off and independent of us, and the process of inquiry is conceived as discovering this world. The truth of this reality is wholly intrinsic to it.

Against this view, Gadamer claims that the human sciences, at least, involve a reality to which the inquirer is not peripheral and in which the effects between knower and known are reciprocal rather than one-way, and he goes so far as to state that "the object of research [is] actually constituted by the motivation of the inquiry" (*TM* 284). The interest we have in the research topic is based on the "light in which it is presented to us" (*TM* 284). The very writing of history becomes part of history itself and will be studied as such by future historiographers (who will themselves be studied, by the successors, and so forth). From Dilthey, Gadamer takes the notion of *Erlebnis*, in which the primary units of the human sciences are simultaneously units of experience and units of meaning (*TM* 65). This view is counterposed to the view, held by Kant and the positivist empiricists, that the ultimate building blocks of knowledge are "sensations" conceived as automatic responses to stimuli and devoid of meaning. For Dilthey, experience is inherently historical, not a fact to which value and meaning get added later (*TM* 221). One of the most important implications of this view for Gadamer is that the object of knowledge can no longer be conceived as autonomous or separable from the process of inquiry or the knower. The object of knowledge is presented in the "light" of *Erlebnis*.

A further reason for rejecting the idea that the subject and object are separable is Gadamer's belief in the linguisticality of all human inquiry. The whole process of inquiry, involving fusion, interpretation, and application, is linguistic (*TM* 383).[9] Gadamer understands his claim that language is a medium of intersubjectivity between persons and between the knower and the known as an ontological claim. He rejects the ontology of the view that the subject or inquirer reaches out to an intrinsic meaning within the text and uses the medium of language as a tool to do so. This would make language a tool of the process of knowing rather than a constitutive part of it. Instead, Gadamer maintains that language is the universal medium within which understanding takes place (*TM* 392–95). Language is the medium of intersubjectivity and inquiry not because it exists in a space between knowers and between the knower and the known, but because it surrounds and permeates them like an atmosphere. The air not only surrounds us; it is inside of us and part of what we are. It is in this sense that language is the medium of the very life-world that is the goal of inquiry in the human sciences.

What is studied in the human sciences is not a world-in-itself (an objective world), but a social reality constructed out of our common meanings or fused horizons, that is, out of tradition. This social reality is not *expressed* linguistically, but simply *is* linguisticality. When we seek to understand a text or a practice, the object of our inquiry is as much ourselves in the process of inquiry as it is the separate text or practice. The constitutive elements of understanding, as we have seen, involve the prejudices of both the text's and the reader's historical horizons, past and present. Truth, or the product of inquiry, cannot therefore refer only to the intrinsic properties of the object of the text or practice as these are set apart from or opposed to language or ourselves. The text has the meaning it has only in

---

9. Gadamer's use of the term "language" here is different from the word's ordinary usage, as in the phrase "the language of English."

relation to the interpreter, involving the interpreter's historical horizon and the application of the inquiry. Both horizon and meaning are linguistic at their most primordial levels, from the ground up. The object of knowledge is not intrinsic or independent, it is not opposed to or separate from the subject engaged in inquiry, and it is not extralinguistic; therefore the separation believed to exist between subject and object (or text and referent) loses its usefulness as these concepts lose the sharpness of their boundaries.

We will explore in more detail Gadamer's reconceptualization of the ontology of truth in the next chapter. A central issue will be whether this alternative ontology can be applied beyond the realm of inquiry in the human sciences to knowledge in general. In the 1960 pre-Kuhnian edition of *Wahrheit und Methode*, Gadamer distinguishes between the natural sciences and the human sciences precisely in relation to this issue—the constitution of the object of research as just discussed. He asserts that in the natural sciences the object of research dictates the process of scientific development, whereas in the human sciences the "motivation of inquiry" has more constitutive powers (*TM* 283–84). This sounds as if Gadamer holds a fairly traditional view of truth and objectivity in the natural sciences, but there are two complications which prohibit such a conclusion. Elsewhere, particularly in his account of linguisticality and the conditions of understanding, Gadamer makes universalist claims about the historical dimension of all knowledge, claims at odds with his neat separation of the natural and human sciences. Moreover, in the later editions of his work, he has added footnotes which admit that, in this post-Kuhnian era, his account of the nature of truth in the natural sciences is too simplistic (see *TM* 283n, 285n). As a result of this tension and uncertainty in his work, there has been a flurry of debate over the universality of Gadamer's hermeneutic claims, as we shall see. My interest in this issue will not be directed toward discerning Gadamer's own views so much as using his views as a springboard to explore the issue of truth in general.

Before we turn to Gadamer's epistemology, however, we need to look at one final aspect of his philosophical hermeneutics. Part of the importance of transcending the subject/object distinction consists in the fact that it is an obstacle to our achieving what Gadamer calls *wirkungsgeschichtliches Bewußtsein* which has been translated variably as "effective-historical consciousness," "historically effective consciousness," "the history of effect," and "consciousness in which history is ever at work."[10] Essentially, the phrase means the awareness that we are "always already affected by history" (*TM* 300). Helping us to achieve this awareness is the point of much of Gadamer's work because he believes it to be necessary for

---

10. Palmer, *Hermeneutics*, p. 191; Gadamer, *Truth and Method*, p. 341.

hermeneutical inquiry, that is, for all understanding in which tradition plays a role (*TM* 341).

The rigid separation and opposition of subject/object must be rejected in order for this historical awareness to be conceived of as possible and in fact enlightening. Conceptualizing the subject as active and the object as passive in the process of inquiry would block rather than facilitate this awareness. Likewise, separation of subject and object hinders if not blocks our capacity to be open to the text, to be modified by it, and to recognize that we share a commonality with it. Therefore it is not enough, Gadamer says, to posit a dialectical relationship between subject and object (*TM* 311). This would keep the metaphysical categories intact, and would "separate what clearly belong together"(*TM* 311). The separation must be altogether transcended.

It is difficult, however, to know precisely what Gadamer means by "being open to what the text says to us," unless it is simply trying to discover the intrinsic meaning of the text. It is clear Gadamer wants to affirm the former and eschew the latter, but how are we to understand the former except as meaning the latter? This problem brings out a pervasive tension that I have already mentioned. On the one hand Gadamer wants to reject notions of intrinsic meaning, but on the other hand he repeatedly emphasizes the role of historical texts, the continuity of tradition, and our need to be open to the truth of a text. I want to end this chapter by exploring this problem.

### The Problem with Tradition

Gadamer defines understanding as the fusion of two horizons, the horizon of the reader and the horizon of the text. Every such fusion is a point in the evolving tradition of the text, and that tradition, seen as a continuum, is a fusion of all the text's moments of interpretation. But what does it mean to describe each moment of understanding as a fusion of two horizons? The horizon of the reader, as we have seen in the discussion on prejudice, can never be rendered totally perspicuous, although aspects of it become observable when there occurs a disruption in the process of interpretation. Given Gadamer's views, however, it is difficult to comprehend how the historical horizon *of the text* is observable at all.

One possible way to ascertain the horizon of the text might be to compare the results of alternative assumptions. If we discover through the process of interpretation that one assumption renders a text unintelligible while another assumption renders it sensible to us, we can plausibly treat that second assumption as an element of the horizon of the text. But whether or not a text is intelligible to us depends on our prejudices as much as or more than it depends on the prejudices of the text. Thus, the *cause* of the fact that the first assumption renders the text unintelligible while the second assumption renders it sensible may be found in the features of our own prejudices rather than in elements inherent to the text. For Gadamer, every element of interpretation involves an interaction between two components that are not identifiable in isolation. If this is the case, we can never ascertain the contribution of the text to interpretation, but only assume that such a contribution is being made.

Gadamer would seem to agree that the past element of tradition cannot be identified when he says that we are unable to appropriate the "author's real intent" and when he denies the very existence of an "authentic, intrinsic meaning" of the text. Meaning changes with changes in its input or constitutive elements—that is, reader, interpretation, application, and historical horizon. But if the historical horizon of the text cannot be appropriated apart from these other elements, through the author's real intent or the essential, authentic meaning of the text, to what can the horizon of the text possibly refer? As Gadamer says, the reader "can, indeed he must, accept the fact that future generations will understand differently what he has read in the text" (*TM* 340). Moreover, he asserts that "the heart of the hermeneutical problem is that one and the same tradition must time and again be understood in a different way . . ." (*TM* 312). If this is the case, then how can Gadamer assert with such assurance the continuity of tradition through history, the "duration" of a work, and the "continuing validity of the classical" (*TM* 290)? If we cannot identify the historical horizon of the text itself, how can we justifiably believe in a continuation of past beliefs and prejudgments or the existence of a continuous—even though only partially continuous—tradition?

Gadamer puts great emphasis on the transmission of tradition: his principal disagreement with the Enlightenment is precisely over the question of tradition's value (*TM* xxv). It is because he wants to revalidate tradition and direct our philosophical preoccupations to traditional, historical texts that he has been labeled a conservative philosopher. Because Gadamer valorizes tradition, he advises us to be "open to the truth of the text, of what tradition says to us." He says we must be able "to open ourselves to the superior claim the text makes and to respond to what it has to tell us" (*TM* 311). By including prejudice in the act of understanding/interpretation, Gadamer demonstrates that traditions continue. Because we use continuously operative prejudices in interpretation, tradition survives into the present and future despite attempts to eradicate it. Through textual interpretations tradition continues to influence us and to flourish, though in many cases it is unseen by us. Gadamer's argument is not simply that tradition and prejudice are unavoidable, but that they provide the necessary groundwork through which alone knowledge is possible. Thus he not only reintroduces tradition and prejudice, but gives them epistemic validity.

This reclamation of tradition is one of Gadamer's most original and significant contributions to twentieth-century thought, and it marks his work as a more decisive break with the Enlightenment than that of many postmodernist contemporaries. But the question remains, if there is no essential or original intent or meaning of a text, how can we assert the continuation even in reinterpreted form of a historical horizon of the past? How do we know that current interpretations carry anything forward from the past? The bare symbols on the page may continue (though of course texts will deteriorate in any manuscript tradition), but these symbols carry no meaning without interpretation. Remember that Gadamer asserts forcefully that interpretation is not an act adjacent or posterior to understanding, and thus we have no prior access to the meaning of the symbols before our own historical horizon begins its process of interpretation through the sieve of prejudice. How then can Gadamer claim that all textual meanings are the product of interpretation, that meaning changes as horizons and applications change, and yet that traditions endure?

This problem, however perplexing, is not debilitating to Gadamer's account because he defines tradition in an unusual way. "Tradition is not simply a permanent precondition; rather, we produce it ourselves, inasmuch as we understand, participate in the evolution of tradition and hence further determine it ourselves. Thus the circle of understanding is not a 'methodological' circle, but describes an element of the ontological structure of understanding" (*TM* 293). Gadamer offers a radically revisionist proposal for what we should mean by the term "tradition," that is, tradition evolves and is reinterpreted at each historical moment. It is therefore impermanent and open-ended. One might object to this and ask why we should call it tradition at all if it is produced anew through each interaction with a new horizon. We have no means to check our interpretation against the historically "authentic" one, and since each interpretation that yields understanding represents a new fusion, we have no means of knowing what elements have endured through the processes of interpretation, or in fact if any have. Given that Gadamer rejects the separation of subject and object, we cannot identify within a fusion the element that is new and the element that has continued. Therefore, it might seem more correct to say that what exists is a continuous series of fusions, rather than an ongoing tradition.

But Gadamer insists that his point is an ontological and not a methodological one. We cannot demand of Gadamer the delineation of a method of access to the text's historical horizon, or a procedure for its identification, without ignoring this shift. Moreover, to conceptualize tradition or the past as an object autonomous from and opposed to oneself as knower would be to assume a subject/object separation. If we accuse Gadamer of not being able to identify the element in tradition that is separate from subjective input, he will respond that the subjective and objective aspects cannot be separated in that way.

Further, Gadamer's claim about the continuation of past horizons is justified in light of his argument that in order to understand a text at all we must be able to share with it some common assumptions. Jürgen Habermas understands Gadamer's account in this way as well: "The interpreter is a moment of the same fabric of tradition as his object. He appropriates a tradition from a horizon of expectations that is already informed by this tradition. For this reason, we have, in a certain way, already understood the tradition with which we are confronted. And only for this reason is the horizon opened up by the language of the interpreter not merely something subjective that distorts our interpretation."[11] The presupposition that the reader's historical horizon yields a subjective interpretation which distorts inquiry is part of the Cartesian ontology of inquiry. Gadamer, as Habermas shows, gives a metaphysical answer to the epistemological objection about the influence of "subjective" elements. His answer is to reconceive the metaphysics of subjectivity in such a way that it is not cut off, separated, or autonomous from the object of inquiry, from tradition, or from the horizon of the text. This claim is justified in part by the fact that we can only explain how understanding is possible, how it is that we can understand a text written a thousand years ago, by asserting the continuation of tradition and the commonality of perspective shared by text and reader.

Such a line of reasoning should not be unfamiliar to analytic philosophers, since it is very similar to a central argument of Kant's. For Kant started out with a question about knowledge and ended up giving a metaphysical answer about categories in the mind. Similarly, the circle of understanding—the infamous hermeneutical circle—which involves two horizons, a text and a reader, and presupposes that the past horizon overlaps into the reader's present horizon without benefit of methodological explanation, is both explained and absolved from epistemological sin via an ontological argument about the structure of understanding. Understanding is not a subject appropriating the intrinsic nature of an object, but an already fused horizon (the present) interacting to produce a new fusion in relation to a text. In this way, Gadamer argues we must *presuppose* the continuation of tradition, and are justified in doing so despite the lack of a

11. Jürgen Habermas, "A Review of Gadamer's *Truth and Method*," in *Understanding and Social Inquiry*, edited by Fred Dallmayr and Thomas McCarthy (Notre Dame: University of Notre Dame Press, 1977), p. 343.

method or procedure for identifying past horizons. Only by referring to tradition or the continuation of the past can we assert or explain the possibility of understanding. Needless to say, such an argument would not convince a skeptic, who does not take it as a given that understanding is possible. Nevertheless, the argument works for those of us who share Gadamer's assumption that understanding, or knowledge, does in fact exist. In form, then, his argument works as a transcendental deduction, deducing what must exist in order to explain the existence of something we already know to exist, which for Gadamer (and for Kant) is knowledge.

There remains a tension in Gadamer's work between his invocation of a kind of permanent truth in tradition on the one hand and his insistence on the impermanence, mutability, and historical mobility of meaning on the other. There is no question that conservative impulses in Gadamer's work remain manifest in the former tendency. But I would argue that if we follow Gadamer's definitions of tradition and of meaning carefully, the mobile and impermanent side must win out, even though this goes against some of Gadamer's own pronouncements. We can reestablish the coherence of Gadamer's account by emphasizing the changing and impermanent nature of tradition, and in so doing we minimize the conservative aspects of his hermeneutics. Thus my interpretation might be called a "left-Gadamerianism," but I would argue that it is based on an openness to the truth of what Gadamer is saying and is a reading guided by a commitment to maximize the coherence and truthfulness of the text—critical elements for any interpretive process, as we shall see.

In the following chapter I will use the basic rubric of Gadamerian hermeneutics as presented here to develop and argue for an interpretation of Gadamer as an epistemological coherentist. The principal arguments will be based on Gadamer's account of the hermeneutical circle and the process of interpretation and understanding. There is, however, a strong motivation evident in Gadamer's whole corpus toward the identification of connections and harmonies between elements often thought of as disparate and distinct, and part of my argument is based on my perception of this motivation. In his critique of the Enlightenment, for example, Gadamer is not interested in enacting a simple reversal of the binary terms Descartes provided. He rejects the Romantic reaction on the grounds that it simply inverted the Enlightenment's repudiation of magic, ancient practices and beliefs, and the affinity with nature (*TM* 273). Where the Enlightenment promoted the conquest of mythos by logos, Romanticism simply wanted to reject the universality and dominance of logos in favor of mythos. Gadamer writes that "the romantic reversal of the Enlightenment's criteria of value actually perpetuates the abstract contrast between myth and reason." He describes his goal as different from this. Instead of reversal, his account of understanding and his reconstruction of reason seek again and again to demonstrate the fundamental connectedness and harmony between the elements we have separated in the concepts of reason and tradition, logos and mythos, truth and prejudice. Thus in his vision, understanding is not only guided by the pursuit of coherence, but also characterized by a pre-existing coherence of various constitutive elements. And it is for this reason that Gadamer moves away from methodology and toward "allowing what is to be."[12] It is to this account that we will now turn.

12. Gadamer, *The Relevance of the Beautiful and Other Essays*, trans. Nicholas Walker (New York: Cambridge University Press, 1986), p. 49.

# CHAPTER TWO

# "*The relationship is primary . . .*": Hermeneutics as Epistemology

Hans-Georg Gadamer's account of justification and truth is an approach with several important advantages, particularly over typical analytic epistemologies. He offers us a way to conceptualize the inevitable locatedness of knowers not as a detriment but as a necessary condition for knowledge. In his account, the act of knowing is modeled on an I/Thou relationship, and in such a relationship the goal is not to eliminate the "I" but to fuse it with the position of the "other." Gadamer gives this feature of relatedness ontological primacy, and to the extent discrete subjects and objects figure in his account at all they are derivative upon the prior relation. Thus, subject and object are never pure; these terms denote useful constructs rather than fundamental entities. Gadamer also develops a plurality of types of knowing, and emphasizes the play of movement without closure that characterizes belief-formation. He portrays a more realistic, and less alienated, conception of reason, one that is more easily reconcilable with a recognition of reason's finite and limited contours.

In this chapter I will try to make good on these claims by presenting a theory of justification and truth based on Gadamer's hermeneutics. I will develop an account more readily familiar to analytic philosophers as an epistemology. Gadamer's views on knowledge are not wholly original. As we have already seen, his account of truth is similar to Hegel's, but has a decided advantage in dropping Hegel's predisposition toward identity and closure and his spiritualistic metaphysics. Gadamer bases his account not in Spirit but in language. Gadamer also builds on the work of Heidegger, though it is mistaken to view Gadamer as basically a warmed-over Heidegger.[1] Unlike Heidegger's, Gadamer's writings encapsulate and present in a particularly clear way the epistemological insights of previous hermeneuts, as well as improving on them. Gadamer borrows from Heidegger's notion of truth as *aletheia*, a disclosing. But where Heidegger relies on an onto-theological account to support his claim that truth is a disclosing, Gadamer develops this account of truth through an analysis of interpretation and the process by which we discern the meaning in a text, thus securing his theory of truth more firmly to familiar human practices. In this way, one need not accept the fully articulated Heideggerian conceptualization of Being and *Dasein*'s proximate relatedness to Being in order to accept the hermeneutic account of understanding and the essence of truth as *aletheia*.

It might be objected at the outset that Gadamer's is a theory of textual interpretation, not a theory of knowledge. But Richard Palmer, Richard Rorty, Joel Weinsheimer, Richard Bernstein, and Charles Taylor have argued that Gadamer's theory is universally applicable to all inquiry, and not just to inquiry into the meaning of texts. I would add that Gadamer's arguments are often excluded from epistemology only because of an excessively narrow and dogmatic account of the necessary presuppositions for epistemology, and that this account ends up begging the question against Gadamer's counterarguments. That is, the fact that Gadamer's theory of understanding eschews method, correspondence, or an intrinsic conception of truth, meaning, and reality cannot mean that it is not a theory of knowledge at all, if Gadamer proposes alternative views about the nature of inquiry, as I argue he does. If we can define epistemology as a discipline that asks and answers questions about the possibility of knowledge, truth, and justified beliefs, and as a project that does not merely describe processes of inquiry but offers an evaluation of them, then it is clear that Gadamer does have an epistemology, or it will become clear by the end of this chapter. I shall address the issue of the universalizability of Gadamer's theory of knowledge later on, because the issues involved in that debate will only become clear once we see how he develops his account.

## Gadamer's Concept of Justification

The object of justification for Gadamer is interpretation rather than belief. Is this more than a terminological point, and could these two terms have the same referents? Gadamer's decision to focus on interpretation, a

---

1. See Francis J. Ambrosio, "Dawn and Dusk: Gadamer and Heidegger on Truth," *Man and World* 19 (1986): 21–53, for a useful discussion of Gadamer's and Heidegger's differences.

term which for him always connotes understanding and application as well, obviously follows from his project to develop a theory of philosophical hermeneutics, which was formulated initially as a theory of interpretation. However, whereas predecessors like Dilthey and Schleiermacher approached hermeneutics as a methodology for uncovering the historical contexts of ancient texts, Gadamer develops hermeneutics as a philosophy of understanding. Within hermeneutics traditionally understood, beliefs we develop about the meaning of a text never result from a mere appropriation of the text's intrinsic meaning; they are always based on an interaction between text and reader, between its horizon and our own. What Gadamer adds to this is the claim that *all* understanding is achieved through just such a fusion of horizons within language. Given this, all understanding can be modeled after the process of interpreting a text. Therefore, the unit to be justified can be represented by the term "interpretation" rather than the term "belief" without implying that the analysis is applicable only in the restricted case of textual interpretations.

In the English translation of *Wahrheit und Methode*, the central terms "interpretation" and "understanding" figure in a similar way as do the terms "belief" and "knowledge" in Anglo-American epistemology. All understanding requires or involves interpretation, just as all knowledge requires or involves belief. Like belief, interpretation can be justified, unjustified, or partially justified, whereas understanding, like knowledge, is either achieved or not. We do not speak of justified or true knowledge or justified or true understanding because these would be redundant expressions.

In Gadamer's philosophical hermeneutics, coherence is involved in the justification of interpretations in two ways: in the actual procedure consciously used by the knower and in the implicit effect of the background meanings or tradition. I will call the first of these Gadamer's procedural argument for coherence and the second his ontological argument. Gadamer's account of justification needs to be understood within the context of his critique of "false methodologism." Much of *Truth and Method* is taken up by this thesis: that we in the twentieth century overemphasize the importance of methodology and exaggerate the extent to which we can exert control over the processes by which we come to know. There are no methodological principles by which we can purify our reason of its prejudices or transcend history and location. Gadamer sees the pursuit of method as based on the belief that, prior to inquiry, we can set out the steps of understanding. Although Gadamer believes that no such a priori method is available, he does attempt to describe the process by which justified interpretations are produced, and we can discern a coherentist movement in his account of both this process and the structure of understanding itself.

What consequences for understanding follow from the fact that belonging to a tradition is a condition of hermeneutics? We recall the hermeneutical rule that we must understand the whole in terms of the detail and the detail in terms of the whole. . . . We know this from learning ancient languages. We learn that we must "construe" a sentence before we attempt to understand the linguistic meaning of the individual parts of the sentence. But the process of construal is itself already governed by an expectation of meaning that follows from the context of what has gone before. It is of course necessary for this expectation to be adjusted if the text calls for it. . . . Thus the movement of understanding is constantly from the whole to the part and back to the whole. Our task is to extend the unity of the understood meaning centrifugally. The harmony of all the details with the whole is the criterion of correct understanding. The failure to achieve this harmony means that understanding has failed.[2]

The process of interpretation consists in the attempt to achieve (1) a coherent reading of the text and (2) the reading that establishes the most comprehensive coherence possible, or that includes as much of the text as possible in its account. Our prior expectations of meaning move back and forth from part to whole in a process of revising and re-revising until both parts and whole are understood in the maximally unified and harmonious way. This goal of maximum comprehensive coherence is the epistemic criterion for an adequate understanding. Thus the test of validity, or criterion of justification, that will be used to evaluate an interpretation is its achievement of coherence. But why should the knower give such priority to the criterion of coherence? Moreover, why should we strive to interpret a text as coherently as possible—what connection does that have to *epistemic* justification?

Gadamer argues that when we begin to read a book, say *The Phenomenology of Spirit*, we come to it with certain preconceptions about its meaning, the significance of its content, and the position it occupies within a larger debate before we ever set eyes on the first page. Even if we have only the foggiest notion of who G. W. F. Hegel was, we approach his text with a body of fore-meanings (Heidegger's term) or prejudgments. Some prejudgments will be operative even if we know absolutely nothing about the text itself or its author before commencing to read it: we then approach it with fore-meanings and prejudices out of our own historical horizon, standpoint, and situation. We might have certain pre- or semiconscious attitudes toward the text simply because it is written by a German, or be-

2. Hans-Georg Gadamer, *Truth and Method*, 2d rev. ed., rev. trans. Joel Weinsheimer and Donald G. Marshall (New York: Crossroad Press, 1989), p. 291. Hereafter quotations from this text will be cited in parentheses after the quotation.

cause it was written by a male, or because we find the title presumptuous or obscure. We approach texts as full human beings with historical specificity and, therefore, with a set of prejudices. These prejudices are variable: we will not bring the same set to every text. Which prejudices will become operable will depend on the elements we can discern about the text itself. In this case, for example, we could assume that German philosophy is profound, or that anything written in the nineteenth century has a depth unknown in the work of our contemporaries, or that this work at least has a certain presumption in its favor because it was written by a European man. These prejudgments need not be consciously articulated to be operative. Thus, before we have read the first page there has already occurred an interaction between reader and text which begins the process of producing meaning.

Understanding a text does not require ridding ourselves of the prejudicial influences of these fore-meanings. It *could* not require this, both because we cannot transcend the human condition of historical locatedness into a neutral standpoint without presuppositions and because, if we could erase all fore-meanings, we would then no longer be able to understand anything. Gadamer stresses that understanding is possible only because fore-meanings exist between every text and reader; a shared sphere out of which differences can be discerned. Just as we come to the text with a horizon, so too the text itself has a horizon of fore-meanings and presumptions embedded within it. The notion that a text itself can be said to have a horizon will require some discussion further on, but here we can simply note its implications for Gadamer's account of justification.

Gadamer's argument for the necessity of shared fore-meanings is reminiscent of Wittgenstein's discussion of ostensive definitions. According to Wittgenstein, ostensive definitions—which involve pointing to an object and repeating its name—rely for their success on a host of unspoken assumptions. If I see a Martian standing in my garden pointing to a tomato and uttering the sound "dervit" I am not justified in surmising that "dervit" means tomato unless I know that the Martian is pointing and not stretching her finger, that she is pointing to the tomato and not the tomato plant or row of plants, and that she is indicating a type of vegetable rather than its color, stage of ripeness, shape, or some other feature. Wittgenstein suggests that unspoken assumptions underlie the success of any ostensive definition and make up part of our culturally specific language game, involving gesture as well as linguistic utterance. W. V. O. Quine also argues that whether someone is pointing to a rabbit or a temporally specific rabbit-stage cannot be determined by simply observing with care what is being pointed at. These arguments are similar to Gadamer's argument that understanding something new begins not with a blank slate and a new text, but with a set of fore-meanings that precede an approach to the text, or with a prearranged structure within which the text is placed.

Despite his focus on the inescapability of prejudice, Gadamer warns that:

> If we examine the situation more closely, however, we find that meanings cannot be understood in an arbitrary way. . . . We cannot stick blindly to our own fore-meaning about the thing if we want to understand the meaning of another. Of course this does not mean that when we listen to someone or read a book we must forget all our fore-meanings concerning the content and all our own ideas. All that is asked is that we remain open to the meaning of the other person or text. But this openness always includes our situating the other meaning in relation to the whole of our meanings or ourselves in a relation to it. (*TM* 268)

Acknowledging the inescapability of our own prejudgments does not, therefore, entail a subjectivist account of interpretation. As an antidote to such subjectivism, Gadamer suggests that if we use the I/Thou relation as a model we will achieve epistemic success as well as an ethical mode of knowing. There are three possible modes of knowing the other, Gadamer tells us, whether the other is another person, a tradition, a natural object, or a single text: (1) treating the other as an object, that is, as predictable and devoid of its own horizon of meanings; (2) claiming to know the other in advance, prior to any contact; and (3) approaching with openness to the other as a Thou, while maintaining an awareness of one's own prejudices (*TM* 359–62). The first mode is typical in the natural sciences. The second mode is characteristic of an authoritarian attitude which would presume to know the welfare of another before asking them. Gadamer accepts neither of these modes as defensible even in specialized spheres. Understanding will be achieved only with the third mode, in which one puts aside the arrogance of believing in one's own epistemic invincibility and accepts a more humble position, acknowledging one's own limits and the need to learn from the other.

Having an open epistemic attitude involves three elements. The first element is to become as aware as possible of our prejudices (*TM* 269). The entire horizon of prejudgments we bring with us can never become perspicuous in all of its contours, but we can develop a partial awareness of it, the first step toward which is of course to acknowledge its existence. The main way in which we can increase our awareness of our prejudices is to develop the second element, which involves being "sensitive to the text's alterity" (*TM* 269). This alterity is ontologically dependent on our prejudices, since the text is only foreign in as much as it differs from our previous conceptions of it. Thus, it is through contact with difference that our prejudices become visible; the alterity or difference of the text, what Gadamer calls its otherness, creates a standard by which we can become aware of our deepest and least questioned assumptions. The third element required for an open epistemic attitude is that, in light of the text, we should be willing to revise our prejudices. This is what Gadamer means when he counsels us to be open to the truth of the text—not simply to its intelligibility, but to its truth.

In this elucidation of openness, Gadamer evokes a dialectical or interactive picture of a process involving both reader and text. Reading a text involves a back-and-forth motion, a play, between the fore-meanings that we ascribe to the text and the text itself. The play gradually develops until we have achieved an interpretation that transcends the limits of our fore-meanings, although they are never left behind entirely. This movement or play must, however, be directed or guided in some way—Gadamer insists that its direction is not arbitrary—and what guides it is the impetus toward coherence. Reading a text involves a constant process of revision, in which both our fore-meanings and provisional interpretation are revised in light of further reading. This revising is guided by the desire to establish the maximum internal coherence of the text and the maximum coherence between the text and our interpretation. If the continued acceptance of a given prejudgment creates incoherence or reduces coherence, it must be discarded. For example, if that Martian in my garden goes on to point to a caterpillar and repeats the word "dervit," I must develop a new interpretation of her behavior. Perhaps she is pointing out things that are alive, or things that are in a garden, or things that she eats. The particular hypotheses I consider will be determined by their ability to preserve the coherence of her behavior.

As we shall see in the next chapter, the argument Gadamer makes in defense of the coherence criterion is analogous to the one that Donald Davidson advances for the necessity of maximizing comprehensive coherence in order to effect a radical translation. It may seem counterintuitive to suggest that the most valid meaning of a text is always the one that maximizes the text's comprehensive coherence, for surely we can imagine texts that are simply incoherent. One might ask, what if the true meaning of a certain text is that it is incoherent or even meaningless? We must remember here that for Gadamer there is no uniquely true, intrinsic meaning of a text, and thus he cannot be required to show that the assumption of coherence will always pick out that one true meaning. In the absence of an intrinsic meaning, Gadamer's defense of coherence might be read (as Bernstein reads it, for example) as an argument based on pragmatism: coherence is the criterion that will maximize a text's sense for us, and is it not pragmatically desirable to increase our understanding of a text rather than decrease it?

But does this argument validate coherence as an *epistemically* significant criterion of justification? In other words, does it demonstrate a link between coherence and truth such that we have some reason to believe that maximizing coherence enhances the likelihood that the interpretation this criterion yields is true? Since this question involves the concept of truth, its answer will have to await our further development of Gadamer's theory of truth. For now we must simply note that in Gadamer's view coherence must be the principle criterion for judging adequate interpretations, given the inevitability of the role of fore-meanings in understanding and given the reciprocating nature of the revising process. As each new section of the text is read, we must be open to a revision of our interpretation in light of its ability to make the text coherent. The coherence of the text is thus a necessary and justifiable presupposition or working hypothesis, required for the interpretive process. Again, this argument resembles standard arguments in Anglo-American philosophy, particularly in the philosophy of science. We must assume there is regularity in the world in order to do science; we must assume the world can be made sense of before we attempt to make sense of it. Even inductive methods of reasoning cannot be absolutely justified, except by showing that it is necessary to assume that the future will be like the past in order to generate any explanatory and predictive theory.

Thus coherence figures into Gadamer's justification of interpretation in the actual process by which the knower develops an understanding of the text. The reader must consciously strive for an interpretation that makes the text maximally coherent. This is what I am calling Gadamer's procedural argument for coherence. But coherence also figures into interpretation in another way: through the effects of tradition and the background of common meanings shared within a social reality. This is Gadamer's ontological argument for coherence, and it will bring us to a greater appreciation of the historicized dimension of Gadamer's epistemology.

I have already discussed Gadamer's view that prejudices are always part of the process of understanding a text, and are in fact necessary if understanding is even to be possible. These prejudices, or prejudgments, are actually the means by which tradition is continued and preserved. All interpretations are historically specific and form part of the evolutionary continuum of a constantly reinterpreted tradition. One implication of this is that coherence is not merely a characterization of the process of interpreting a text, but also an ontological component of understanding. Gadamer's ontological claim is that understanding involves a mediation of elements. It is not possible for there to exist incommensurable, and therefore incoherent, interpretations of a tradition: radical differences will always contain commensurate elements. Moreover, it is also not possible for us to assume an independent position outside of the developing tradition. Let us recall how Gadamer describes our relationship to tradition: "Our usual relationship to the past is not characterized by distancing and freeing ourselves from tradition. Rather, we are always situated within traditions, and this is no objectifying process—i.e., we do not conceive of what tradition says as something other, something alien. It is always part of us, a model or exemplar" (*TM* 282).

We engage in the process of interpreting and understanding from within a tradition which is itself constantly in the process of revision. Because it is not possible to break totally free of this tradition, it is not possible to produce an understanding that is radically incoherent with it. This is not to say that tradition is static, that it never undergoes revision and change, and that our attitude toward it is thus never one of negation. It is to say that, even if our attitude is a negating one, it negates from the inside. It is impossible for us to stand outside the tradition and negate it in its entirety.[3]

The way in which this argument contributes toward a theory of epistemic justification may not become fully clear until we discuss Gadamer's ontology of truth. But I seek to demonstrate that because understanding is ontologically dependent on an evolving tradition, for Gadamer our beliefs subsist within an ever-evolving web of belief with no privileged, absolutely unrevisable core. This suggests that they cannot be represented by a pyramid schema that would rest all justified beliefs on some secure foundation. The process of evaluating interpretations involves establishing their coherence to a web of belief, a process that maintains tradition and the influence of prejudgments. To mix metaphors again, one might say that our raft is afloat within tradition, which Gadamer conceptualizes as a sea of possibilities.[4]

Gadamer's epistemology thus bears a striking resemblance to the coherence models of Quine, Nelson Goodman, and Thomas Kuhn, who likewise believe in systems of coherent beliefs (webs or worlds or paradigms, respectively) which serve as the tribunal to which new beliefs are subjected. The primary criterion of revision for both prejudices and the web of belief is coherence. Gadamer's advice to be "open to the alterity of the text" is like Quine's directive to be open to new experience: both counsel against a conservatism or antifallibilism which would slow down the evolutionary development of the web.

3. See Gadamer, *Truth and Method*, pp. 270–71, 276. This argument denies the possibility of a total skepticism in which we would doubt all of our beliefs at once. A similar argument is made by Ludwig Wittgenstein, *On Certainty*, trans. Dennis Paul and G. E. M. Anscombe (Oxford: Basil Blackwell, 1969).
4. See David Linge, introduction to *Philosophical Hermeneutics*, by Hans-Georg Gadamer (Berkeley: University of California Press, 1976), p. liv.

Another point of contact with Gadamer's views is the *positive* contribution such presuppositions and previously established tribunals are claimed to have on the production of knowledge. For example, Kuhn argues that paradigms do not play a merely distorting role, obscuring certain issues and dictating the range of acceptable hypotheses. Paradigms exert their peculiar power because of their generative capacity to *produce* a research agenda. On this sort of view, a process in which new accounts are epistemically evaluated according to their coherence to paradigms or traditions is not an unfortunate situation to which we must be resigned given our human limitations—it is what *makes possible* the achievement of knowledge.

At this point we need to return to some of the problems identified with this account that were raised in the last chapter. One such problem concerned whether we have any criteria with which to judge and evaluate those prejudices of which we can become aware. I have been arguing that Gadamer offers coherence as the principal criterion of justification for interpretations. Remember that the prejudices we bring with us to inquiry will become identifiable when an incoherence between a prejudgment and the text disrupts the smooth flow of reading and blocks the fusion of horizons that Gadamer calls understanding. Thus, only those prejudices that decrease the text's coherence will be identifiable.

Gadamer says that these prejudices—the ones that are identifiable—are precisely the ones we must be willing to revise because they block our ability to establish the text's meaning as comprehensively coherent. But should we always revise our prejudices whenever they conflict with a text? If not, how are we to decide when they should be revised and when they should be retained? As Georgia Warnke asks, "When do we give up the attempt to learn from *Mein Kampf?*"[5] The desire for an answer to such questions need not be based on the fetishizing of methodology. Quine tells us that such decisions should be based on whether the assumptions or beliefs in question are in the core or periphery of our web of belief. Kuhn advocates using the criterion of maximizing problem-solving ability to revise assumptions. Gadamer provides no guidance at all.[6]

5. Georgia Warnke, *Gadamer: Hermeneutics, Tradition, and Reason* (Stanford: Stanford University Press, 1987), p. 90.
6. Thomas Kuhn, *The Structure of Scientific Revolutions*, 2d ed. (Chicago: University of Chicago Press,1970); W. V. O. Quine, *From a Logical Point of View* (Harvard University Press, 1953). There is reason to believe, however, that Gadamer does not think revision of prejudice in favor of a text's increased coherence should always win out. The thrust of Gadamer's work is toward the revalidation of tradition and an openness to the possibility of truth even in ancient texts. Gadamer sees this as a necessary corrective to the modern Enlightenment prejudice going in the opposite direction, which maligns tradition and presumes

Still, Gadamer gives us coherence as the criterion with which to evaluate prejudice, though he is vague in explaining exactly how it is to be used. The unit whose coherence requires maximization is not simply an isolated text, but the continuum of interpretations or fusions we know as tradition. This means that when we interpret *Mein Kampf*, what is at stake is not simply the plausibility of Hitler's perspective on his life and society, but our understanding of how we and Hitler can exist along the same continuum and partake in the same, however evolving, cultural and social traditions. The use of coherence as a criterion of valid interpretation is motivated by Gadamer's desire to emphasize our commonality with the past. This suggests that perhaps the easy self-satisfaction we may achieve by denying any commonality with *Mein Kampf* is less valid than a recognition that there are elements in common between our respective horizons. This recognition may serve better political ends than any smug denials, in revealing anti-Semitic or profascist elements which have persisted in our own fore-knowledges.

Does this account allow for the possibility of progress in understanding? Can we say that inquiry is progressing if it is merely an evolving process of establishing coherence between historical horizons? On the face of it, it is difficult to see how the mere establishment of coherence between one's prior assumptions and a text can have epistemic significance. An insistence on the historical finiteness of understanding and the use of coherence alone as the criterion of validity seem to lead inevitably toward relativism, antirealism, or even skepticism. We must be wary, however, of begging the question against Gadamer by posing questions and problems that presuppose an Enlightenment or positivist framework. If we see prejudice as only capable of distorting inquiry, or if our desire to believe in progress determines what theory of understanding sounds plausible, then we are letting our own prejudgments dictate the meaning of Gadamer's text, without being open to their revision. On the other hand, it would be self-contradictory for Gadamer to oppose Anglo-American philosophers for raising such queries, since such concerns reflect their own historical horizon and their attempts to apply Gadamer to their own theoretical context. We should keep these issues in mind as our own horizon is tested in an analysis of Gadamer's theory of truth, rather than let Anglo-American prejudices serve as indefeasible objections to his theory.

---

against the validity of ancient texts. Thus, whereas the Enlightenment would favor (in Gadamer's terminology) holding onto present prejudices against the claims of a text, Gadamer promotes revising prejudice in favor of the text. Since the latter pull is characterized as a corrective, however, it seems plausible that Gadamer wants to bring the two into balance, rather than replace one with the other. This does not, of course, solve the problem I am raising about the need for guidance in determining when to revise prejudices.

## Gadamer and Epistemology

My basic argument has been that Gadamer's concept of how an interpretation is justified relies principally and fundamentally on considerations of comprehensive coherence. The use of the criterion of coherence is given pragmatic justification by the claims that there is no intrinsic meaning within the text and hence that a procedure of interpretation cannot ensure discovery of such a meaning. The argument has four steps. (1) There is no uniquely true meaning intrinsic to the text. (2) Therefore, ascertaining this meaning cannot be the criterion of a good procedure for interpretation (or meaning-acquisition). (3) This allows us to move to a pragmatic approach in choosing a criterion of interpretation. (4) Maximizing the comprehensive coherence of a text is the pragmatically optimal criterion of interpretation in that it maximizes the intelligibility of the text. A pragmatic rendering of Gadamer's argument would be misleading, however, if it implied that meaning is an arbitrary invention constructed solely from the subjective consciousness of the reader (conceived as an autonomous and independent consciousness). A justified interpretation of a text will bring together into a coherent whole the various constitutive elements of meaning: horizons of past and present, text and reader. Coherence figures into the procedure of interpretation which Gadamer argues the reader should and in fact must use for understanding to occur, and coherence figures into the ontology of the *event* of understanding, the ontological background upon which justification occurs.

What is the relationship between this theory of justification as it applies to the interpretation of texts and the more general theories of justification in Anglo-American epistemology? In the latter context, justification is normally approached as a theory of the procedure or method for forming, confirming, and revising beliefs. Actually existing doxastic practices generate beliefs in any number of ways: the purpose of a theory of justification is to identify epistemically reliable beliefs as well as processes for generating beliefs. Some epistemologists insist that justification entails the believer's conscious use of dependable processes; this position is known as internalism. The intuition here is that if a process confers justification on a belief but the believer does not know that this process is operative, it seems wrong to say that the believer is justified. Other epistemologists argue that all we need for justification is to establish the belief's connection to truth; this is known as externalism. The intuition here is that the main reason to have a theory of justification is to show how a belief is true or likely to be true, and unless a theory of justification provides a link to truth, it cannot serve as an *epistemological* justification for a belief.

The discussion about justification among Anglo-American epistemologists can be divided along these lines, and the concerns of both positions need to be addressed in a complete theory of justification. Without a link to truth it is unclear what epistemic benefit a justification-conferring property could bestow on a belief. Yet if justification is completely external to and independent of the believer's awareness, it seems counterintuitive to say that the believer is justified in holding that belief.

Gadamer's theory of philosophical hermeneutics addresses both of these tasks, through his procedural and ontological arguments for coherence. The procedural argument pays attention to the interpreter's conscious actions, while the ontological argument conceptualizes how an interpretation is linked to the true. It is obvious throughout, however, that Gadamer wishes to emphasize the second task. Thus, the body of his work resembles to a much greater extent externalist theories of justification, and might in fact be classified as an externalist account.

Gadamer himself is as confused about his relationship to Anglo-American epistemology as Anglo-American epistemologists are about his work and its irrelevance to their concerns. For example, throughout *Truth and Method*, Gadamer emphasizes that his is a descriptive rather than a prescriptive agenda.[7] He seems to believe that philosophers of science and epistemologists try to articulate an ideal and abstract method of inquiry. His agenda, in contrast he thinks, is to describe the process of inquiry in the sciences as it actually *occurs*: "In other words, I consider the only scientific thing is *to recognize what is*, instead of starting from what ought to be or could be. Hence I am trying to go beyond the concept of method held by modern science (which retains its limited justification) and to envisage in a fundamentally universal way what *always* happens" (*TM* 512). Gadamer is referring here to Anglo-American epistemology and philosophy of science, but he misdescribes the project of those disciplines. They aim not to tell scientists what correct methodology to use, but to explain why the method used in science yields truth. This project corresponds to the externalist task in theories of justification, to Kant's project in the first *Critique*, and to the focus of Gadamer's *Truth and Method*. Thus, Gadamer's belief that his nonprescriptive approach to inquiry demarcates his work from Anglo-American theories of knowledge is quite mistaken. If his is primarily an externalist theory of justification, then it is a theory which links justification to truth-conduciveness. In the next section we will explore just what Gadamer means by "truth."

---

7. See, for example, Gadamer, *Truth and Method*, pp. xxiii, 512. In these passages Gadamer contrasts his view with "modern science," but given the context he can only mean philosophers of science or epistemologists of science.

## Gadamer's Concept of Truth

Though truth figures prominently in the title of Gadamer's text, it is an elusive concept within. In this section I try to explicate this term in Gadamer's usage "as far as the subject matter permits," as Kant might counsel. Gadamer holds that there are three distinct forms of knowledge: the scientific knowledge of nature (which is based primarily on sensory experience), moral rational knowledge, and aesthetic knowledge (*TM* 97–98). Each of these forms conveys truth. Moreover, the sensory knowledge so important for the sciences is itself mediated, not an automatic response to stimuli as in the mechanistic model of sensation adopted by Kant and the positivist empiricists (*TM* 65). Gadamer takes from Dilthey the notion of *Erlebnis*, an account of experience which holds that even at its most basic perceptual level, experience is not devoid of meaning. Thus, the primary units of scientific knowledge are simultaneously units of sensation and units of an experience imbued with meaning. This view already suggests that the natural sciences are not ontologically prior in any way to the human sciences, and that they do not achieve an ontologically simpler, more direct form of knowledge. It also suggests that a reductionist program that would reduce other forms of knowledges to knowledge in the natural sciences is mistaken. We must keep this meaningful character of sensory experience in mind when we consider whether Gadamer's concept of truth is objectivist.

Before we move to that issue, we must look at Gadamer's argument for the assumption of truth. We have already seen how Gadamer argues that in the process of interpreting a text we are required to assume from the outset its coherence in order to check our fore-judgments, to have a standard for revision, and to achieve the most adequate and comprehensive understanding. We must also assume its truth. "Since we are now concerned not with individuality and what it thinks but with the truth of what is said, a text is not understood as a mere expression of life, but is taken seriously in its claim to truth. That this is what is meant by 'understanding' was once self-evident" (*TM* 297). Gadamer repeatedly admonishes us to be "open" to what the text "says to us," that is, to presume from the outset its truthfulness. Ontologically, such openness involves, as in Heidegger, the notion of clearing a space, making an opening, in which the truth of the text can reveal itself. This requires a kind of passiveness, a suspension of assessment and categorization, so that the newness and difference of the text will not be obscured totally by our prior judgments. But the motivation to clear an open space must come, not from a prior judgment, but from a prior assumption that the text's claim to truth must be taken seriously.

Gadamer's reasoning here for assuming truth parallels his argument for assuming coherence. If one does not assume the truth of the text, one has no standards of interpretation, no reason to discard an initial prejudice that makes the text appear false, and no means of deciding between alternate interpretations. Gadamer implies that if we do not assume the text's truth or adopt an attitude of openness toward it, we cut off the possibility of understanding it at all. If we assume the truth of the text, if we take its claim to truth seriously (and what text does *not* make a claim to truth, however indirectly?) then we will seek an interpretation that maximizes the plausibility of the text's claims. In some sense Gadamer's maxim here amounts to giving the text an epistemic benefit of the doubt, or practicing an epistemic charity. This approach does not require that we continue to accept the text's claim to truth throughout the entire process of interpretation. If we presume truth and coherence as a working hypothesis in the interpretation, but the text fails to achieve any plausibility, then we are justified in discarding this hypothesis or modifying it. Certainly our conclusion that the text's claims are largely erroneous will be more persuasive after we have practiced epistemic charity than if we had come to the same conclusion after a process of interpretation in which we initially did not take the text's claim to truth as a serious and sincere claim.

The requirement that we assume truth, however, or that we try to maximize the truth of a text in our interpretation of it, does not yet explain what exactly it is we are assuming when we assume a text to be true. We still do not know what Gadamer means by "truth." When he writes, "We are now concerned not with individuality and what it thinks but with the truth of what is said" (*TM* 297), the "individuality" he is referring to is the subjective intention of the author of a text. Gadamer's point is that hermeneutic understanding does not seek the meaning of a text within the subjective understanding of the author. The true meaning of a text transcends this in every case. The meaning of a text results from an interaction between it and an interpreter, in which the text is applied to a particular historical context. It emerges from an open space cleared by the reader in which the text's substance can present itself. The meaning of a text is not arbitrary, subjective, or relative, and there is only one true meaning for each such interaction. The *true* meaning will be found through careful attention to the text's claim to coherence and truth, and will consist of the most comprehensively coherent interpretation. Thus, it is possible for a given interpreter to be wrong, through sloppy reading or lack of attention to detail, and it is reasonable to assume that in every specific case, there will be a unique best interpretation.

Now this uniquely best interpretation is obviously indexical rather than universal, and therefore not generalizable. The historical specificity of all interpretation yields an indexical account of truth. My interpretation of Jean-Paul Sartre's *La Nausée* may be the most comprehensively coherent and therefore the uniquely true interpretation of *La Nausée*, but it is uniquely true *for* the particular and historically specific elements involved in the interpretation at the time I make it. Thus five years from now I may make a very different interpretation of *La Nausée*, and my interpretation may again be true, true for the specific elements involved in the interpretation at that later time. This may seem counterintuitive. After all, is it not likely that my interpretation of *La Nausée* now, after I have taught the text for several years and studied more of Sartre, is better than the initial interpretation I developed as an undergraduate? As a practical matter, how can I justify my criticisms of students' papers on this text if we relativize all interpretations?

First of all, Gadamer is not relativizing all interpretations. If I critique student papers on the grounds that their interpretation of *La Nausée* did not take into account its relationship to another text by Sartre that I did not assign or discuss in class, this is hardly a justifiable method of evaluating their interpretations. On the other hand, I can reasonably critique their papers on the grounds that they do not take into account all of the elements of the texts we have read together, thus using Gadamer's coherentist criterion to judge the adequacy of their interpretation. But the criteria we use to judge student papers may not have any necessarily epistemic relevance, since we may not be judging the truth of their interpretation so much as their ability to develop an argument or explore a philosophical problem.

Consider other sorts of interpretive differences. When I first read *La Nausée*, its misogynistic portrayals of women went unnoticed and unremarked, either by my professor or by myself. Today these themes stand out and I insist on addressing them in class discussions. Would not my feminist inclinations motivate me to say that the interpretation I now have is epistemically better? There are two possible answers. On the one hand, as I have said, Gadamer is not relativizing all interpretations or suggesting that all interpretations are equally adequate or justifiable. Suppose the misogynist metaphors and sexist assumptions of a philosophical text are treated as unfortunate digressions irrelevant to any serious issues the author was addressing. Judged by the criterion of comprehensive coherence, such an interpretation would be deemed less justifiable than an interpretation that took all of the text's components into account. Thus a feminist could apply Gadamer's criterion more broadly to philosophy classrooms and philosophical scholarship, showing that the common tendency to dismiss "lapses" of fairmindedness in our canonical texts is unjustifiable, or perhaps indicative of a shared set of prejudgments between readers and texts.

On this first answer, then, Gadamer's account of interpretation might be used without contradiction to justify my later interpretation of *La Nausée* as superior to my former one.

On the other hand, or in another case, a second answer might be more appropriate. If there is no single true interpretation of a text across historical and cultural contexts or horizons, then we need not repudiate former interpretations as a necessary prerequisite before we can justify later interpretations. We need not, for example, repudiate Augustine's reading of Plato in order to argue for our (different) reading of Plato, because the two are not in competition. The justifiability of Augustine's reading should be judged in accordance with his historical horizon. This does not imply that if Augustine's reading of Plato is found to have merit, that we must then adopt it in place of our own or any other. New considerations which we may wish to bring to bear on Plato's texts, such as issues of class, are legitimate within Gadamer's account of interpretation as involving application and the fusion of horizons, and will most likely yield new meanings in our context. Thus, here we might want to say that both Augustine's and Elizabeth Spelman's interpretations of Plato are justified, even though they are different, and that Spelman's does not negate Augustine's. To the extent we share Spelman's horizon, however, her reading will be a more adequate one than Augustine's writings can provide us today. The indexical status of the truth-value of interpretations means that we must accept a plurality of justified interpretations, but it also allows us to make evaluative discriminations within this plurality based on contextual considerations.

An indexical account of truth, expressed sometimes as "true for," is applicable to all cases in which unspecified temporal and subject or object references are made. For example, the truth of the proposition "I am now sitting down" must be indexed to a particular "I" and "now," and the truth of the proposition "This chair is broken" must be indexed to a particular chair. These simple examples reveal that the concept of indexical truth involves both objectivity and relativism, since a statement's truth-value is relative to a particular speaker at a particular time, and yet the truth of the proposition is not subjective or arbitrary but quite objective. Objectivity of truth does not, therefore, require universality or the generalized applicability of a claim across temporal or spatial variables.

Gadamer's concept of truth is indexical in this sense. The proposition "The Alcoff interpretation of *La Nausée* is true" is an objectively determinable proposition *and* specific to a finite range of elements involving the interpreter and the text. One interesting question about such a view is whether the truth-value of an interpretation is intersubjectively determinable, as I seemed to imply in the above discussion. Can anyone determine whether or not the Alcoff, Spelman, or Augustine interpretations are true? The answer to this question will depend on whether the horizons, prejudgments, and contexts of particular interpreters can be discerned by others, since these elements are constitutive of the truth-value of any interpretation. Gadamer does not provide answers to these questions, nor does he delineate the degree of specificity of an indexical claim to truth. We know that for Gadamer the claim to truth is specific to certain elements, but we do not know *how* specific or limited the range of such truth is—whether, for instance, it can include several individuals or be ascertained by others besides the interpreter herself.

Another issue to consider is whether Gadamer means for the concept of truth to apply to a single interpretation of a text or to the evolving continuum of interpretations of a given text. On this point Gadamer says the following: "The discovery of the true meaning of a text or a work of art is never finished; it is in fact an infinite process. Not only are fresh sources of error constantly excluded, so that all kinds of things are filtered out that obscure the true meaning; but new sources of understanding are continually emerging that reveal unsuspected elements of meaning" (*TM* 298). In this passage truth refers to an infinite process of interpretation, a process that subsumes within itself the successive singular interpretations made at specific historical moments by specific readers. But it is not the case that just any interpretation can be included in the process which is called "true." Only the best interpretations, defined as the most comprehensively coherent in light of all the relevant elements involved, should be included in the chain of interpretations making up this process. It would seem that these best interpretations should be called true if they contribute to the infinite process of discovering the true meaning of a text. On the other hand, we may want to say that only the infinite process deserves the claim to truth, since it is more comprehensive than any single interpretation. Gadamer's own writings are ambiguous on this point.

There is no necessary incompatibility between labeling the process true and labeling the individual interpretations true, so one resolution to this problem might be to assert that both can be so labeled. In each case truth refers to something different, but given that Gadamer's truth is indexical, the ensuing relativity is not a problem. The truth of an individual interpretation depends on the relevant elements involved. If some one were to ask, "What is the true meaning of the text in relation to elements $x$, $y$, and $z$?" we could answer with a given interpretation and this interpretation would have a specific truth-value. Now, what if someone were to ask, "What is the true meaning of the text in relation to all possible historical horizons?" Or simply, "What is the true meaning of the text?" without specifying a limited range of application. Here we should answer, according to Gadamer, that "the true meaning of the text" refers to the infinite process of interpretations. In both cases the criterion of truth for Gadamer is comprehensive coherence, but this criterion can be applied to a single interpretation or to the process that includes succeeding interpretations. Thus "the unit of truth" for Gadamer need not refer to the individual interpretation or to the process of interpretations: it can refer to both. Moreover, it can refer to both cases without losing the indexical property outlined earlier.

We have established that Gadamer's concept of truth is indexical and therefore relative (or specific) to a certain collection of elements, and that its criterion is comprehensive coherence. Now is this concept a coherentist one or a correspondence one? The fact that Gadamer's concept of truth is indexical and unique to specific elements suggests that it might be interpreted as a correspondence theory and does not automatically fall into the coherence camp. For a true interpretation is the one that corresponds, one might say, to the true meaning given the specific elements involved. Moreover, Gadamer says that the movement of truth is determined by the activity of the thing itself rather than the conscious choices of the knower, and that truth asserts itself, that it is evident or lit up (*TM* 485–86). Such notions of truth as a kind of disclosedness or *aletheia* seem perfectly compatible with correspondence accounts that would define truth as a correct match between belief (or interpretation) and the thing itself.

The correspondence theory of truth is typically associated with the belief that the object of truth is an independent reality, or a reality independent of human interpretation. But Gadamer, as we have seen, rejects the claim that the object of inquiry is a thing-in-itself, ontologically separate from knowers. All that is strictly required by the correspondence theory of truth, however, is that there exist a reality conceptually distinct from the body of cognitive propositions such that we can distinguish between true and false propositions by their correspondence, or lack thereof, to that reality. Correspondence theories of truth have been linked to foundationalist epistemologies and realist metaphysics, but this relationship is historical rather than conceptual, and thus is not exclusive.[8] Nonfoundationalist proponents of correspondence include (arguably) Kant, Rorty, Laurence BonJour, Davidson, and Nicholas Rescher. The notion of correspondence is sufficiently vague and ambiguous that it has no necessary link to foundationalism. Its connection to realism seems less arbitrary, given its need to establish a distinct reality as discussed above, but even here the varieties of realist metaphysics indicate the plasticity of correspondence rather than its rigidity. For example, correspondence figures in Kant's theory of truth as a relation between propositions and phenomenal reality, which is not inde-

8. See, for example, Michael Devitt's attempt to disassociate realism from semantic correspondence in *Realism and Truth*, 2d ed. (Oxford: Basil Blackwell, 1991).

pendent of human interpretation. The variability possible in the correspondence theory seems to allow us to characterize Gadamer's conception of truth as a correspondence one. We could say, for example, that there is a true interpretation of *La Nausée* given my historical horizon and application, and through the process of establishing comprehensive coherence and revising my prejudgments I can discover this true interpretation, in which case my belief in the Alcoff interpretation will correspond to the true interpretation or it will not.

In my view, however, such an interpretation of Gadamer's account of truth would be a mistake. For Gadamer the true interpretation of a text is the one that is the most comprehensive and makes the most sense of it, that is, the interpretation that establishes the most comprehensively coherent fusion between the horizons of text and reader. What best captures this idea is not truth as correspondence but truth as coherence. Consider the following passages:

> Inasmuch as the actual object of historical understanding is not events but their "significance," it is clearly an incorrect description of this understanding to speak of an object existing in itself and of the subject's approach to it. The truth is that historical understanding always implies that the tradition reaching us speaks into the present and must be understood in this mediation—indeed, *as* this mediation. (*TM* 328)

> Neither is the mind of the interpreter in control of what words of tradition reach him, nor can one suitably describe what occurs here as the progressive knowledge of what exists. . . . [The knower is not] seeking an object, "discovering" by methodological means what was really meant and what the situation actually was, though slightly hindered and affected by his own prejudices. . . . But the actual occurrence [of understanding] is made possible only because the word that has come down to us as tradition and to which we are to listen really encounters us and does so as if it addressed us and is concerned with us. (*TM* 461)

The idea of correspondence entails the existence of two separate entities that preexist their encounter and that can then enjoy a correspondence relation. The separate elements involved in correspondence theories are most often a proposition and a fact in the world. It may be the case that there is a causal connection between the proposition, when it is a belief, and the fact in the world, but the two are nevertheless distinct and separable. One thinks of a mind-independent reality with a fact true about it and a knower who holds a propositional belief trying to attach this to the world or gauge its attachment. The knower and the propositional belief are on one side,

and the fact in the world and the human-independent reality are on another, and truth ensues whenever there is a relation of correspondence between elements from different sides, however these sides are portrayed.

As the passages above reveal, this ontological picture is precisely the one
Gadamer wants to transcend. In his picture, the subject/object schism is replaced by an interactive model in which truth is conceived of as a "play"
or an "event" (*TM* 490). A true interpretation does not preexist the interaction between reader and text but *comes into existence in the event of interaction.*[9] The elements that interact to produce truth cannot be
ontologically identified prior to their interaction. "There is no question of
a self-conscious spirit without world which would have to find its way to
worldly being; both belong originally to each other. The relationship is primary" (*TM* 459).

Gadamer's ontology of truth must be distinguished therefore from the ontologies presupposed by most correspondence theories of truth, which are
committed to the existence of intrinsic features and things-in-themselves. It
would distort his account and mislead readers to call it a correspondence account, with correspondence's ontological baggage of intrinsicality. The fundamental criterion or prerequisite of truth is the coherence of elements
involved in the interactive process of understanding, not the attachment of
a proposition with the world.

### Subjectivist or Constructivist?

Despite Gadamer's emphasis on historicality, he does not wish to embrace a radical subjectivist or irrationalist theory of knowledge. I have tried
to take this aspiration seriously by interpreting his position as an indexical
theory of truth. In an indexical theory, however, truth must entail a certain
degree of relativism. A true interpretation is always only true for a certain
set of interactive elements; it is not generalizable. In this sense Bernstein is
incorrect when he asserts that Gadamer transcends objectivity and relativism; rather, he embraces both.

Gadamer's metaphysics of truth is not purely constructivist à la the work
of Peter Berger and Thomas Luckmann or the Strong Programme of sociology of knowledge developed by David Bloor and Barry Barnes.[10] These

9. Lawrence Schmidt also characterizes Gadamer's concept of truth as an experience of enlightening which collapses the subject/object distinction. See his "Das Einleuchtende: The Enlightening Aspect of the Subject Matter" (paper presented at the Conference of the Society for
Phenomenology and Existential Philosophy, Villanova University, October 1990).
10. Peter L. Berger and Thomas Luckmann, *The Social Construction of Reality* (Garden City,
New York: Doubleday, 1966); Barry Barnes, *Scientific Knowledge and Sociological Theory*
(London: Routledge and Kegan Paul, 1974); David Bloor, *Knowledge and Social Imagery*

views construe truth in the social sciences as determined principally and fundamentally by the community of knowers, and they refuse the evaluative distinction that epistemology would make between true and false beliefs. For them, both sorts of beliefs are subject to the same process of sociological analysis, which seeks to determine how believers actually come upon their beliefs and discounts the possibility that, sometimes, beliefs are generated because they are true.

*Truth and Method* seems to have been written in part for a particular audience: those twentieth-century thinkers who are arrogantly satisfied that the appropriation of reason and the method of science are all that is necessary for successful inquiry. Gadamer's goal appears to have been to persuade those readers that success in inquiry is principally caused by the continuous tradition of assumptions within which all inquirers operate. We must therefore remain open to what the ancient texts say to us and we must acknowledge our presumptive reliance on this continually evolving web of belief. This repeated invocation of the need to be open to the being or the truth of the text cannot be intelligibly construed as a constructivist theory of truth. The principal difference between Gadamer and the constructivists, however, is in ontology. For Gadamer the continuation of tradition produces success in inquiry not because human beings construct truth, but because truth is an event mediated by inquiry. Gadamer does not repudiate the existence of a human-independent reality, nor does he oppose the idea that this reality participates in the event of mediation and exerts constraints on the "true".

In Anglo-American epistemology, a false dilemma is too often posed between the metaphysics of intrinsic features and things-in-themselves on the one hand and the metaphysics of subjective idealism on the other. On the former view, true descriptions of entities reflect the inherent features of those entities as they exist in themselves apart from all possible contributions of human beings, whereas on the latter view, true descriptions are in some significant way dependent upon human constructions or those human categories that organize perception. The debate over coherence has largely been a debate over which of these metaphysics is entailed by coherentist epistemology. Opponents of coherentism have generally argued that there is no way coherentism can coexist with a realist metaphysics, which is often defined as coextensive with the metaphysics of intrinsicality. Advocates of coherentism have been left with the nearly impossible task of demonstrating that coherentism can be combined with such a meta-

---

(London: Routledge and Kegan Paul, 1976); Barry Barnes and David Bloor, "Relativism, Rationalism, and the Sociology of Knowledge," in *Rationality and Relativism*, ed. Martin Hollis and Steven Lukes (Cambridge: MIT Press, 1984).

physics.[11] These two alternatives do not, however, exhaust all possible ontologies of truth.

## Immanent Metaphysics

Gadamer's ontology of inquiry can be read as the development of a new metaphysics or ontology of truth, which might be called an immanent metaphysics. It poses an interaction between knower and known out of which truth is produced, and thus truth is immanent to the domain of lived reality rather than completely transcendental to any human practice or context. Because it posits a human-independent reality which exerts constraints on the "true," such that what is true is not arbitrary or under the complete control of the knower, Gadamer's account is not strictly subjectivist. But selection based on the knower's horizon goes on at every instant, as does an interaction with the knower, who is historically contextualized. In Kuhn's famous example of the astronomers before and after Herschel, each is constrained by the human-independent world to see an incandescent globule in the sky, and each is also directed by his respective paradigm to see that globule as a star or a planet. This means that our "true" propositions are neither wholly false nor wholly true in the sense of correspondence. To the extent that they are said to refer wholly to the human-independent reality, there is no absolute sense of correspondence. Of more concern to us is the mediated reality of the human context within which truth is an event. Let me develop this conception a bit further.

How would such a view apply to clear-cut propositions such as "This table is two meters long"? Is not the length in meters of this table an intrinsic fact about it? Even this, however, involves mediation since the unit of measurement is human-constructed. The case is even more obvious for such propositions as "Black holes exist," "Neutrinos are colored," "Electrons have no mass," "Capitalism oppresses large numbers of people," "Women have second-class status," and "All knowledge is expressible in propositional form." These claims are more clearly the product of interpretation, an interaction between theories and models constrained by independent reality. But the constraints reality offers allow for the play of selection. Gadamer's argument is that the particular selection we make will be connected in interesting ways to our historical context.

One possible way to understand Gadamer is to conceptualize knowledge as existing along a continuum from a human-independent reality to human

11. For example, the coherentism of Laurence Bonjour tries to establish that coherence will yield truth about things in themselves. See his *Structure of Empirical Knowledge* (Cambridge: Harvard University Press, 1985).

contexts. Particular propositions fall at particular points along this continuum, some closer to the human-independent reality and some closer to the human. Most of the really interesting propositions—the ones we fight about the most, the ones on the frontiers of the natural sciences, and perhaps the whole body of propositions in the social sciences—exist somewhere near the middle of the continuum, as products of an interaction between humans and world. The propositions on the frontiers of science exist near the middle because they are so highly theoretical: we must borrow heavily from our conceptual apparatus and theoretical commitments for their construction, and our perceptual data is heavily dependent on our experimental, conceptual, and theoretical constructs.

On this view, all knowledge is contextual to some degree and the truth of a proposition is never simply a matter of correspondence to human-independent reality. What are the implications of such a continuum of knowledge for the propensity of philosophers to base their epistemologies on propositions that express simple perceptual beliefs and that exist on or toward the human-independent end of the continuum? Such propositions guarantee that the resulting epistemologies will be applicable only within a relatively small range of propositions, and perhaps not applicable at all to any of the really interesting and troubling propositions. Such propositions as simple perceptual beliefs should therefore not be used as decisive test cases for fundamental questions in epistemology. Gadamer's epistemology, on the other hand, is focused toward the broad middle of the continuum of knowledge, that is, those beliefs in the human and social sciences.

To say that beliefs like "Capitalism oppresses large numbers of people" or even "Neutrinos are colored" are *approximations* of an intrinsic truth about reality because they are the product of interpretation would be misleading. For Gadamer there is no uniquely true interpretation that captures the intrinsic meaning of a text, and so there is no absolute standard by which approximations can be measured. There just *are* interpretations, or events of mediation. Instead of forcing all of our beliefs down toward the human-independent end of the continuum (or proving to ourselves that they reside there already), we should accept their position in the middle. Moreover, we should stop using only that end of the continuum as a test for epistemologies. Human-independent reality is not the only sharp and clear standard for demarcating acceptable and unacceptable interpretations, and in fact because of its inaccessibility and indeterminateness it may not be a useful standard of demarcation at all. The important point here is that when we say that propositions about a mediated reality are not discoveries about human-independent reality but interpretations open to practical judgment, we are not committed to saying that such propositions are arbitrarily selected. We can still devise criteria, standards, and methods for correctly generating propositions, though these methods may be historically bound, and the propositions that result will still be eligible for the honorific title of truth.

If we let go of the "discovering human-independent reality" conceptual picture, do we open a Pandora's box of subjectivism? Will foolproof arguments against racist genetic theories or other pernicious falsehoods no longer be possible? Such worries may be caused by the grip of the old metaphysics and its false dilemmas, and the unfamiliarity of the new. We can still argue against false truth-claims on epistemic grounds. On Gadamer's interactionist view, there is not an infinite number of ways to characterize an event (contra Goodman or the constructivists), but there is more than one. They will be constrained by reality but given form by the knower and by the historical context. Context may be seen as a particular level of conceptual and theoretical development—the knower will borrow from that context, or seek to transcend it, but ultimately be constrained within it. Thus truth, in the interactive sense, is contextual. Why must we reserve the term truth for intrinsic truth, for truth at the human-independent end of the continuum? This sketch of immanent metaphysics remains in need of further clarification and development. In the final chapter of this book I will return to the topic.

## Subjects and Objects

The notion that Gadamer's ontology of inquiry can be represented by the idea of a continuum contains an obvious problem. A continuum bounded on one end by the human horizon and on the other end by a human-independent reality seems to preserve the subject/object opposition that Gadamer wants to transcend. The two ends of the continuum, if they could be neatly designated as points or segments, would correspond to the traditional conception of subject and object. If this is the case, then a continuum model cannot be said to be an accurate represention of Gadamer's views, or to put it another way, it does not achieve a maximum level of comprehensive coherence since it contradicts one of Gadamer's central points.

Let us look at Gadamer's discussion of the subject/object separation again. He writes: "Our line of thought prevents us from dividing the hermeneutic problem in terms of the subjectivity of the interpreter and the objectivity of the meaning to be understood. This would be starting from a false antithesis that cannot be resolved even by recognizing the dialectic of subjective and objective. To distinguish between a normative function and a cognitive one is to separate what clearly belong together" (*TM* 311).

What Gadamer denies here is that meaning, as the goal of inquiry and the referent of "true," is an object. Meaning cannot be understood as objective or as an element intrinsic to a text. There can be no dialectical interplay between an interpreter and the intrinsic meaning of the text because there is no such intrinsic meaning. Likewise, there is no pure subject because the subject shares a common tradition with the text and cannot therefore be conceptualized as totally autonomous and apart, capable of complete freedom in choosing an attitude toward the text. This suggests that it is not the oppositional dichotomy of human/world that Gadamer wishes to transcend by rejecting the subject/object separation, *unless* the world is conceived as containing intrinsic *meaning*. For Gadamer meaning is not a feature of the world, but a feature that comes into existence through the fusion of its constituent elements. This is why he accepts Dilthey's conception of *Erlebnis*, which posits the most basic level of experience as containing meaning. Because Gadamer does not reject a human/world distinction, however, it remains consistent with his views to maintain that a continuum model fairly characterizes Gadamer's ontology of truth.

## Truth as Coherence

I hope I have established that Gadamer's account of truth is coherentist and connected to an immanent metaphysics. This does not solve all of the difficulties with Gadamer's epistemology, however, if we may judge by the history of criticism to which coherence theories have been subject. Coherentist epistemology has been attacked precisely for leading to coherence theories of truth, and two principal problems have been raised with such theories.[12] The first is that a coherence theory of truth entails antirealism and is therefore unacceptable. This criticism assumes that all realist ontologies of truth posit truth as referring to an intrinsic reality. I have argued that Gadamer rejects both of these ontologies of truth and forges a third: an interactionist ontology of truth which does not reject realism, but also does not posit truth as a property of an intrinsic reality. Gadamer's position may still be associated with an antirealism, however, if the latter is construed as a semantic theory about meaning.

The second problem with the coherence theory of truth is said to be that, because coherence cannot be established as a truth-conducive criterion of justification, those who want to adopt a coherentist account of justification are forced to tack on a coherence theory of truth as an ad hoc solution to

---

12. Ibid., pp. 88, 109, 158; Michael Williams, "Coherence, Justification, and Truth," *Review of Metaphysics* 34 (1980): 243–72.

this problem. Bonjour argues that coherence theories of truth must have independent arguments in their favor or be subject to this critique. Gadamer's work provides an example of such independent arguments. Given Bonjour's own metaphysical commitments, he may not be persuaded by Gadamer's arguments for an interactionist ontology of truth, but he must admit that the focus of Gadamer's work is to build this new ontology in its own right, and not simply to solve the problems involved in a coherence theory of justification. It is Gadamer's focus on the historical dimension of understanding that leads to his interactionist metaphysics and coherence theory of truth, rather than problems he has in justifying his coherence theory of justification. He is thus one of the few philosophers in the history of philosophy to have developed independent arguments for truth as coherence.

David Linge explains Gadamer's views on ontology as follows: "Like the game, the text or art work lives in its presentations. They are not alien or secondary to it but are its very being, as possibilities that flow from it. . . . The variety of performances or interpretations are not simply subjective variations of a meaning locked in subjectivity, but belong instead to the ontological possibility of the work. Thus there is no canonical interpretation of a text or art work; rather they stand open to ever new comprehensions."[13] There is no intrinsicality of truth because the text itself resides in its interpretations. Thus, the coherence theory of truth follows not from Gadamer's desire to expiate coherence as a justificatory criterion but from his conceptualization of the ontological status of interpretation.

There are still problems and questions outstanding, most notably about relativism. But before we can turn to these, we must address the critical question whether Gadamer's ontology of inquiry in the human sciences can be more universally applied as a general theory of knowledge, as my arguments in this chapter have assumed. We have now have covered enough of the features of Gadamer's account to address this issue with some clarity.

## Philosophical Hermeneutics as Coherentist Epistemology

Is Gadamer's theory of philosophical hermeneutics universally applicable to all inquiry and to all knowledge? Or are the claims he makes about inquiry uniquely or primarily relevant to the human and perhaps the social sciences? Gadamer develops his hermeneutics through an exploration of the process of textual readings, aesthetic analysis, and interpretive exegesis. He has limited his own application of philosophical hermeneutics to

13. Linge, introduction to *Philosophical Hermeneutics*, by Gadamer, pp. xxv–xxvi.

analyses of Plato and Hegel.[14] Moreover, throughout *Truth and Method* Gadamer makes a categorical distinction between the natural and social sciences, a distinction he bases on a fairly conventional understanding of their objects of inquiry (*TM* 283–85). In other places, however, Gadamer states that hermeneutics seeks to clarify the conditions necessary for all understanding, conditions that precede and make science possible (*TM* xxix, 295). This universal nature of the hermeneutic condition results from the linguistic nature of all understanding (*TM* 476). Gadamer argues that linguisticality is a universal and irreducible ontological feature of the human relationship to the world.

This ambiguity in the extent to which Gadamer himself would universalize his claims has given rise to a debate among Gadamer scholars. Jürgen Habermas, Hubert Dreyfus, and Warnke have argued that Gadamer's hermeneutic analysis has a restricted range of application, while Rorty, Palmer, Weinsheimer, Bernstein and Taylor have argued for its universality.[15] Not surprisingly, the positions these philosophers take with respect to the universality of Gadamer's hermeneutics parallel their positions in the debate among philosophers of science concerning the specificity of social science and whether its separation from natural science is based on a difference in kind or a difference in degree. That debate takes its relevance from Gadamer's own initial distinction between natural and social science, which in his view differ in their objects of analysis. Gadamer writes that, in the social sciences, "an 'object in itself' clearly does not exist at all. This is precisely what distinguishes the human sciences from the natural sciences. Whereas the object of the natural sciences can be described *idealiter* as what would be known in the perfect knowledge of nature, it is senseless to speak of a perfect knowledge of history, and for this reason it is not possible to speak of an 'object in itself' towards which its research is directed"

14. Hans-Georg Gadamer, *Dialogue and Dialectic: Eight Hermeneutical Studies on Plato*, trans. P. Christopher Smith (New Haven: Yale University Press, 1980); Hans-Georg Gadamer, *Hegel's Dialectic: Five Hermeneutical Studies*, trans. P. Christopher Smith (New Haven: Yale University Press, 1976).

15. See Jürgen Habermas, "The Hermeneutic Claim to Universality" in *Contemporary Hermeneutics: Hermeneutics as Method, Philosophy, and Critique*, ed. Josef Bleicher (London: Routledge and Kegan Paul, 1980), pp. 181–212; Hubert L. Dreyfus, "Holism and Hermeneutics," *Review of Metaphysics* 34 (1980): 3–23; Georgia Warnke "Hermeneutics and the Social Sciences: A Gadamerian Critique of Rorty," *Inquiry* 28 (1985): 339–57; Richard Rorty, *Philosophy and the Mirror of Nature* (Princeton: Princeton University Press, 1979); Richard Rorty, "A Reply to Dreyfus and Taylor," *Review of Metaphysics* 34 (1980): 39–46; Richard Palmer, *Hermeneutics: Interpretation Theory in Schleiermacher, Dilthey, Heidegger, and Gadamer* (Evanston: Northwestern University Press, 1969); Joel C. Weinsheimer, *Gadamer's Hermeneutics: A Reading of "Truth and Method"* (New Haven: Yale University Press, 1985); Richard Bernstein, *Beyond Objectivism and Relativism: Science, Hermeneutics, and Praxis* (Philadelphia: University of Pennsylvania Press, 1983); Charles Taylor, "Understanding in Human Science," *Review of Metaphysics* 34 (1980): 25–38.

(*TM* 285).[16] Some have interpreted this distinction as supporting their view that, while the natural sciences seek to describe and explain the intrinsic facts of a reality separate from us, the social sciences study meanings in the life-world, that is, the human-made world of institutions, practices, and language. Meanings in the human sciences are not located in our ontology of truth in the same way that we locate the objects of inquiry in the natural sciences; in the former case, meanings exist on an interactive level and are dependent on human consciousness in a way that rocks and electrons are not. For these and other reasons social science, and indeed any study of meanings, is said to have a hermeneutic dimension. Warnke allows that Gadamer's claims about the universality of linguisticality in all inquiry suggest that there is a hermeneutic dimension in the natural sciences as well, but that the degree and nature of this dimension differs significantly.

Against these sorts of views, Palmer has argued that the decisive point about hermeneutics in the universality debate is not the *object* of inquiry in the sciences but the *process* of human inquiry. Palmer says that according to Gadamer this process is "historical, linguistic, dialectical"[17] in *all* instances, and that therefore a hermeneutic awareness is relevant to all forms of inquiry. Palmer's argument does not require a reinterpretation of or a counterresponse to Gadamer's claim that there is a distinction between the natural and social sciences in their objects of inquiry. The objects may indeed be different, but if all inquiry follows a similar historical, linguistic, and dialectical process, then all the sciences are hermeneutic.

Weinsheimer offers an interesting alternative to Palmer's view. He defends hermeneutic universality not by arguing that the distinction between the sciences is irrelevant, but by arguing that it is mistaken. Weinsheimer maintains that Gadamer's account of method in the natural sciences, as well as his understanding of dominant views held among philosophers of science, is determined by the fact that Gadamer is still working with a logical positivist account of science.[18] The claim that Gadamer understands natural science through logical positivist accounts of it has far-reaching implications. Weinsheimer points out that the most important of these is that Gadamer's views are in fact less divergent and less irrelevant to the debates in Anglo-American philosophy of science *since 1960*, when *Truth and Method* was first published, than Gadamer himself and others believe. Weinsheimer's claim here is controversial.[19] A less controversial implication

16. Again, in the second revised edition of *Truth and Method* Gadamer suggests the outdated status of this view in light of post-Kuhnian philosophies of science.
17. Palmer, *Hermeneutics*, p. 212.
18. Weinsheimer, *Gadamer's Hermeneutics*, pp. 2–4.
19. See, for example, Jerald Wallulis's review of Weinsheimer, *Gadamer's Hermeneutics*, in *Canadian Philosophical Review* 6 (1986): 86–88.

is that Gadamer's perception of the distinction between natural and social science is based on a naive conception of natural science—a positivist brand of empiricism that has been superseded. More complex and sophisticated conceptions have been developed of how science operates, of the relationship between the scientist and theories on the one hand and theories and the world on the other, and of the usefulness of distinctions such as the one between observable and theoretical entities. If some of the more current conceptions of natural science are used to define it (and here you can take your pick among the widely variant accounts of Kuhn, Imre Lakatos, Larry Laudan, and others for significant departures from positivism), then the basis for Gadamer's distinction between natural and social science falls and a universally applicable hermeneutic dimension to knowing becomes more plausible.

Weinsheimer's analysis is persuasive but is now partly out of date. In the second edition of the English version of *Truth and Method*, Gadamer has inserted some footnotes which indicate that he has revised his position "in light of the past three decades of work in the philosophy of science" (*TM* 285n). In particular, he now questions his previous assessment, quoted earlier, that the object of the natural sciences can be described as an "object in itself," and that a neat distinction can be drawn between different branches of inquiry on the basis of their object of research. Although this makes Weinsheimer's analysis of Gadamer's mistake out of date, it supports Weinsheimer's conclusion that there exists a significant hermeneutic dimension to all forms of inquiry.

The strongest argument in favor of the claim that Gadamer's theory of philosophical hermeneutics is applicable to all forms of inquiry is that all inquiry is historically embedded and linguistic. Hermeneutics in general represents the position that these facts cannot be transcended but must be incorporated into any analysis of inquiry (and it is for this reason that Rorty positions hermeneutics outside of epistemology, which he defines as the attempt to transcend such limitations of knowledge). Even if we grant, however, that there is a hermeneutic dimension to all inquiry, it remains possible and perhaps plausible that the hermeneutic dimension plays a stronger role in the social and human sciences than in the natural sciences.

To decide this issue we need to look once again at the four basic arguments for a hermeneutic dimension to inquiry. (1) Both the object of inquiry and the process of inquiry are irreducibly linguistic.[20] (2) All inquiry is historically specific. (3) The existence of a shared common tradition in

---

20. To say that the object of inquiry is irreducibly linguistic is to say that inquiry cannot exist apart from language and that the object of inquiry is the product of an interaction rather than something which preexists inquiry intact; as a product of an interaction involving the inquirer, inquiry comes into being as a linguistic object.

which both text and reader participate is the only way to explain our ability to understand texts, especially texts from the distant past. (4) Understanding requires interpretation and application to manifest itself. Claims 2 and 4 are unquestionably universal in scope. All inquirers are historically situated within a particular trajectory of research programs and theoretical (and perhaps technological) developments, no matter what their discipline. Gadamer's account of the historical specificity of the knower refers us to his claim that all understanding involves an interpretation from the knower's particular horizon and an application to her particular context.

Claims 1 and 3, however, may have especial relevance to the social and human sciences. As Warnke has argued, we can agree with Gadamer that both fossils and actions are constituted within a linguistic interaction (that is, fossils *as fossils* rather than as undifferentiated objects are constituted linguistically), which leads us to accept Claim 1. But there is a further distinction between fossils and actions that needs to be made. Fossils as objects of inquiry come into existence via the linguistic community of scientists. Actions, however, come into existence as objects of inquiry via the linguistic community of scientists and the linguistic community of actors. "The difference is crucial here because it means that natural science involves one 'web of meaning' whereas social science involves two."[21] If this is the case, then the object of inquiry in the social sciences is constituted to a greater extent by linguisticality. Since hermeneutical analysis focuses on uncovering the historical dimension of the study and construction of meaning, hermeneutics would have greater relevance to the social sciences. The special relevance that Claim 3 has for the social sciences follows from this point. To the extent that the linguistic project of the social sciences studies the linguistic actions of human beings, shared prejudices may come into play at two levels in the process of inquiry rather than one.

I am persuaded by this line of thinking that hermeneutics has special relevance to the social sciences. It continues to have some relevance for all forms of inquiry, however, because all human inquiry is linguistic; we have no extralinguistic methodology or procedure. Both kinds of science depend on theories; both build on or reject past theories and develop lines of research within theories. The development of science is in some measure the development of theories, and the meaning of any theory can only be fully enunciated if its *historical* development is taken into account. Thus historical specificity is significantly relevant to all science. Moreover, all beliefs are interpretations, a translation of the "other" into something we can understand within our horizon of prejudicial assumptions. The irregular markings on a sheet of computer printout which a scanner observes

21. Warnke, "Hermeneutics and the Social Sciences," p. 346.

as the track of a uranium atom accelerated through a carbon target involve interpretation, as do the data collected in surveys on voting behaviors. Data does not preexist interpretation: it comes into existence *as data* through the act of interpretation. If all understanding involves interpretation and historical specificity, then Gadamer's theory that hermeneutics is the condition that makes understanding possible has universal applicability to all inquiry.

The degree of relevance, however, might not be the same for all sciences. If we distinguish the social sciences as involving to a greater extent elements that Gadamer includes in his hermeneutic analysis, then hermeneutics is more relevant to the social sciences. The object of inquiry in the natural sciences may be linguistic, but it is a single-order linguisticality rather than a double-order one, as in the social sciences. Natural science studies the movement of nonlinguistic entities linguistically; social science studies human practices, that is, the movements of linguistic entities, linguistically. Whether or not this difference implies that the constraints imposed on interpretation and belief in the natural sciences by the human-independent reality are greater or more forceful is a topic we will explore in the final chapter.

Let me stress that Gadamer's account of prejudice also applies to natural science. Is there a more fundamental aim in the development of theories in the natural sciences than the achievement of an explanation that provides a comprehensive coherence for all the elements involved—previously accepted theories and prejudices of the scientific community as well as data? Allowing the social sciences a special relevance in no way weakens hermeneutics' universal relevance for all forms of human inquiry.

## Relativism

Gadamer's ontology denies that the human-independent reality can provide a standard for adjudication of competing knowledge claims. He rejects the possibility of canonical or universally true interpretations. What kind of relativism are we getting into here? In any discussion of relativism as a generic problem, we run the risk of leaving intact outside of the discussion that which most requires analysis.[22] This is because the nature of relativism as a problem takes its shape and its significance from the theory of justification and more importantly from the ontology of truth it assumes. Therefore, we must discuss the problem of relativism as it arises

22. See Joseph Margolis's illuminating recent book on this topic, *The Truth about Relativism* (Oxford: Basil Blackwell, 1991).

*within* Gadamer's epistemology, rather than assume the problem to have generic characteristics or universal significance for all epistemology.

We have already discussed how, to the extent Gadamer's theory of truth is indexical, it is committed to some degree of relativism. There can be no universal or generalizable truth-value for a particular proposition, given the mediating structure of understanding and the role of particular, historically specific elements within it. For Gadamer, "true" must always mean "true for." Such a conception of truth would be inimical to most epistemologies (unless restricted to trivial subjective or temporally located statements) but not so for Gadamer's, because of his interactionist ontology of truth. The beliefs or interpretations given a "true for" truth-value are not relegated to "approximations of truth" status, since all truth is indexical, and its referent is a mediation of elements rather than the intrinsic nature of a thing-in-itself. Truth exists all along the continuum, and not just at the human-independent end. (To make truth a referent only for the human-independent end of the continuum would likely lead to all the sorts of problems encountered by logical positivism.)

Keeping in mind Gadamer's interactionist ontology helps us to understand that the relativism of indexical truth in his epistemology does not lead to the idealism or ontological anarchy it might within other systems. But what about the task of adjudicating competing knowledge-claims? If all truth is indexical, there is a sense in which knowledge claims would not be *competing* unless they shared every constitutive element. But the practical problem of disagreement remains nonetheless. If I say, "Women have second-class status in society X," and you say, "No they don't," these claims refer to the interaction between a certain horizon (mine or yours) and another horizon of practices, texts, and institutions within society X. It would be easier to adjudicate such a disagreement if Gadamer had clarified his position on the degree of specificity of horizons (or even *taken* a position). If you and I share the same horizon, adjudication between our competing claims would seem to be possible. But if you and I do not share a horizon, and we disagree, how can we possibly resolve our differences?

What if you live in society X and say, "Women are not second-class citizens here," and I am a social theorist from another society and hold the reverse? Both our claims are about the women who live in society X, and so it would seem that both claims cannot have the same truth-value. But according to Gadamer's ontology, my claim may be true for the fusion of my horizon from society Y and the horizon of society X (that is, my claim may maximize the comprehensive coherence between these two horizons better than any alternative), while your claim may be true for your horizon within your society. Does this mean that both claims can be true for Gadamer? This perplexing conclusion would not entail breaking the law of noncontradiction, because of the indexical nature of Gadamer's concept of truth. But knowing this fact does not alleviate our desire or need for adjudicating these claims.

The claim of indexicality has little substance until we can specify and identify what the indexical elements *are*, and here Gadamer provides us with little help. If we could identify the constitutive elements of truth in the social sciences, say, such as different types of prejudice, classificatory schemes, methodologies, background expectations, political values, and so on, then we might be able to offset the dilemmas caused by what look to be conflicting and relative knowledge-claims. It is likely that there exists here a serious problem of complexity which would undermine our efforts to identify all the constituents of truth, but we certainly should be able to explicate the concepts of tradition and horizon in further detail. Doing so would make it easier to ascertain the relevant differences between (apparently) conflicting claims and thus to understand how to resolve conflict where possible.

Another way Gadamer tries to avoid a radical relativism is to argue that tradition represents a continuity from past horizons into present ones, and that there is thus no incommensurability of horizons. Remember his argument that without presupposing a shared commonality between horizons we could not explain how understanding is possible. This element of commonality should guard against constant, radical, and anarchistic interpretations cropping up everywhere. But there are two problems with this response. First, it does not offer guidance in adjudicating conflicts of belief that remain despite the commonalities. It is not a method of adjudication but an argument that the problem will not be as serious as it might be. Second, the response relies on our ability to identify the continuity in tradition with some reliability, an ability which I earlier challenged. I will turn to this issue next.

## The Problem of Tradition Revisited

The gist of the problem of tradition as it was set out in the last chapter was that Gadamer cannot both deny the intrinsicality of meaning and assert the continuity of tradition, where tradition is defined as the fusion of past and present horizons of meaning. Gadamer's response to this problem is to deny that tradition is an object or something that can be procedurally identified or, worse yet, discovered. Continuity is a legitimate presupposition for maximizing the coherence of our understanding of inquiry, rather than an entity we believe in because it can be pointed to. Gadamer's account works not just as a pragmatic justification but also as a transcendental deduction, given that we must infer the continuity of tradition to account for the existence of present knowledge.

We must, however, look again at this problem if we are to assess the issue of relativism in Gadamer's work. If a significant (that is, significantly pernicious) truth-relativism does not follow from his theory, it is because of his insistence upon continuity. Within a shared and continuously evolving tradition, indexical truth loses the full force of its bite. It is between incommensurable webs of belief that truth-relativism looks like anarchy; within a single, continuous web of belief it is more manageable. This is because if I and my doxastic opponent share large parts of our respective horizons then it is possible that we can effectively communicate and perhaps establish an interpretation that we can both accept. Continuity between horizons increases the likelihood of potential agreement. Gadamer does not, however, give us sufficient information on how to describe the contents of horizons and thus to judge continuities in content. Without identifiable continuity, his indexical relativism could become a serious problem.

Gadamer's system embraces both the objectivity of truth and its relativism. Perhaps he is right. Certainly it would account for the proliferation of ideas, theories, and commitments that do exist in some other way than by endorsing the claim that "I'm right and they are all wrong." Gadamer might say that such a heterogeneity is evidence of a kind for the interactive nature of knowledge, the constitutive role of horizons, and the absence of any decisive standard or procedure for adjudication. His philosophy gives us no explanation of how adjudication can occur, and he attacks most procedures currently acceptable. But if Gadamer *is* right that truth is the product of a mediation between elements, there may be other ways to adjudicate competing claims. One way would be to use noncognitive arguments that rely on moral, political, or religious commitments to justify our views. Another would be to bring the constitutive elements of competing claims more into harmony.[23] We might go through an experience with our opponent, show them some experiences they may not have had yet, and seek out some analogue of their prior experiences. Of course, we already use these procedures and they are not successful in all cases. Moreover, merely achieving agreement is a controversial method of adjudicating competing cognitive claims. How can we know that such procedures of persuasion will ensure the triumph of the epistemically better view?

Obviously, Gadamer's epistemology leaves us with an unsettling amount of relativism. This alone cannot, however, be a decisive objection

---

23. Obvious examples of such attempts are Rawls's veil of ignorance and Habermas's theory of universal-pragmatics.

to his epistemology unless we assume (1) that there is an alternative epistemology available with less relativist implications, or (2) that, if no alternative exists, skepticism is preferable to Gadamer's epistemology. Given Gadamer's analysis of the ontology of truth, it is not self-contradictory to accept, perhaps with some resignation, the relativism implied by Gadamer's views: the theory as a whole is not reduced to incoherence simply because it involves some relativism, as is usually charged. Perhaps, as I have said, that is just the way things are. If it is, Gadamer has correctly described the situation.

## Conclusion

Gadamer's theory of philosophical hermeneutics is a coherentist epistemology. There are, however, unresolved and perhaps unresolvable tensions in his work between the continuity of tradition and the universality of interpretation, and between objectivism and relativism. Moreover, Gadamer is frustratingly unclear on many points. He does not specify the range of application for a horizon. Is it different for each individual or for each epoch? His ontology of truth is vague, though I have tried to reconstruct it in more detail than he offers. Coherentism pervades his system, he uses the term himself, and yet he never defines it in explicit detail.

Moreover, Gadamer's conception of justification as a cognitive procedure is relatively meagre and unhelpful. Anglo-American epistemologists need not read Gadamer to come across the idea that maximum coherence is a necessary presupposition for understanding. Increasingly, we do not need to read him to find arguments defending the legitimacy (or at least the inevitability) of prejudice or prior theoretical commitments for all cognitive inquiry.

Gadamer does, however, offer a way to conceptualize the inevitable locatedness of knowers not as a detriment but as a necessary condition for knowledge, and thus he provides a highly realistic account of reason. His ontology of truth could be most useful for Anglo-American debates because it provides a means to transcend the dilemma between a metaphysics of things-in-themselves and a metaphysics of constructivism. Gadamer's ontology of truth also provides an independent argument for the coherence theory of truth, besides a novel explication of truth as mediation. It offers the hope that we can remain realists and retain an objective conception of truth even in the face of positivism's demise. I am far from asserting that Gadamer's epistemology can solve all the problems in Anglo-American epistemology or serve as an exemplary paradigm of coherence epistemology. My claim is simply that Gadamer's ontology of truth provides a hint of where to begin, an original and alternative conception of reality, and a profusion of possibilities with which to strengthen coherentist theories of knowledge. I will return to this point in the final chapter.

# CHAPTER THREE

# "No *man is the lord of anything . . .*": Davidson's Charitable Truth

With its emphasis on formal elaborations of truth-conditional semantics, action, and events, the work of Donald Davidson may seem as far
from Hans-Georg Gadamer's hermeneutics as one could get. As much as
Gadamer is embedded in the tradition of continental philosophy, Davidson
is paradigmatic of an analytic philosopher in style, approach, and preoccupations. Yet Davidson's work has also presented a radical challenge to
accepted assumptions favored by many if not most philosophers working
in the Anglo-American tradition. In the area of philosophy of language
Davidson has argued that we can dispense with such long-standing concepts as reference and representation. In epistemology Davidson has asserted that all that is necessary to develop a theory of belief and
justification is to understand the requirements for being a successful field
linguist. He has further claimed that truth is a primitive and that attempting to theorize or explicate truth will lead to a "transcendental metaphysics," a phrase he uses pejoratively. Following W. V. O. Quine's sparse
empiricism, Davidson has attempted to do semantics and, more recently,
epistemology without most of the usual metaphysical encumbrances. In
this sense his work has exemplified both a stylistic and a substantive form
of philosophical minimalism.

Davidson's recent move into epistemology proper has only increased his
iconoclasm. His persuasive and widely influential articles on action, events,
and conceptual schemes written in the 1960s and 1970s have led to more
fundamental claims about epistemology and a coherentist account of justification. Davidson's epistemology is still developing, and each new article
seems to distance itself from the one that came before, but the move of

such an influential philosopher away from traditional accounts of foundationalism and in the direction of coherence signals a growing trend among analytic philosophers toward one or another form of antifoundationalist epistemology.[1] An exploration of the reasons for Davidson's move should therefore yield some insight into the new, more self-reflexive and creative developments in analytic philosophy.

In the essay, "A Coherence Theory of Truth and Knowledge," Davidson developed an argument to support the claim that "there is a presumption in favor of the truth of a belief that coheres with a significant mass of belief" and that therefore "every belief in a coherent total set of beliefs is justified" even though every belief is not necessarily true.[2] While Davidson did not characterize his position as coherentist in earlier work, he has been championing holism for many years. For example, in "On the Very Idea of a Conceptual Scheme" he held that "it is sentences . . . that face the tribunal of experience, though of course they must face it together."[3] Thus, some of the arguments he later used to defend a coherence theory of justification can be traced throughout his work on interpretation from the last twenty years, although their connection to coherentism has been made explicit by Davidson only recently.

Because Davidson keeps reconstructing and recharacterizing his epistemological positions, it is impossible to offer a general account and evaluation of his epistemology. I will not try to incorporate all of his varying positions in this account. My interest focuses on certain themes that run throughout his writings, such as holism, charity, and the relationship between language and truth, and on recent attempts, beginning in the 1980s, to develop an epistemology consistent with his work in semantics. Even this later period contains shifts, but I shall argue that in some cases these shifts are not as fundamental as Davidson thinks, and that in particular, despite current protestations, his account of knowledge remains fundamentally coherentist.

In the first section of the chapter I will focus on Davidson's account of justification and discuss how it arises out of his views on radical interpretation. On the basis of the analogy he makes between radical interpretation and knowing, Davidson argues that coherence is a truth-conducive crite-

---

1. I am not claiming here that all forms of coherentism and foundationalism are mutually exclusive. See Ernest Sosa, "The Foundations of Foundationalism," *Nous* 14 (1980): 547–64. The versions of coherentism I am examining are, however, each motivated by a rejection of foundationalism.
2. Donald Davidson, "A Coherence Theory of Truth and Knowledge," in *Truth and Interpretation: Perspectives on the Philosophy of Donald Davidson*, ed. Ernest LePore (Oxford: Basil Blackwell, 1986), p. 308.
3. Donald Davidson, "On the Very Idea of a Conceptual Scheme," in *Inquiries into Truth and Interpretation* (Oxford: Clarendon Press, 1984), p. 193.

rion of justification. Part of his argument for coherence also involves the Principle of Charity, which he advances as a universal prerequisite for successful interpretation and understanding. This principle has generated much controversy concerning whether its application is actually as ubiquitous as Davidson claims. Davidson also applies the Principle of Charity to the truthfulness of beliefs, to argue that we cannot *not* assume the general truthfulness of the majority of any actual coherent set of beliefs. But he refuses to draw idealist conclusions from this claim and insists on the veridical nature of belief. I want to explore the ontology of truth that is engendered by Davidson's attempt to reject metaphysical realism and yet maintain that belief is veridical. He has characterized his views on truth as developing a third alternative between a traditional realism—which he says involves a correspondence theory of truth and the intuition that truth is ultimately unconnected to belief—and epistemic concepts of truth—which he says "humanize" truth to make it more accessible but end up reducing "reality to so much less than we believe there is."[4] His new alternative concept of truth is thus meant to be extra-epistemic and yet nontranscendental, and Davidson believes that it can accommodate at least a version of realism and avoid epistemic relativism. Whether or not Davidson's project is fully successful, his attempt to develop an alternative epistemology will be instructive for the immanent, coherentist model we are exploring in this volume.

In the final section of this chapter I will reintroduce Gadamer in order to explore the relationship between his version of coherentism and Davidson's. In actuality, Gadamer and Davidson have remarkably similar arguments for coherence. They both come to a coherentist position through a preoccupation with the problems of interpretation, they make use of transcendental arguments reminiscent of Kant to develop their ontologies, they both collapse interpretation and understanding, and they both end up defending a principle of epistemic charity.

My purpose in this chapter, then, as in the earlier chapters on Gadamer, is not primarily to defend or reject Davidson's coherentist epistemology, but to explore it as an example of the current state of coherentism, and to demonstrate its essentially close relationship with some of the epistemological positions advocated by important continental philosophers, here focusing on Gadamer. At the least, this relationship would seem to indicate that the philosophers who never read each other should begin doing so. We may also find that some of the obstacles facing a coherentist account of knowledge are intractable even across differences of philosophical tradition.

---

4. Donald Davidson, "The Structure and Content of Truth," *Journal of Philosophy* 6 (1990): 279–328.

## Davidson on Justification

In order to understand Davidson's argument for a coherence theory of justification, we must explore his work in semantics and his efforts to extend Alferd Tarski's semantic theory of truth to natural languages. Besides his work on applying Tarski, Davidson has also pursued a related project to develop an account of truth that posits no "unnecessary" metaphysical entities such as reference, experience, sense data, or facts (positivistically understood).[5] He has attempted to explicate meaning in terms of truth conditions, thus again avoiding unnecessary metaphysical baggage. This taste for a barren ontological landscape has assuredly been influenced by Quine. But because Davidson shares a minimalist agenda with Quine, he must also share some of the problems Quine has had in developing a plausible explanation of the possibility of successful interpretation and translation without recourse to the usual conceptual tools.

When meanings were thought to exist behind words, and reference behind propositions, interpretation and translation could easily be explained by saying that these processes involve matching up meaning and reference between linguistic items in different languages. You could translate cat into *gato* by attaching both words to an object in the world, namely a cat, via a realist theory of meaning or reference. You could also interpret the speech patterns in a different language by demonstrating the reference of the terms. Along with Quine, Davidson repudiates such extensionalist approaches to meaning and has attempted to use a Tarski-style theory of truth to develop a theory of meaning that applies to natural languages and will not require reference. Both Davidson and Quine also use the situation of a field linguist who is trying to understand a foreign community's speech as the test for an adequate theory of translation and interpretation. But unlike Quine, Davidson rejects a behaviorist formulation, which would have the linguist translate meanings via observable reactions to stimuli. Given this rejection, however, Davidson had to be able to offer an alternative account of translation and interpretation, and the alternative he developed was a coherentist one, thus beginning his evolution toward coherentist epistemology.

In the case of what Davidson calls "radical" interpretation, where a linguist is out "in the field" hearing an unfamiliar language for the first time, the only data the interpreter has to go on are the body of sentences assented to by the speakers (assuming that sentences can even be demarcated). All that can be surmised without a prior ability for communication are the sen-

---

5. See Davidson, "On the Very Idea of a Conceptual Scheme," p. 194. See also Donald Davidson, "In Defense of Convention T," in *Inquiries into Truth and Interpretation*, p. 72.

tences which the speakers apparently believe to be true. "I hope it will be granted that it is plausible to say we can tell when a speaker holds a sentence to be true without knowing what he means by the sentence, or what beliefs he holds about its unknown subject matter, or what detailed intentions do or might prompt him to utter it."[6] Thus, initially all we can know is the attitude a speaker holds toward certain expressions, an attitude of "holding true." This provides a starting place from which to develop a theory of meaning in the absence of an already developed understanding of the content of the speaker's beliefs.

Davidson then argues that, given this initial situation, the field linguist can only proceed to translate the beliefs of the speaker and interpret the meanings of the speaker's utterances by using a holistic and coherentist procedure that develops hypotheses about the meaning of specific utterances on the basis of their relation to other utterances, always assuming their internal coherence. There is no independent test or stable standard (such as reference) to which we might appeal, since the very rules of reference operative in a foreign language may be different from those operative in our own. In "Belief and the Basis of Meaning," Davidson writes: "If we know only what sentences a speaker holds true, then . . . to interpret a particular utterance it is necessary to construct a comprehensive theory for the interpretation of a potential infinity of utterances. The evidence for the interpretation of a particular utterance will therefore have to be evidence for the interpretation of all utterances of a speaker or community" (148). Since we have no standard by which to justify our interpretations other than the utterances themselves, we can only appeal to further utterances and on the basis of these try to develop an interpretation of specific utterances by creating a coherent network of interpretations that provide mutual evidential support for one another (146). Davidson has thus built a requirement for comprehensiveness into his conception of the coherentist procedure of interpretation. In order to develop an account of meaning, a coherentist approach must work toward maximizing the comprehensiveness of its interpretive theory, and thus be able to yield further successful interpretations when it is extended to cover more and more utterances. Coherence works as a criterion to yield justifiable interpretations because it establishes a comprehensive network of meaningful utterances whose sense is derivable from their interrelationships.

Davidson is not advocating that we adopt this methodological model; rather, his argument is that this procedure is inevitable for any successful radical interpretation. In radical interpretation, such as the situation of the

6. Donald Davidson, "Belief and the Basis of Meaning," in *Inquiries into Truth and Interpretation*, p. 144.

field linguist "interpreting utterances from scratch" (144), a Principle of Charity is required which actually involves several "charitable" assumptions: not only that the speakers' beliefs are generally coherent but also that the speaker is rational and that there is a large range of agreement between the speaker's beliefs and our own. The field linguist need not consciously make such assumptions and yet, Davidson argues, they will be implicit and inevitable throughout the process of interpretation, certainly if it is to be successful. Davidson makes this argument as follows:

> If all we know is what sentences a speaker holds true, and we cannot assume that his language is our own, then we cannot take even the first step towards interpretation without knowing or assuming a great deal about the speaker's beliefs. Since knowledge of beliefs comes only with the ability to interpret words, the only possibility at the start is to assume general agreement on beliefs. We get a first approximation to a finished theory by assigning to sentences of a speaker conditions of truth that actually obtain (in our opinion) just when the speaker holds those sentences true. The guiding policy is to do this as far as possible, subject to considerations of simplicity, hunches about the effects of social conditioning, and of course our common-sense, or scientific, knowledge of explicable error. The method is not designed to eliminate disagreement, nor can it; its purpose is to make meaningful disagreement possible, and this depends entirely on a foundation—*some* foundation—in agreement.[7]

In some ways, charity (that is, the assumption of rationality, coherence, and agreement) provides the stable standard or hidden yardstick whose existence Davidson denies but which makes possible the adjudication of interpretive conflicts. Obviously, knowing what sentences a speaker holds true is not enough to produce a unique interpretation of the content of those sentences. They could be translated in any number of ways, more or less coherent or rational. Simply stipulating that our translation must produce a coherent account of the speaker's utterances is not enough either: more than one coherent account is probably always possible.

In light of this problem, Davidson adds that we must also know the conditions under which a speaker will assent to a given sentence. Thus if a speaker says "conejo" every time a rabbit comes within view, we can begin to hypothesize that "conejo" means rabbit. Of course, such a singular claim would have little plausibility unless embedded within a larger theory interpreting a significant number of utterances. But Davidson notes that more than comprehensiveness is required here. If we know that the

---

7. Davidson, "On the Very Idea of a Conceptual Scheme," pp. 196–97.

speaker's vision is good and that the rabbit is within range of that vision, we are assuming that the speaker is not delusionary, psychotic, or (what is arguably the same thing) a global skeptic. Thus we must assume that the speaker would not assent to a sentence meaning "An elephant has passed by" or "Beware the ides of March" every time a rabbit passes by. We must assume that the speaker is both rational and largely shares our beliefs about the world, such as the belief that when a rabbit crosses our path in clear view it is indeed a rabbit and not an elephant, mythical monster, or drinking partner. According to Davidson, this assumption cannot be corroborated by independent tests: thus its status as an *assumption*. If we have no coherence-based reasons to believe the speaker to be delusionary, and if under identical conditions *we* would say that a rabbit has passed, then we must ascribe this meaning to the speaker's utterance as well. Since a knowledge of the conditions under which a speaker utters the word "conejo" underdetermines our translation of the word, interpretation and translation require the operation on our part of a number of charitable assumptions about the speaker.

The relationship between the coherentist method of interpretation and the principle of charity—which involves assuming that the speaker is rational and shares with us a significant range of beliefs—is thus a close one. Coherence alone is insufficient for radical interpretation without the assumption of rationality and agreement. On Davidson's view, then, there are four requirements for successful interpretation: (1) knowledge of the sentences assented to by the speaker, or, in other words, knowledge of the speaker's beliefs; (2) knowledge of the conditions under which the speaker assents to particular sentences; (3) an assumption that the speaker is rational, which is by necessity an assumption that the speaker conforms to our understanding of rationality; and (4) an assumption that the speaker shares many or most of our beliefs.

If these four requirements obtain, the field linguist then uses a coherentist method to produce an interpretation and translation of the speaker's utterances. That is, he or she strives to produce a comprehensive account of the speaker's utterances in which interpretations of particular sentences gain credence from the interpretation of other sentences until the whole forms a coherent web of beliefs. Davidson's purpose in pointing out the necessity of the Principle of Charity is then not to persuade us to adopt it, since he considers it unavoidable, but rather to show how it undermines the possibility of conceptual relativism (and later on, global skepticism) through its constraint on the production of alternative theories of interpretation.

To get from this line of argument to a coherence theory of epistemic justification only one further premise is needed: that the situation of the field linguist is the universal situation of all knowers in relation not only to other knowers but even to our own beliefs. This is indeed Davidson's claim. His strategy is to offer radical interpretation as the basis for a universal semantics. As far back as 1967 Davidson argued that "if sentences depend for their meaning on their structure, and we understand the meaning of each item in the structure only as an abstraction from the totality of sentences in which it features, then we can give the meaning of any sentence (or word) only by giving the meaning of every sentence (or word) in the language. Frege said that only in the context of a sentence does a word have meaning; in the same vein he might have added that only in the context of the language does a sentence (and therefore a word) have meaning."[8] Davidson's position here is that linguistic meaning is derivable from the same sort of method we have been outlining for radical interpretation, where the meaning of one sentence is derived from and justified via a comprehensive theory developed about the meaning of a significant range of sentences or, as he puts it here, a language. The implicit premise in the above passage (which Davidson makes more explicit later) is that there is no way to get at meaning through a method of comparing or checking sentences against the world.[9] If this is the case, then it is indeed true that all of us are in the same position as the field linguist. We know only our beliefs, or those sentences held true, and the beliefs held by others with whom we are communicating, and we have no independent yardstick by which to measure these beliefs against the world. Thus, as Davidson and others have often said, we cannot get outside of the circle of our beliefs.

Moreover, following C. I. Lewis, Frege, and P. F. Strawson, Davidson now also argues that correspondence accounts of truth cannot be valid because "if true sentences correspond to anything at all, it must be the universe as a whole; thus, all true sentences correspond to the same thing."[10] This is because the correspondence theorist cannot locate a fact or part of reality to which a true sentence corresponds without such a location involving a frame of reference, but by extension the frame of reference will eventually include the whole universe. Thus each true sentence corresponds to the same thing: the universe. On Frege's version of this argument, any sentential operator with the same truth value can be substituted for another in a sentence that allows the substitution of coextensive terms (such as is allowed in ordinary English). If the sentence is " 'S' corresponds to the

8. Donald Davidson, "Truth and Meaning," in *Inquiries into Truth and Interpretation*, p. 22.
9. See, for example, Davidson's introduction to his *Inquiries into Truth and Interpretation*, p. xviii.
10. Davidson, "Structure and Content of Truth," p. 303. Simon Evnine gives a very helpful summation of Frege's argument in *Donald Davidson* (Stanford: Stanford University Press, 1991), pp. 136, 180–82.

fact that Frege was a logician," any set of sentences with the same truth-value can be substituted for S, such as "Hypatia was a philosopher" or "Kant never married." All facts, then, correspond to the same true sentence, which renders useless the notion of truth as correspondence to the facts.

Davidson's rejection of correspondence does not lead him to accept some version of idealism or to give up a conceptual distinction between belief and truth. He continues to reject antirealism on the grounds that it would deprive "truth of its role as an intersubjective standard."[11] But he also rejects the claim that the causal connection between reality and true belief can provide the justification our interpretations require. "I . . . reject the doctrine that either reality or truth depends directly on our epistemic powers. There is a point in such a rejection. But it is futile either to reject or to accept the slogan that the real and the true are 'independent of our beliefs.' The only evident positive sense we can make of this phrase, the only use that consorts with the intentions of those who prize it, derives from the idea of correspondence, and this is an idea without content."[12] So on the one hand, the field linguist's trust that the speaker's beliefs are caused by the world helps to indicate how an interpretation of those beliefs should go. In a concrete sense, certainly the linguist checks beliefs against the world, or the conditions in which the belief occurs. But Davidson resists the move which would make this practice the basis of a metaphysical claim about an extralinguistic method of checking the reference of beliefs with the world, where the world is conceptualized as completely independent or external. We have no *need* of such a claim to explain the field linguist's practice, nor does such practice provide justification for such a claim.

Clearly, Davidson makes a persuasive case about the epistemic situation of the field linguist who is engaged in radical translation. But just as clearly, the epistemological arguments that he attempts to draw from this situation—the defense of coherentism, the rejection of correspondence—will only be persuasive to the extent that he can show that the field linguist is analogous to every human knower. In some of his more recent articles Davidson has tried to develop a stronger case for a general coherence theory of justification. His case essentially involves eliminating the main alternative to coherence: direct epistemic justification for our beliefs through experience and/or perception. Against this view, Davidson holds that, although we have good reason to suspect that many of our beliefs are *caused* by experience or perception, we cannot provide an epistemological link be-

11. Davidson, "Structure and Content of Truth," p. 309.
12. Ibid., pp. 304–5.

tween such causes and our beliefs. He explains this as follows: "It should be clear that no appeal to perception can clear up the question what constitutes a person's ultimate source of evidence. For if we take perception to consist in a sensation caused by an event in the world (or in the body of the perceiver), the fact of causality cannot be given apart from the sensation, and the sensation cannot serve as evidence unless it causes a belief. But how does one know that the belief was caused by a sensation? Only further beliefs can help."[13] Here, Davidson is not denying perception and experience a role in belief formation, but he does deny that they can provide *direct epistemic* support. When we say that perceptions justify beliefs because they cause beliefs, we are actually using a coherentist method— that is, justifying beliefs via other beliefs—because our claim that perceptions cause beliefs *is itself a belief.* In "Empirical Content," Davidson continues:

> Neurath was right in rejecting the intelligibility of comparing sentences or beliefs with reality. We experiment and observe, but this is not "comparing" in any but a metaphorical sense, for our experimentation bears no epistemological fruit except as it *causes* us to add to, cling to, or abandon our beliefs. This causal relation cannot be a relation of *confirmation or disconfirmation*, since the cause is not a proposition or belief, but just an event in the world in our sensory apparatus. Nor can such events be considered themselves evidence, unless, of course, they cause us to believe something. And then it is the belief that is properly called the evidence, not the event. (331)

Because we cannot compare beliefs with reality (in this abstract, metaphysical sense), we cannot claim that perceptions or experience *simpliciter* justify our beliefs. We can only say that perceptual events cause us to have certain perceptual beliefs which are epistemically justified via coherence relations.

For example, our belief that all ravens are black cannot be supported by our seeing a black raven because our seeing a black raven cannot give us a reason to believe that all ravens are black unless we *"believe* that here is a black raven" (323). Thus it is not that the existence of the black raven is irrelevant to the belief that all ravens are black; "What should be denied is that these mundane events are to be analyzed as involving evidence which is not propositional in character—evidence which is not some sort of belief" (324). One might conjecture that a baby who perceives a black raven should not be said to have epistemic support for the belief that all ravens are black because the baby's perception did not produce in the baby the belief in the

---

13. Donald Davidson, "Empirical Content," in *Truth and Interpretation,* ed. LePore, p. 324.

existence of a black raven but rather the belief (perhaps) in the existence of an interesting moving object. Perceptions do not always produce the sort of beliefs that can confer justification. In the case where a perception of a black raven by an ornithologist, say, produces the sort of belief necessary to support the belief that all ravens are black, then that perception plays a causal role in justifying her or his belief. But the only sort of role that perception and experience can play in the formation of belief is a causal role, and causation needs to be kept distinct from epistemic justification.

Why cannot perceptions play a justifying role? Davidson claims that our actual perceptions are so fleeting and private "as to lack connection with the sentences of the public language which alone are capable of expressing scientific, or even objective, claims" (327). If perceptions are made to be the "foundation of knowledge," then our knowledge so conceived rests on "something so private that even its meaning could only be given at a moment for an individual" (326). On the basis of this phenomenological argument, Davidson agrees with the many critics of logical positivism that subjective perceptual experiences are just too thin and unsubstantial to provide a bedrock large and strong enough to hold up the weight of our whole body of beliefs.

Davidson's reasoning here, while persuasive, only works to the extent one adopts an internalist account of epistemic justification. He is assuming that a theory of epistemological justification must require believers to be able to give an account of what justifies their belief, and therefore that justification is internally accessible to the believer. It is this requirement more than any other that keeps perceptual experience from being able to provide epistemic justification. If one held an externalist position on justification, requiring of a justified belief only that it exist in a proper relation to its cause, for example, then perception could provide epistemic justification to the extent that it provided the proper relation between the belief and the belief's cause.[14]

So Davidson's more general argument for coherence as the criterion of epistemic justification takes the form of eliminating the main alternative to

14. It could be argued that Davidson eschews this line of thinking, and externalism along with it, because he repudiates the possibility of a confrontation between knowers and a world conceptualized independently of belief. In this case he would not merely be assuming internalism, he would have an argument against externalism. For this to work, however, we would have to show that externalism, or at least the view that perception can justify beliefs, necessarily involves a belief in confrontation. This seems unlikely, to the extent that confrontation involves an extralinguistic or outside perspective on our relationship to the world (as both Davidson and Richard Rorty claim), which is a truly absurd thesis that in fact no one holds. Alternatively, externalism could be understood as the view, not that such a confrontation confers justification on our beliefs, but that the fact that the world causes our beliefs (a claim that Davidson parts company with Rorty in accepting) confers justification without needing any outside perspective as corroboration.

coherentism: the claim that we can provide a foundational justification for our beliefs via perception or experience. On Davidson's view, we believe because we see, but we are not justified in believing because we see. This is because (1) the fact that our beliefs are caused perceptually only confers justification by virtue of our believing it, and thus all our beliefs are justified via other beliefs (rather than via experience), and (2) perceptual experience is just too fleeting and private to provide a warrant that is communicable in the public realm of belief which Davidson's interest in language places at the center of his epistemological considerations. Thus, perception must be built up into a suitable warrant-conferring belief through inferences, which entails that the evidence that is used to justify beliefs always amounts to a set of beliefs.

But this view does not entail coherentism unless coherentist theories and foundational/perceptual theories exhaust the possibilities of epistemological justification. There are in fact other alternatives which Davidson fails to mention except to dismiss them rather cavalierly without argument. The most notable of these is pragmatism. The only argument he offers against a pragmatist account of epistemic justification is that the notion of "warranted assertability" reduces truth to an epistemic concept that "invite[s] skepticism" and relativism by making truth dependent on what we can know.[15] We will explore this argument further in the next section.

Nonetheless, on the basis of his argument that no perceptual foundation can provide epistemic justification for our beliefs, and that our beliefs can only get justification from other beliefs, Davidson concludes that only a coherence theory of justification is defensible. This version of the argument for coherence does not rely on facts about radical interpretation but on rather conventional considerations within epistemology. The argument hangs on assuming an internalist account of justification: that for a belief to be justified a believer must be able to give an account of how the belief came to be justified. The existence of some external epistemic connection between the belief and the cause of or object of that belief is implicitly taken as insufficient.

How does Davidson respond to the objection that a coherentist account will engender epistemological relativism by allowing for conflicting but equally coherent and therefore equally justified systems of beliefs? He tries to derail this objection by insisting throughout that the only unit of justification he will entertain is an actual belief, that is, a belief that he or some other real believer actually holds. He explains this insistence by the following: "It's not clear what it means to say I could 'arrive' at various systems, since I do not invent my beliefs; most of them are not voluntary."[16]

15. Davidson, "Structure and Content of Truth," p. 298.
16. Davidson, "Empirical Content," p. 331; see also his criticism of Neurath, p. 327.

If real beliefs rather than fairy tales or novels are the subject of our investigation, Davidson seems to think that the philosopher's worry over the possibility that coherentism will produce a proliferation of different belief systems is a specious concern. He acknowledges that this answer alone does not establish that coherence yields truth, and so it does not answer the skeptic, but it does go a certain way toward answering the charge of relativism.

Davidson actually has two reasons for believing that his coherentist account of justification can avoid succumbing to relativism. The first involves his stipulation as stated above that the unit of justification must pertain to real beliefs. This avoids the charge that a coherence account would offer epistemic license for the production of a plethora of imaginary coherent systems: no one would seriously entertain such imaginary systems and so, Davidson argues, they cannot be used as a trump card against coherentism. The possibility remains, however, that there exist equally coherent systems of statements that people actually believe and about which a coherentist account would seem to be able to offer no help in adjudicating. But Davidson has a counterargument to this scenario as well. Given that the operation of the Principle of Charity is a necessary part of all interpretation, and given that the principle mandates the assumption of large-scale agreement between our beliefs and other's beliefs, the possibility of a coherent (or incoherent) system of beliefs completely different from our own is unintelligible.

Echoing Gadamer here, Davidson argues that in understanding we assimilate. This claim conforms to many "everyday" experiences of understanding. Who of us has not sat through a philosophical paper on an unfamiliar topic in a daze of confusion, struggling to assimilate the author's statements into some line of argumentation we have heard before? When we do not know what the person means to say—that is, if we cannot effect an assimilation—then we are unable to determine whether we agree with them or not. Philosophical disagreements in fact flourish where agreement between speakers is maximized. Among analytical epistemologists one finds forceful and clearly articulated differences; between analytic and continental philosophers one usually finds awkward silence, vague dismissals, and mean jokes rather than specified disagreements.

Davidson claims that disagreement is only intelligible against a background of agreement. As many have pointed out in relation to Thomas Kuhn's theory of scientific revolutions, truly incommensurable paradigms (or incommensurable conceptual schemes that are internally coherent) could never disagree with or refute one another, since there must be shared terms in which to express and identify such disagreements. Without the ability to establish differences between paradigms, it is also impossible to establish the scientific progress Kuhn apparently believes to exist. Davidson extends this argument to say that not only can incommensurable paradigms not disagree with one another, it is not even intelligible to entertain such a possibility.

The application of the argument concerning conceptual schemes to the problem of relativism does not show that a more small-scale version of relativism between particular beliefs which different speakers hold is not possible. The argument only establishes that such disagreements cannot constitute the majority of our beliefs. There is more than one type of relativism, and ruling out global relativism does not suffice to rule out more local forms. A simple coherence criterion of justification might provide a thin requirement with inadequate means to adjudicate disagreements. We will need to return to the issue of relativism when we address Davidson's account of truth.

Before turning to truth, however, I want to summarize once again the ways in which Davidson defends a coherence theory of justification. First, he uses the meager evidential resources of the field linguist and the necessity of the Principle of Charity to provide a transcendental deduction, as Carol Rovane has shown, to the effect that the coherentist method of justification follows from the fact of successful communication.[17] The argument takes as a given the fact of effective communication between speakers and successful interpretation and translation (at least some of the time), and then deduces what must be the case for this to occur. Second, Davidson shows that the coherence theory of justification provides us with a plausible account of interpretation and translation, an account that can show why particular interpretive claims are advanced over others. Third, Davidson argues that noncoherentist, foundationalist accounts of justification cannot be defended by grounding belief on direct perceptual experience.

We have seen, however, that Davidson's arguments depend on his ability to generalize from the case of the field linguist over all possible knowing practices, that he assumes an internalist account of justification, and that there remains some legitimate concern that relativism cannot be decisively avoided. Another question that might be raised concerns the *epistemic* status of Davidson's argument for coherentism. If a method is unavoidable, we might be said to have a kind of justification for its use (since the attempt to avoid using it would be foolish and doomed to failure). But in what sense is his an epistemic justification, that is, in what sense does it link coherence to truth?

---

17. Carol Rovane, "The Metaphysics of Interpretation," in *Truth and Interpretation*, ed. LePore, pp. 417–29.

Of course, stipulating that epistemic justifications must establish truth-conduciveness is contentious. There are other possible ways to explicate the term "epistemic." For example, if we held Peirce's view that the goal of inquiry is the elimination of doubt, then a method of epistemic justification would be justified if it demonstrably aided us in eliminating doubt (this is precisely the metajustificatory argument that Peirce used to defend the abductive method of science). Even if we reject Peirce's account, there is more than one possible criterion for an adequate epistemic justification, or more than one possible way to cash out what it means for a justification to be an epistemic one. Davidson, however, along with Laurence BonJour and other coherentists, appears to take truth-conduciveness as the criterion of epistemic justification and claims that coherence is in fact truth-conducive. What sense of the term "truth" underlies this claim?

### Davidson on Truth

Davidson's work on truth developed out of his attempt to apply Tarski's theory of truth to problems in the semantics of natural languages. He was not concerned with explicating truth itself and has consistently held that the concept of truth is a primitive, meaning that there is no more basic concept by which it might be defined. His motivation in dealing with truth originated entirely from a concern with semantics and interpretation. Davidson believed that by utilizing Tarski's disquotational theory of truth he could explicate meaning without having to postulate some metaphysical relation like reference or some metaphysical entity like sense-data, proposition, or experience. He wanted to avoid the metaphysical baggage of an intermediate level between beliefs and the world or of entities behind or beyond doxastic utterances, but to do this he had to show that such assumptions were unnecessary for an explanation of meaning. Davidson believed he could show this by using a Tarski-style semantic concept of truth in order to explicate meaning without the postulation of metaphysical constructions. His aim, if anything, was antimetaphysical.

At the same time, however, Davidson has wanted to hold onto an extra-epistemic version of truth, a version which holds that true statements are caused by a world irreducible to what is warrantedly assertable or epistemically ascertained. Whether this latter claim makes Davidson a realist is controversial, not only among his commentators but even with himself. His views on the relationship between belief, language, and reality have not substantially changed in thirty years, but he has alternately characterized himself as a correspondence theorist, a coherence theorist, a realist, and then none of the above.[18] Until very recently, Davidson avowed a commitment to both realism and correspondence. He now says that this was a mistake based on the false belief that the only alternatives to realism and correspondence would involve antirealism and an epistemic concept of truth. Interestingly, Davidson has not disavowed the substance of his earlier views, only the way he located them within existing categories. I think he is right to avoid aligning his views with either traditional realism or antirealism, and it strikes me that many of the charges against and misunderstandings of Davidson result from an excessively narrow epistemological imagination, incapable of considering alternative ontological configurations for the meaning of truth. Michael Devitt, for example, cannot conceptualize how Davidson can reject the concept of an uninterpreted reality without rejecting the existence of a theory-independent reality.[19] Thus he, like others, wonders how Davidson can continue to call himself a realist. I will try to defend Davidson's self-understanding on this score, but I will also argue contra Davidson that his alternative configuration of the ontology of truth is best represented within a coherentist framework, as I have broadly envisioned it.

Although for Davidson truth is a primitive, the term still has some metaphysical bite since he claims that it is not reducible to an epistemic concept. This makes his argument that the coherence criterion of justification is truth-conducive both more interesting and more difficult to understand. Davidson holds that particular beliefs gain epistemic justification when they are seen to cohere with a large body of coherent beliefs. We have already gone over his explanation of why this is the case. What remains to be established, however, is whether Davidson's claim that we cannot identify a largely false set of beliefs is sufficient to provide an epistemic justification for the truth-conduciveness of coherence as a criterion of knowledge.

The unit of concern here for Davidson is the web, not the particular belief. Although we can give justifying reasons for particular beliefs, reasons that rely ultimately on their coherence to the web of beliefs, we cannot give reasons why particular beliefs must be true beyond this. Therefore "each of our beliefs may be false. But of course a coherence theory cannot allow that all of them can be wrong."[20] The "of course" follows from the fact that if all of our beliefs can be wrong, then coherence with the web cannot

18. Donald Davidson, "True to the Facts," in *Inquiries into Truth and Interpretation*, pp. 37, 54; Davidson, "On the Very Idea of a Conceptual Scheme," p. 198; Davidson, "Coherence Theory of Truth and Knowledge," pp. 307, 316–19; Davidson, "Empirical Content," p. 331; Davidson, "Afterthoughts, 1987," in *Reading Rorty*, ed. Alan Malachowski (Cambridge, Mass.: Basil Blackwell, 1990), pp. 134–37; Davidson, "Structure and Content of Truth," pp. 298–99, 302–9.
19. Michael Devitt, *Realism and Truth*, 2d ed. (Oxford: Basil Blackwell, 1991), p. 201.
20. Davidson, "Coherence Theory of Truth and Knowledge," p. 309.

confer epistemic justification. Only if the web is largely true does it have the power to provide justification of particular beliefs, or to establish that they have a high probability of truth. So for Davidson's coherentist epistemology to work, the unit he must establish as (largely) true is the web or set of beliefs.

Davidson could make the following case for such a claim. If our web of beliefs includes literally millions of statements of the kind "I am seeing a computer screen right now," "I saw a computer screen one minute ago," "I saw a computer screen two minutes ago," and so on, thus including all our trivial perceptual beliefs, then it seems plausible to hold that most of them are true. In other words, we could still allow for a pretty large degree of error, perhaps all of our highly speculative beliefs in developmental psychology for example, and yet hold that the majority of our beliefs remain true. If this is what Davidson means by the assertion that "most of our beliefs must be true," then only someone who considers global skepticism a serious possibility would argue against his claim. This strategy, however, reduces the claim to a triviality; it is more likely that what he means to say is that most of our substantive beliefs must be true. Why should we believe this?

In giving up the possibility of confrontation between beliefs and the world Davidson believes that he has given up any possibility of providing *evidence* for his claim that our beliefs are mostly true. "What we have shown is that it is absurd to look for a justifying ground for the totality of beliefs, something outside this totality which we can use to test or compare with our beliefs. The answer to our problem must then be to find a *reason* for supposing most of our beliefs are true that is not a form of *evidence*."[21] To provide evidence would be to furnish information external to our web of belief about how our web connects to the world. For Davidson, however, we have no way of appropriating an external vantage point in order to check the belief to see whether or not it actually obtains. So all we are left with being able to provide are *reasons* coherent within our web of beliefs which indicate that our beliefs are mostly true.

Davidson gives three basic reasons for accepting the claim that most of our beliefs are true. First, beliefs are supervenient on nonepistemic events; they are caused by the world.[22] The *fact* of supervenience cannot provide epistemic support for the claim that the web must be largely true because Davidson has ruled out the possibility of nonepistemic events providing epistemic justification, for reasons we have already seen. Only beliefs can confer justification. But insofar as it is a *belief*, the claim that the world causes our beliefs can provide epistemic support for believing that most of

21. Ibid., p. 314.
22. Ibid., p. 314.

the web of coherent beliefs must be true. But it can only provide such epistemic confirmation to the extent that the claim itself is justified, since only justified beliefs can confer epistemic confirmation. And the only way in which Davidson can justify his belief that the world causes our beliefs is by establishing its coherence within the web, which makes the argument looks viciously circular. For coherent inclusion in the web only provides justification if the web itself is justified, and the argument Davidson gives in defense of the web's justification is itself justified only by its coherent inclusion within the web. We cannot argue that the web is largely true because our beliefs are caused by the world, when the only justification we have for this latter claim is its coherence to a web that is largely true. This problem of circularity might seem to beset any reasons Davidson could offer for the epistemic justifiability of the web, since a coherentist is by definition committed to a circular process of justification. All of the reasons he offers, however, are not as apparently weak as the one just given.

Davidson's second reason seems to have a better chance of success, since it is not based on what appears to be a simple assertion but on a transcendental argument. This reason involves the Principle of Charity. Davidson's arguments for holding that in order to interpret a foreign speech we must assume some large level of agreement between us and the speaker also entails that we must assume some large level of truth in any large and systematic web of belief. The argument in both cases is the same.

> Of course it cannot be assumed that speakers never have false beliefs. . . . We can, however, take it as a given that *most* beliefs are correct. The reason for this is that a belief is identified by its location in a pattern of beliefs; it is this pattern that determines the subject matter of the belief, what the belief is about. Before some object in, or aspect of, the world can become part of the subject matter of a belief (true or false) there must be endless true beliefs about the subject matter. False beliefs tend to undermine the identification of the subject matter; to undermine, therefore, the validity of a description of the belief as being about that subject. And so, in turn, false beliefs undermine the claim that a connected belief is false.[23]

In other words, a critical mass of true beliefs is needed in order to identify false beliefs. If the content of a belief—and therefore how we interpret and translate it—can only be acquired through a background pattern of beliefs, then we cannot, without sacrificing the intelligibility of the whole enterprise, throw into question too many of the beliefs in a web (at least all at once). To

---

23. Donald Davidson, "Thought and Talk," in *Inquiries into Truth and Interpretation*, p. 168.

achieve understanding requires the acceptance of most beliefs as true. There is no way to identify a totally false set of beliefs, ours or anyone else's. It follows that everyone that we can understand holds mostly true beliefs.

Notice that the central methodological requirement here is that a large background of beliefs be held stable in order to provide a way to identify the meanings of other, newer beliefs. If all parts of the web are constantly changing, the coherentist method of assigning interpretations cannot hope to succeed, because "a belief is identified by its location in a pattern of beliefs; it is this pattern that determines the subject matter of the belief." Interpretation thus requires a stable background, and Davidson's claim here is that only truth can confer such stability: "It is the pattern of sentences *held true* that gives sentences their meaning."[24] Without the assumption of truth Davidson thinks we have no means to create the stability needed to judge new beliefs, identify meaning, or articulate disagreements and errors. Davidson therefore takes the Principle of Charity to justify the belief that a coherent web of beliefs is largely true.

From a traditional realist perspective, however, this argument cannot work. Even if Davidson is right that a large set of stable background beliefs is necessary to identify error and disagreement, a traditional realist would not allow that *truth*-claims can be justified in this way. Davidson's explanation of the methodological prerequisites for identifying the content of belief could be readily accepted by a skeptic who would then simply point out that identification of content is different from verification of truth. The fact that there may be methodological limits on how much error we can identify in our web of belief does not entail that there are corresponding metaphysical limits on how much error our web can actually hold. The Principle of Charity provides epistemic constraints on what we can *know*, but does not establish what there must *be*.

Further, it could be argued that, even if a stable background of beliefs is required to establish meaning, there are other ways to achieve stability than making a claim to truth. We could hold these beliefs to be warrantedly assertable, or simply core-constituents of the web. Or we could be Humean skeptics and say that we have many beliefs for psychological reasons, and that these can be divided between the ones that are relatively easy to relinquish and the ones that are not. We could achieve a stable background of beliefs in any one of these ways and be able to effect interpretation and translation without ascribing truth to most of our beliefs. Thus, the fact that we need some stable beliefs for the coherence theory of justification to work does not require an ascription of truth, and therefore does not confer a reason to believe that most of our beliefs are true.

24. Ibid., p. 162 (my emphasis).

These objections, however, miss the mark. Davidson is not attempting to show that the necessity of charity establishes a means of discovering the real meaning of statements or the correspondence of belief to a theory-independent reality. To get at what he *is* trying to show, Rovane has helpfully demonstrated that Davidson's project is fundamentally parallel to Kant's, in that it is not trying to disprove skepticism so much as explain why skepticism is obviously false. "Davidson's approach to metaphysics is at bottom, i.e. in its very general features, a Kantian stand in metaphysics, the aim of which is to expose the metaphysical significance of the conditions on the possibility of judgement or belief."[25] Kant begins with the given fact that we have knowledge and then inquires what must be true about us and about the world for this to be the case, eventually locating the necessary preconditions of knowledge in the nature of experience. Davidson begins with the given fact of successful communication and locates the preconditions necessary for communication in a general agreement, rationality, and truth.

But even if we share Davidson's presumption in favor of the existence of successful communication, do we really then need to posit the truth of our web of belief? It seems that in order to understand others all we really need to posit is the existence of shared beliefs and some large percentage of beliefs held stable during the interpretive process. We could then successfully communicate with others even if all of these beliefs were in reality false. Furthermore, does successful communication, or communication that appears to be successful, really require that we actually share beliefs or only that we *assume* shared beliefs? Consider Wittgenstein's example of the beetle box.[26] If we each possess a beetle box into which the other can never look, we might consistently mistake the content of another's beetle box, or the meaning of another's sentence. But if our misunderstanding is systematic enough that it produces no or few anomalies in the theory of interpretation we construct, how could we ever find out? Communication could appear to be happening, but all we need to explain this is the assumption of shared agreement between communicating speakers, and not the existence of actual agreement or the truth of most of our beliefs. Of course, we are fudging a bit here. The imagined, skeptical interlocutor in this case is not actually going along with Davidson in assuming that successful communication exists. But this is precisely the point. Why should we make this assumption if, given the beetle-box problem, we have no way of really knowing or checking to see whether communication is actually or only apparently successful?

25. Rovane, "Metaphysics of Interpretation," p. 419.
26. Ludwig Wittgenstein, *Philosophical Investigations*, 3d ed., trans. G. E. M. Anscombe (New York: Macmillan, 1958), remark 293.

From a traditional realist perspective, then, Davidson's use of a transcendental deduction does not seem to strengthen his position. Nor does his third justificatory argument for the link between coherence and truth, which goes as follows: "Imagine for a moment an interpreter who is omniscient about the world, and about what does and would cause a speaker to assent to any sentence in his (potentially unlimited) repertoire. The omniscient interpreter, using the same method as the fallible interpreter, finds the fallible speaker largely consistent and correct. By his own standards, of course, but since these are objectively correct, the fallible speaker is seen to be largely correct and consistent by objective standards."[27] The argument here is that even an omniscient interpreter would be bound to adopt the Principle of Charity in interpreting a speaker's beliefs, and therefore would have to assume that most of their beliefs are true. Given that this would apply to any set of beliefs held by a speaker, Davidson concludes that most of our beliefs must be true.

This is a curious argument. It might seem that an omniscient observer by definition would not be bound to observe a Principle of Charity since she or he could have access to other, external information, such as a confrontation between a speaker's beliefs and reality. Why should we assume that an omniscient observer would be stuck in the circle of its beliefs and therefore be forced to adopt the Principle of Charity as we mere mortals are? Moreover, the argument only works if the antecedent is in fact true, that is, if there is an omniscient observer engaged in interpreting our beliefs. But clearly we cannot rest a theory of epistemic justification on that assumption, without returning epistemology to the problems of Descartes.[28]

The omniscient interpreter argument can do no better to convince a traditional realist than Davidson's second metajustificatory argument, since they both rely on the Principle of Charity. If one can dispense with classical realist assumptions, however, the structure of Davidson's case becomes much clearer. The omniscient interpreter is as bound to the Principle of Charity as we fallible interpreters because, as Davidson said even in 1973, meaning itself is "a theoretical construction. Like any construct, it is arbitrary except for the formal and empirical constraints we impose on it. In the case of meaning, the constraints cannot uniquely fix the theory of interpretation."[29] Meaning does not exist prior to the act of interpretation,

---

27. Davidson, "Coherence Theory of Truth and Knowledge," p. 317.
28. These and other criticisms of Davidson's argument have been developed in Richard Foley and Richard Fumerton, "Davidson's Theism?" *Philosophical Topics* 48 (1985): 83–89. They compare the appeal to an omniscient interpreter to Descartes' predicament in which only the belief in the existence of an omniscient, omnibenevolent God can hold off skepticism.
29. Donald Davidson, "The Material Mind," in *Essays on Actions and Events* (Oxford: Clarendon Press, 1980), pp. 256–57.

waiting for discovery; meaning is an entity that emerges within processes of interpreting speakers. Ontologically, therefore, meaning is an emergent entity. The omniscient interpreter has no more access to meaning than do fallible interpreters, because there is no more access to be had than what may be reached through processes of interpretation, and those processes require use of a Principle of Charity. This is why Davidson can deduce metaphysical conclusions from methodological considerations—because he rejects a transcendental realist account of meaning that assumes meaning to be independent of the process by which it is ascertained.

Because meaning is interdependent with belief and truth, Davidson's rejection of a realist account of meaning has important implications for his epistemology as a whole. Of meaning, truth, and belief he says "each of these concepts requires the others, but none is subordinate to, much less definable in terms of, the others."[30] Neither he nor most of his commentators have seemed able to face these implications: until recently Davidson persisted in declaring himself committed to a correspondence theory of truth, even though the position he developed on meaning and articulated as early as 1973 would make such an overall account puzzling.

It has been taken as a truism that epistemologists who hold coherence theories of justification inevitably find that they cannot provide noncircular arguments for the truth of our web of beliefs once they stipulate that nothing nonepistemic or outside the web can confer justification. If it were the case that all metajustificatory arguments for coherence are ultimately question-begging or specious, then coherentism would indeed be a dead-end epistemology. Davidson presents an alternative to this familiar impasse, however, by proposing a third position between transcendental or traditional realism and epistemic accounts of truth. In the objections to Davidson's metajustificatory arguments considered above, I assumed that Davidson must establish the link between coherence and truth by realist standards, that meaning exists inside the beetle box whether or not it is interpreted or communicated to others, and that global skepticism is a viable option.

How do Davidson's arguments look if we dispense with such assumptions, and instead interpret them within an antifoundationalist position that eschews traditional realism and correspondence? (To some extent this involves reading his works backward, approaching the earlier discussions of coherence through the later works which take a more radical position.) The arguments about the need for the Principle of Charity show that we must assume the stability of most of our beliefs in order to express ourselves meaningfully. Global skepticism is therefore incomprehensible be-

---

30. Davidson, "Afterthoughts, 1987," p. 136.

cause it requires us to attempt the impossible project of identifying erroneous beliefs without any background of stable beliefs. Even stories about evil demons and brains in vats produce their effect of destabilizing our beliefs because they propose another set of beliefs—a fairly large set including the story itself, how we came to find out about the story, what must be the case for us to believe the story, and so on.[31] So there is no way in which we can intelligibly throw out or suspend all or even most of our beliefs. Nor can we provide a foundational justification of the web of belief through perception, conceptualized as prior to belief. The only tenable position left is to hold onto our web of beliefs, articulating errors and true beliefs against its background and developing a coherent theory with as much internal support as possible to explicate our position. This view of Davidson as a sort of robust antifoundationalist has been suggested by Marie McGinn.[32]

According to McGinn, Davidson's antifoundationalism can be ascertained in his refusal to entertain seriously objections against his positions that might be made by a global skeptic. As we have seen, Davidson argues that global skepticism is incomprehensible because errors cannot be identified without a background of belief, and therefore the postulation of total error is simply unintelligible. Now, not everyone thinks this argument works (Devitt, for example),[33] but even if it does work the skeptical question would be whether what it shows is that our web of belief is mostly true. McGinn argues that the argument works, not through "proving" the truth of the web, but by showing where epistemic justification must end.

> It is not . . . that the anti-foundationalist simply chooses dogmatically to treat some judgments as a stopping point, in order for the practice of justification to get off the ground. Rather, he claims that it is commitment to a background of unquestioned beliefs that gives the beliefs we do question their sense, that makes it possible for those beliefs to be challenged, justified, undermined, and so on. . . . Thus, without claiming that any belief is metaphysically certain, and without submitting to dogmatism, the anti-foundationalist has shown why, in a given context, the process of justification must end where it does.[34]

31. Hilary Putnam has argued along these lines that skeptical stories such as the one about "brains in a vat" require reference to real entities, and therefore that our talk presupposes or entails that we are not brains in vats ourselves. See his *Realism, Truth, and History* (New York: Cambridge University Press, 1981), chap. 1.
32. Marie McGinn, "The Third Dogma of Empiricism," *Proceedings of the Aristotelian Society*, 1981–82, pp. 89–102.
33. At least in his earlier, first edition, incarnation. See Michael Devitt, *Realism and Truth*, 1st ed. (Princeton: Princeton University Press, 1984), pp. 174–76.
34. Marie McGinn, "Third Dogma," pp. 96–98.

The point of antifoundationalism is precisely that our beliefs are foundationless. This does not somehow *prove* them, but indicates rather that they are not lacking anything, since there is nothing intelligible for them to lack. Thus what the argument shows is that no further justification is required. Such an approach, which rejects skepticism without refuting it, can also be found in the work of Peirce and Wittgenstein.[35] If we do interpret Davidson along the lines McGinn suggests, how can we square an apparent antirealist approach to meaning with his insistence that truth is extra-epistemic and that belief is veridical or supervenient on reality? To sort out his view, we need to look further at Davidson's ontology of truth.

On the one hand, Davidson has presented himself as a fairly traditional realist, claiming that the world causes our beliefs, that we have direct perceptual access to the world, and that truth is correspondence with a mind-independent reality.[36] On the other hand, Davidson has held some very nontraditional views about meaning and truth; that truth is a primitive which needs no explication, that there is no intermediary level between us and the world, no scheme/content or observation/theory distinction, and that all we need for a theory of truth is Tarski's Convention T.[37] This odd combination of views is evidenced in the following: "Truth emerges not as wholly detached from belief (as a correspondence theory would make it) nor as dependent on human methods and powers of discovery (as epistemic theories of truth would make it). What saves truth from being 'radically non-epistemic' (in Putnam's words) is not that truth is epistemic but that belief, through its ties with meaning, is intrinsically veridical."[38] What alternative conception of truth can reconcile these various commitments?

We can begin by becoming clear on what Davidson is rejecting. To Rorty's dismay, truth for Davidson is not a human construction or an epistemic notion, capable of being fully elucidated via justification or assertability. For Davidson truth is metaphysical: "The truth of an utterance depends on just two things: what the words as spoken mean, and how the world is arranged."[39] Thus, to say that a sentence is true is to make a metaphysical claim about what is the case and not merely an epistemic claim

35. See Stanley Cavell's discussion of Wittgenstein in his "Emerson, Coleridge, Kant," in *Post-Analytic Philosophy*, ed. John Rajchman and Cornell West (New York: Columbia University Press, 1985) p. 84; I have argued this about Peirce in "Charles Peirce's Alternative to the Skeptical Dilemma," *Auslegung* 13 (Winter 1986): 6–18. Davidson has finally admitted, after much prodding from Rorty, that he too is telling the skeptic to "get lost." See Davidson, "Afterthoughts, 1987," p. 134.
36. Davidson, "Coherence Theory of Truth and Knowledge," p. 309.
37. Ibid., pp. 312–13, 316.
38. Davidson, "Afterthoughts, 1987," p. 136.
39. Davidson, "Coherence Theory of Truth and Knowledge," p. 309.

about what we know or can know to be the case. However, Davidson wants to keep the "metaphysics of truth" beautifully simple and transparent: no noumena, no phenomena, no need for correct representations of the given, just words and things. As Simon Evnine puts it, "Davidson goes straight to the world itself to help fix what mental states and sentences are about."[40] This refusal to posit any intermediary entities such as "sensations," "experience," or "ideas," which empiricists from Locke through Quine have used as the basis of knowledge, marks Davidson's break from the empiricist tradition and his most radical difference with Quine.

Curiously, the reason Davidson cites for rejecting such empiricist constructions along with traditional realism and epistemic theories of truth, is that they "invite skepticism,"[41] this despite Davidson's admission that "I should not pretend that I am answering the skeptic when I am really telling him to get lost."[42] Even though his approach to the problem of skepticism is not to attempt a refutation, Davidson wishes to develop a theory of truth that will avoid skepticism, and thus he avoids both traditional realism and epistemic theories as inadequate in light of this goal.

This position might seem contradictory, since on the one hand Davidson tries to sidestep skeptical challenges yet on the other he is clearly concerned about skepticism as a real issue. In fact, when he offers a concern about skepticism as his reason for rejecting traditional realism and epistemic theories of truth, he may even appear to be following Barry Stroud's advice that addressing the possibility of global skepticism should be a central task of epistemology. I think, however, that Davidson's position with regard to skepticism is fundamentally different from what Stroud has in mind. Davidson does not want to refute the skeptic by proving that knowledge is possible; he wants to reroute epistemology around the skeptical impediments without falling in the trap. Thus he aims to devise a concept of truth that avoids "inviting" skepticism in the way he sees previous theories as doing. How does he attempt this?

Davidson's ontology of truth begins with language, and more particularly, with linguistic communication toward the goal of interpersonal understanding. This is his "given": the fact that language is spoken, understood, and communicated. What must be the case for understanding and communication to exist? Basically, all we need posit are meanings, beliefs, and truth; all else is unnecessary. Beliefs are the attitudes of speakers toward their utterances; meanings are the propositional content of utterances; and truth is the normative character of doxastic attitudes. Before we can use these conceptual tools to produce an account of understanding and com-

40. Evnine, *Davidson*, p. 145.
41. Davidson, "Structure and Content of Truth," p. 298.
42. Davidson, "Afterthoughts, 1987," p. 134.

munication, two further crucial ingredients are necessary: rationality and coherence. We must assume that speakers are rational, that their beliefs are caused by the world, that they are logically consistent and strive for coherence between their multiple commitments. With these assumptions we have all we need to generate an account of linguistic communication.

But what sort of truth does this yield? Could not the above framework operate as well in a fantasy world as in a world where speakers know and speak about their world in ways that are accurate and true? Davidson's answer is no, because when an interpreter attempts to discern the meaning of an utterance but only knows that the speakers hold the utterance to be true, then the interpreter must go "to the world": "What the interpreter has to go on, then, is information about what episodes and situations in the world cause an agent to prefer that one rather than another sentence be true."[43] Determinations of rationality and coherence involve a world-context in which utterances are made. Meaning is determinable by relating the speaker's belief to the world and to the specific network of causal relations within which the speaker is located and formulates beliefs. This is why Davidson claims that the concepts of meaning, truth, and belief each require the others, but that none is reducible to the others. Without the concept of truth as the veridical nature of belief, the Principle of Charity could not work to generate a theory of interpretation for any given set of utterances. Without a context for belief in which the truth of its propositional content inheres, meaning could not be ascertained.

Truth, then, is more than a simple assumption or heuristic device. It is not simply that which we must take as an unavoidable but unfounded postulate in order to begin the process of understanding. Rather, the belief in truth gains support from its existence within an interdependent set of working elements, including meaning, belief, and rationality as well as truth. Truth is not unsupported, but neither is it supported by a linear foundation; it exists within a coherent web all of whose elements stand or fall together. This makes Davidson's conception of truth a coherentist conception in the sense I have been using the word, for Davidson's truth is immanent rather than transcendent.

How does he then escape the charge that his concept of truth devolves into just the sort of epistemic theory he wishes to avoid? He rejects the strategy of avoiding skepticism that would bring truth "within the scope of human powers by cutting the concept down to size."[44] Indeed, Davidson has most recently distanced his views from coherentism because, in his view, it adopts that strategy and ties "truth directly to what is believed," a

---

43. Davidson, "Structure and Content of Truth," p. 322.
44. Ibid., p. 280.

thesis he rightly calls "mad."[45] But it seems to me that his views on both truth and justification remain coherentist in important ways even though he correctly separates his account from those of coherentists who would make truth a purely epistemic concept.

Clearly, truth is not purely epistemic for Davidson: it is an attribution involving the relationship between belief and world, between an utterance and its context. The meaning of truth itself, or what it is "about," is not simply a psychological condition, intensional state, or doxastic attitude. Yet Davidson rigorously eschews any hint that such a relationship can be characterized by correspondence or transcendence, and he makes truth a supporting term within his coherentist account of understanding. It is truth that offers the normative structure of thought, speech, and action imposed on all interpretive attributions. This fact "not only ensures that there is a ground level on which speakers share views, but also that what they share is a largely correct picture of a common world. The ultimate source of both objectivity and communication is the triangle that, by relating speaker, interpreter, and the world, determines the contents of thought and speech. Given this source, there is no room for a relativized concept of truth."[46] If the worry over skepticism has been a main reason why many philosophers like Davidson have been motivated to avoid correspondence and realist pretensions, relativism has been a major reason for avoiding coherentist accounts. Is Davidson warranted in believing that he has solved this puzzle?

### Davidson on Relativism

Davidson gives three reasons why his account successfully avoids relativism, some of which we have already discussed, but it is worth summarizing them here. First, the possibility of a proliferation of alternative coherent webs of belief is not a serious likelihood because, as stated earlier, Davidson is only concerned with webs of beliefs that real speakers of a language actually hold, and not with the imagined possibility of webs of belief some science fiction writer could dream up. His concern with epistemology, remember, begins from a concern with linguistic communication rather than an abstractly formulated inquiry into the nature of knowledge. Certainly if we restrict our study to actual beliefs people hold to be true rather than possible belief systems, the proliferation of relative webs of belief is reduced considerably.

45. Ibid., p. 305.
46. Ibid., p. 325.

But it remains possible, even likely, that there exist different webs of belief with significantly disparate truth-claims, as between, for example, speakers from very different cultures around the world. Moreover, Davidson's holistic account of the determination of meaning entails an indeterminacy of interpretation similar to the one Quine proposes for translation. If all we have to go on are knowledge of the sentences assented to by the speaker, knowledge of the context in which a speaker assents to a given sentence, and the Principle of Charity, clearly there will be more than one way to explicate the meaning of the sentences. There is nothing we can use to determine decisively in some situations whether "rabbit" or "undetached rabbit-part" is the true meaning of the speaker's words.

Davidson argues that the indeterminacy that results from this account is trivial and not at all pernicious. "This doctrine of indeterminacy of translation, as Quine called it, should be viewed as neither mysterious not threatening. It is no more mysterious than the fact that temperature can be measured in Centigrade or Fahrenheit. . . . And it is not threatening because the very procedure that demonstrates the degree of indeterminacy at the same time demonstrates that what is determinate is all we need."[47] It may seem unclear at first how the significant semantic difference between "rabbit" and "undetached rabbit-part" is analogous to describing the same temperature along two different systems of linear progression: in the first case there is a true difference in meaning whereas in the second case it is just that there are different ways of expressing the same meaning. Davidson's point, however, is that there is no relevant or significant difference between "rabbit" and "undetached rabbit-part" when in a given situation a speaker's words can be translated equally well using either term. "Equally well" here must mean with equal coherence to the rest of the system of translations, equal ability to predict future sentences held true by the speaker, and so on. If the two terms perform equally well within the holistic theory of meaning the interpreter has developed for the speaker, then any remaining possible indeterminacy is trivial, according to Davidson. Any serious concern over this would have to be based on the belief that meaning exists prior to the process of interpretation, and that if interpretation yields indeterminate results then somehow we have not got it "right": there is some determinate meaning behind the utterance which we have not been able to discover. On Davidson's view, however, meaning is a theoretical construction with arbitrary constraints. The constraints we impose on meaning are precisely those needed within processes of interpretation and understanding, and therefore the desire for a meaning that somehow exceeds those constraints, a meaning considered to exist outside those processes, is unintelligible. This, then,

---

47. Ibid., p. 313. See also Davidson, "Belief and the Basis of Meaning," pp. 151–54.

might be thought of as Davidson's second argument against relativism: the concern that relative ascriptions of meaning are inadequate presupposes a realist account of meaning. In actuality, indeterminate meaning-ascriptions are no more significant than temperature readings which vary from Fahrenheit to Centigrade. The difference is not ontological; thus it is trivial. The relativism involved in indeterminacy of translation is thus not the relativism that worries epistemologists.

Third, Davidson believes that many relativistic conclusions will be avoided by the necessity of seeking a comprehensive theory of interpretation or translation. For instance, in an attempt to translate an individual foreign speaker's utterances, the level of indeterminacy may indeed loom large:

> A theory for interpreting the utterances of a single speaker, based on nothing but his attitudes towards sentences, would, we may be sure, have many equally eligible rivals, for differences in interpretation could be offset by appropriate differences in the beliefs attributed. Given a community of speakers with apparently the same linguistic repertoire, however, the theorist will strive for a single theory of interpretation: this will greatly narrow his choice of preliminary theories for each individual speaker.[48]

Thus, if the unit of interpretation is not an individual speaker but a community of speakers, or the largest group we can manage, the possibility of relativism subsides because the criterion of comprehensive coherence will effectively eliminate the contradictory attributions of meaning which existed on the individual level.

These last two arguments, however, pertain to the situation, again, of the field linguist seeking to understand the utterances of a foreign group of speakers. But the issue of relativism which usually burdens coherence theories is not that of avoiding the attribution of contradictory beliefs within a language or web of belief but of relativism between languages or webs of belief, as in the case of the field linguist and the foreign speaker. Davidson's solution to this predicament, of course, is to deny the possibility of it ever occurring. Because the Principle of Charity operates at every step of the process of understanding, interpreting, and translating, it just is not possible for there to exist two significantly different webs of belief or conceptual schemes.

We have already discussed one objection to this argument, namely that it can yield conclusions only about what we can know, not about what there must be. Davidson's account of meaning as a theoretical construction and of truth as immanent answers this objection by denying the separation it as-

48. Davidson, "Belief and the Basis of Meaning," p. 153.

sumes between epistemic and metaphysical considerations. There remain, however, other problems with Davidson's attempt to outmaneuver relativism by invoking the Principle of Charity. First of all, how much difference versus agreement is allowed? All Davidson argues is that we need a "background" of shared beliefs in order to highlight our differences. Exactly how much difference does this allow? If a coherentist account of understanding and communication works by erasing or minimizing existent differences, perhaps it does entail the totalitarian effects Jean-François Lyotard might accuse it of. Can the Principle of Charity allow for and even encourage the identification, acknowledgment, and examination of differences? Are we in a dilemma here between relativism and the acknowledgment of difference on the one hand, and a totalitarian coherentism on the other?

A second problem is that Davidson's argument does not seem to preclude the possibility that I might come upon an alien culture whose utterances make so little sense to me that the best hypothesis I can offer is precisely that they are operating from within a different conceptual scheme or worldview from my own. Except for the fact that Davidson expressly denies this possibility, it would not contradict his claims to the extent that no real understanding or interpretation would have been effected and so no Principle of Charity would apply. If Davidson's starting premise is that understanding requires some level of agreement, then a situation in which no understanding and no agreement occurred would not refute his position. Of course, in such a situation, I could not with certainty affirm the fact that lack of agreement existed, since without understanding I could not say what the other beliefs were about at all.

Despite this difficulty, Davidson's approach to the problem of relativism has considerable merit. The above example does not show that relative belief systems can coexist with mutual understanding, so he has still avoided a scenario where one is left saying "True for you but not true for me," every epistemologist's nightmare. If we accept Davidson's ontology of meaning and truth, then I think we have to admit that the problem of relativism does not arise. The only serious problem attending his account in my view is the conflict that exists between the Principle of Charity and the acknowledgment of difference, but we will have to look elsewhere for an attentive discussion of this issue.

## Gadamer and Davidson

At this point we need to shift gears a bit in order to compare Davidson's version of coherence epistemology with Gadamer's and assess where our general comparison of coherentisms stands. Others have also recog-

nized the striking similarities between these apparently disparate philosophies. Devitt remarks that "the Davidsonian interpretative perspective is
interestingly reminiscent of the European *Verstehen* tradition, according to
which the social sciences differ from the natural ones in requiring a sort of
empathetic understanding."[49] In reference to Gadamer this is half right: as
we have seen, Gadamer does not make such a strict distinction between the
natural and social sciences, but his characterization of knowledge does
have important empathetic aspects. It is interesting that Devitt also attributes this view to Davidson, a philosopher who does not exactly use the "I
and Thou" terminology.

The similarities between their views should by now be obvious. Both
Gadamer and Davidson come to a coherentist or holistic understanding of
beliefs and justification through a prior concern with the dynamics of interpretation. Gadamer's work on hermeneutics was of course responsible
for his interest in interpretation, and I earlier advanced a theory that
Davidson's concern with interpretation resulted from his need to explain
how successful interpretation and communication could occur once reference was dropped. In any case, both Davidson's works and Gadamer's deal
in large part with the process of interpretation, and it is from a consideration of what is necessary for successful interpretation that each is led to coherence.

Davidson's work on interpretation could be seen as advancing a theory
of the method we must use to interpret foreign utterances successfully. The
method involves using the Principle of Charity, taking the community of
speakers as our unit of analysis rather than the individual speaker, and attributing meaning on the basis of a comprehensive theory that shows the
utterances' internal coherence and their rationality through their agreement with our own beliefs. Gadamer, on the other hand, opposes the idea
that methods consciously appropriated are always operative in understanding. There is a point at which method comes to an end, but beyond
which knowledge keeps going. The hermeneutic analysis of understanding
seeks to account for just this knowledge that transcends method.

Both Davidson and Gadamer, however, articulate coherence as part of
the ground upon which successful interpretation is possible. That is, both
imitate Kant's project of seeking to explain, not the method we must appropriate, but the conditions that operate beyond our conscious control in
knowledge-acquisition, that is, the ontological features of the knowing situation. This project emphasizes the importance of the background that
makes our beliefs justifiable, a background whose contours are hidden if
not imperceptible. Davidson's Principle of Charity, in which we assume

49. Devitt, *Realism and Truth*, 2d ed., p. 191.

both maximum agreement between the speaker's beliefs and our own and the rationality of the speaker, operates inevitably to assimilate the speaker's world to our own when we seek to understand the speaker's utterances. This is not a principle we can choose or not choose to adopt; it is endemic to the process of understanding. For Gadamer, interpretation requires that our horizon fuse with the horizon of the text, thus producing an assimilation between the horizons of reader and text. This is the condition that makes understanding possible. Thus, both Davidson and Gadamer are interested in the background necessary for understanding to be possible, both parallel Kant, and both incorporate coherence, assimilation, and agreement in their conceptions of the grounds of understanding.

Gadamer formulates what I have called a procedural and an ontological component to the way coherence figures into the process of interpreting texts and justifying interpretations. On the conscious level, we can seek the maximum internal coherence of the text, thus producing interpretations of individual statements that preserve rather than disrupt this maximum coherence. This procedure uses coherence to adjudicate between interpretations that differ in the amount of disunity they portray within a text. Coherence also operates ontologically through the assimilation of the reader's horizon to the horizon of the text. Understanding occurs when this unreachable layer of background meanings fuses, thus making the text understandable from within the horizon of the reader. For Davidson also, coherence has a double meaning. We consciously strive, on the one hand, to maximize the coherence of the foreign community's speech, and consider ourselves successful when our interpretation produces a coherent reading of their utterances, with as few internally contradictory beliefs as possible. But this is not the only way coherence figures into the process of understanding for Davidson. It is also the case that understanding requires an assimilation of others' beliefs to our own. This is not something we can choose or not, according to our epistemological assumptions. The assimilation is ontologically necessary in order for the process of understanding to occur. Thus Davidson and Gadamer each posit coherence both as something involved in the procedure we use when we engage in interpretation, and as something that exists in the background, making successful interpretation—and thus understanding—possible. Given his concern to reduce the inflated importance of method, Gadamer predictably emphasizes the latter of these two aspects of coherence, but surprisingly, so does Davidson.

Gadamer and Davidson both argue that we must assume the truth and the coherence of other's beliefs. Davidson claims that we are forced to assume this because agreement, coherence, and rationality are all necessary if the field linguist is to have any hope of making sense of the foreign speaker's utterances. For Gadamer we are in an identical position vis-à-vis

a text we are trying to interpret. Since there is no privileged authorial interpretation, no objective reference to go on, we can only achieve an interpretation by assuming the text's maximum coherence and truth. We must
seek an understanding that preserves these assumptions, without which
there are an indefinite number of possible candidates we could offer as interpretations of the text, each equally valid. Davidson similarly holds that
without these assumptions the field linguist could offer any number of
competing translations of the speaker's utterances, with no hope of adjudication.

Notice that both of these philosophers adopt this line of reasoning once
they have turned their back upon the usual or traditional way interpretation has been explained, that is, through some concept of objective reference or foundational justification. Because neither one of them has much
faith in a noncontroversial link between the belief and the world or text
transcendentally understood, or in the existence of some "true" meaning
beyond the text or utterance, they come to see interpreters as having nothing to go on besides the text or speech to be interpreted and their own prior
beliefs. It is in this situation, the situation of radical interpretation, that coherence must necessarily come to the fore. Both Davidson and Gadamer
universalize this situation to cover all instances of understanding, so that
coherence must play a role, even if only a background role, in all instances
where we come to know. For Davidson, all instances of interpretation are
instances of radical interpretation, and the Principle of Charity must be applied even to our own beliefs. For Gadamer, the hermeneutic of understanding is always in the background of even methodological processes of
acquiring knowledge.

Thus, the overall structure of Davidson's and Gadamer's arguments for
the importance of coherence in interpretation and understanding are the
same. Both argue that the assumption of the text's or speaker's coherence
is inevitable and that we must strive to maximize coherence as the only
means we have for achieving a determinate understanding of meaning.
Neither holds that we have access to some foundation or bedrock which
would provide us with a privileged route to the "true" meaning of the text
or utterance. All we have to go on is the text or utterance and our own web
of belief. Both try to establish the connection between using coherence in
interpretation and using it to determine truth. Gadamer does this by formulating an interactive metaphysics in which the fusion of horizons, or the
coherence between my web of belief and that represented by the text, is
what constitutes the truth of the text or the true interpretation. Davidson
does it by arguing that the web of beliefs his coherentist procedure tells us
to assume to be largely true must in fact be largely true because even an
omniscient observer would have to accept it as largely true. Thus, both

Davidson and Gadamer argue in defense of coherence that (1) it is inevitable, and (2) it is truth-conducive (or at least linked to truth in some significant way). On my interpretation, both offer new accounts of the meaning of truth that can be characterized as immanent.

Perhaps the most important similarity between Davidson and Gadamer is their preoccupation with language, whether spoken, written, or heard. For Davidson, language is both the ground of truth and its necessary limit, and he quotes Shakespeare's Ulysses approvingly when the latter says:

> . . . no man is the lord of anything, though in and of him there be much consistency, till he communicate his parts to others.[50]

Coherentism involves relationships between linguistic items, and even Davidson's concern with belief reduces it to that which can be uttered in linguistic form. But can the whole arena of knowledge be captured by an epistemological account that focuses exclusively on language? Is knowledge always expressible in propositional form? This myopic tendency of coherentist accounts toward the linguistic is a problem I raised in the Introduction. In the next two chapters we will explore the development of a concept of knowledge that, whatever other problems it may have, offers a richer, more practice-oriented version of coherence: Foucault's power/knowledge.

50. Quoted in Davidson, "Thought and Talk," in *Inquiries into Truth and Interpretation*, p. 170.

# CHAPTER FOUR

# "The 'games of truth' . . .":
# Foucault's Knowledge

The idea that the writings of Michel Foucault could make a productive contribution to the project of epistemology is anathema to most of his commentators. He is more often read as attempting to deconstruct epistemology by undermining its principal questions and founding premises. For example, Hilary Putnam attributes to Foucault the view that "all schemes of thought and all points of view are hopelessly subjective" and that beliefs are "mainly determined by unreason and selfish power."[1] If this were true, the projects of understanding how knowledge is possible and of formulating normative accounts of justification would lose their rationale. Richard Rorty and Charles Taylor have argued that Foucault is caught in the self-defeating dilemma of wanting to do "something like epistemology" after having rejected all the premises necessary to make such an enterprise intelligible.[2] On Jürgen Habermas's view, the epistemological content of Foucault's genealogical analysis must collapse in the end to "power effects," thus reducing the power/knowledge dyad that Foucault invents to, simply, power.[3] Even sympathetic readers such as Barry Allen understand Foucault to be claiming that there is nothing more to "being true" than "passing for true."[4] Paul Bové, another sympathetic reader, therefore suggests that any

1. Hilary Putnam, *Reason, Truth and History* (Cambridge: Cambridge University Press, 1981), pp. ix, 162.
2. Richard Rorty, "Foucault and Epistemology," in *Foucault: A Critical Reader*, ed. David Couzens Hoy (New York: Basil Blackwell, 1986), p. 43; Charles Taylor, "Foucault on Freedom and Truth," in *Foucault Reader*, ed. Hoy, pp. 69–102.
3. Jürgen Habermas, *Philosophical Discourses of Modernity*, trans. Frederick Lawrence (Cambridge: MIT Press, 1987), p. 279.
4. Barry Allen, *Truth in Philosophy* (Cambridge: Harvard University Press, 1993), chap. 8.

attempt to reconstruct Foucault's historical accounts as epistemological theses will only "blunt any awareness of how different his project might be."[5]

The account of Foucault's work advanced here will argue against each of the preceding positions. François Wahl reads Foucault as offering a reproach against *a* philosophy rather than philosophy per se, and I will read Foucault's oblique appraisal of epistemology in an analogous vein.[6] Moreover, I shall argue that Foucault's account of power/knowledge might be used to refashion rather than demolish epistemology, and to move it onto more productive terrain. This argument will be advanced in two ways: in this first chapter, I shall demonstrate key lines of continuity between Foucault's account of knowledge and the coherentist tradition in Anglo-American epistemology, and in the following chapter, I will take up the more general questions of what can count as an epistemology and how should Foucault's work be positioned with respect to this area of inquiry.[7] I oppose the view prominent among many continental theorists that Foucault represents such a radical rupture with epistemology that we cannot interrogate his own claims about knowledge in terms of traditional epistemological questions without distorting his project, begging the question against it, or rendering it unintelligible. I also reject the view prominent among many analytic philosophers that Foucault's repudiation of intentionality, reference, or an autonomous characterization of reason and truth places him outside the language game of epistemology. My strategy here as elsewhere in this book is to privilege the questions and founding premises of neither the analytic nor the continental problematics but to initiate a mutual interrogation of these, in this case, across the corpus of Foucault's writings. In this chapter I will try to establish that Foucault is a kind of epistemological coherentist, describe the kind of epistemological coherentist he is, and show how his version of coherentism contributes productively to the development of a coherentist account of knowledge.

The contrast that is often made between coherentist and foundationalist epistemologies is based on the fact that coherentism offers what I have been calling an immanent account of knowledge in contrast to founda-

---

5. Paul Bové, "Foreword, The Foucault Phenomenon: The Problematics of Style," in Gilles Deleuze, *Foucault* (Minneapolis: University of Minnesota Press, 1986), esp. p. xviii.
6. François Wahl, "Inside or Outside Philosophy?" in *Michel Foucault: Philosopher*, trans. Timothy J. Armstrong (New York: Routledge, 1992), p. 77.
7. It is dangerous to attempt a general account of Foucault's "theory of knowledge" that spans his diverse periods. His writings were discontinuous and contradictory, and no one theory can represent the whole, if indeed there is any "theory" to be found in Foucault. I will develop some themes in Foucault's work that remained important throughout, but the following is more of a reconstructive project than an attempt to depict accurately the whole of Foucault's work.

tionalism's transcendental account. For coherentism, knowledge is ultimately a product of phenomena which are immanent to human belief systems and human social organizations, whereas for foundationalism, if a belief is to count as knowledge it must ultimately be able to establish some link to a transcendent phenomenon or to something extrinsic to human belief systems. Thus, foundationalism ties justification to an external realm beyond beliefs and belief sets, and understands truth as a relationship of a certain sort with this external realm, while coherentism holds to an understanding of knowledge as immanent. On a coherentist account, justification is an immanent feature of beliefs in that it refers only to their interrelationships; truth, if it is defined as what coheres, is also emergent from immanent relationships rather than from an external or transcendent realm.

Foucault's account of knowledge is coherentist in that (1) it is an immanent account of knowledge, and (2) it understands both justification and truth as dependent on systemic interrelationships of mutual support between specified elements. As Wahl says, Foucault is "not concerned with truth such as it is posited *before* (and beyond) experience, but such as it *comes into play* in practices and through the interpretation of these practices."[8] For Foucault truth is "a thing of this world," produced within a constellation of elements immanent to the plane of human action.[9] As we shall see, however, Foucault confers the attribution "knowledge-constitutive" on a more varied group of elements than do the traditional analytic versions of coherentist epistemology, which treat only beliefs and belief sets this way.

## A Historical Account of Knowledge

Foucault has characterized his project as exploring "the history of the relations between thought and truth" or the history of reason.[10] This project grew out of an exploration of the conditions of possibility for particular bodies of knowledge: for example, the knowledge of madness, criminality, sexuality, and the self. From an essentially localized exploration of specific systems of knowledge Foucault developed a more general analysis of the processes in which systems of knowledge (or webs of belief) are constructed, including both the rules for inclusion within the systems

8. Wahl, "Inside or Outside Philosophy," p. 71.
9. Michel Foucault, "Truth and Power," in *Power/Knowledge: Selected Interviews and Other Writings 1972–1977*, ed. Colin Gordon (New York: Pantheon Books, 1980), p. 131.
10. Michel Foucault, "The Concern for Truth," in *Michel Foucault: Politics, Philosophy, Culture*, ed. Lawrence D. Kritzman (New York: Routledge, 1988), p. 256.

and the rules for constructing the systems themselves.[11] His concept of a discursive formation can be thought of as a system of possibility for a web of belief.[12] Along these lines, Ian Hacking has usefully suggested how a discursive formation can be understood as offering a "style of reasoning" which bears on the class of propositions considered to have a truth-value and the background assumptions operative in delimiting this class and epistemically categorizing its contents.[13] In his case studies in the human sciences, Foucault argues that, within these "styles of reasoning," the way in which the reasonable has been demarcated from the unreasonable, the true from the false, and the justified from the unjustified, is ultimately *historically contingent*, specifiable only in reference to a cultural space-time rather than a universal rule formation or progressivist epistemic teleology. His work shows that the operable epistemic criteria of demarcation for knowledge consist of a historically specific confluence of a host of interrelated elements, rather than transhistorical teleologies or relationships to transcendent phenomena.

Two points need to be made about Foucault's formulation of the historical aspect of this argument. The first is that Foucault recognizes the unique referential problem that must attend any historical account of reason. It is this problem to which he is alluding when he asks the question, "How can thought, insofar as it is related to truth, have a history?"[14] Given a conception of truth as correspondence to an independent reality, talk about a history of truth can only be understood as talk about a history of the increasing appropriation of truth and perhaps about the history of different attempts to mark out a route to truth. We can explore the history of

11. Foucault's interpreters debate just how general his analysis is. Some, for example, Gary Gutting, understand it as rather narrowly circumscribed, and others, for example, Rorty, see it as applicable to all claims whatsoever. Gary Gutting, *Michel Foucault's Archaeology of Scientific Reason* (Cambridge: Cambridge University Press, 1989); Rorty, "Foucault and Epistemology."

12. Michel Foucault, *The Archaeology of Knowledge*, in *The Archaeology of Knowledge and The Discourse on Language,* trans. A. M. Sheridan Smith (New York: Pantheon Books, 1972), pp. 67, 182. The terms "discourse" and "discursive formation", as well as others, are not treated in Foucault's works with the consistency and exactness analytic philosophers have come to expect. In *The Archaeology of Knowledge*, however, Foucault generally sticks to the rule of using "discourse" to refer to an actually existing group of statements that belong to the same discursive formation. "Discursive formation" refers to formative rules which govern that group and regulate the generation and distribution of new statements within the discourse. Because Foucault himself does not stick to this usage strictly in every essay or interview, some of his commentators have also used the term "discourse" to refer to a discursive formation, or made other variations. I will try to keep my usage consistent with that of *The Archaeology of Knowledge*.

13. Ian Hacking, "Language, Truth, and Reason," in *Rationality and Relativism*, ed. Martin Hollis and Steven Lukes (Cambridge: MIT Press, 1984), p. 48. See also Ian Hacking, "The Archaeology of Foucault," in *Foucault Reader*, ed. Hoy.

14. Foucault, "Concern for Truth," p. 256.

conceptions of justification and systems of belief, but within a correspondence tradition the notion of a history of truth per se can only signify a conceptual confusion. While he is aware of the anomalous status of his project within Western discourses, Foucault insists that we must not dogmatically preempt the question of the history of truth but include its very anomaly as an object of analysis. In other words, the "cognitive dissonance" created within our own discourse by the question of the history of truth should not dissuade us from broaching the subject. Foucault's "historicizing" of truth is therefore neither flippant nor naively unaware of the problems of self-reference that must attend it, but instead is designed to explore the very conditions of possibility that render the question *unaskable* within our own discourse.[15] This is not to say that the problems of self-reference will be simply set aside, but that they will not be allowed to function as unanalyzed assumptions or indefeasible objections to the project.[16]

The second point is that Foucault's histories are of course never supposed to remain, as it were, in history: the purpose of his historical forays is always to give a "history of the present," to understand how our criteria for knowledge evolved, to come to recognize their contingency, and thus to be freed from dogmatic attachments to our own discursive or belief-generating formations. These are the same goals Nietzsche had in mind in developing his genealogies of religion and morality, and it is for this reason Foucault appropriates both the term and the method. For Nietzsche and Foucault, providing a genealogy of present day "absolute" truths will have a liberating effect, dislodging their power and thus freeing us to imagine new possibilities. The point of Foucault's genealogies, then, is to multiply and deepen our practice of critical self-reflection.

But, one might be tempted to ask, why do our present-day beliefs about knowledge need to be dislodged? Without at least a provisionally persuasive answer to this question, one might not be motivated to go any further. For Nietzsche, the problem with Christian morality and religion was that, briefly put, they had become obstacles in the way of a certain type of human flourishing. By valorizing weakness and excusing ressentiment, Christianity blocks the development of a creative courage necessary for philosophical development. Foucault similarly suggests, along with philosophers of the Frankfurt School, that the will to truth exemplified in

15. Gutting offers an insightful discussion of the issue of self-reference in Foucault and why it is actually not a debilitating problem for his account. See Gutting, *Michel Foucault's Archaeology of Scientific Reason*, esp. chap. 7.
16. For useful rejoinders to the self-refuting charge against Foucault, see Thomas R. Flynn, "Foucault as Parrhesiast: His Last Course at the Collège de France," in *The Final Foucault*, ed. James Bernauer and David Rasmussen (Cambridge: MIT Press, 1988), p. 112; and Gutting, *Michel Foucault's Archaeology of Scientific Reason*, pp. 272–87.

the human sciences has led to an increased subjection of individuals to hegemonic power/knowledges and a corollary increase in domination. The fact that power is operative in this story alongside knowledge is clear once one acknowledges the disparity between the incredible authority enjoyed by the human sciences over our lives and the fact that their theories are only tenuously grounded by commonly accepted scientific standards.[17] The human sciences are "dubious, still imprecise disciplines" which rarely enjoy a consensus on methods, suffer constant intrusion of moral and political commitments, and generally obtain only weak, indirect support from the kind of evidence that is not vulnerable to contestatory interpretations.[18] And yet, despite the fact that these disciplines have not achieved the stage of "normalcy" in Kuhn's sense, they are accorded an inordinate authority in criminal and judicial matters, legal determinations of competency for a range of behaviors, and the promulgation of "universal human norms" imposed as measures of judgment on us all. They are used to justify everything from forced institutionalizations to removing children from their parents. Foucault's question thus becomes, how might one account for this disparity between their social authority and their scientific status?

Foucault attempts to offer an explanation that does not rely on a progressive or realist account of science, that is, that does not explain the rise of the authority of the human sciences on the basis of an unexamined assumption about their enlarging reference to reality. He wants to explore the development of the human sciences in a way that does not refer to the truth-value of their claims or epistemically evaluate the content of their theories, and thus he tries to enact what Hubert Dreyfus and Paul Rabinow have dubbed an epistemological bracketing. But such a bracketing requires that we be able to distance ourselves from the "compelling feel" of these theories and dislodge their presumption of epistemic adequacy. This returns us to the genealogical method, by which Foucault pursues a dual purpose: to disabuse his readers of their attachment to transcendent epistemological formulations and to create the conditions whereby a different epistemological project might emerge.

In order to discern this different project we need to begin by taking a closer look at Foucault's central concept: the discursive formation. In general, the discursive formation, as already stated, denotes for Foucault the conditions of possibility for webs of belief. Whereas discourses involve a set of written and spoken statements, both of which may be referred to as "texts," the discursive formation is the structure or system that engenders

---

17. See Michel Foucault, "Two Lectures," in *Power/Knowledge*, p. 107.
18. Foucault, *Archaeology of Knowledge*, p. 178.

the possible articulation of certain statements and not others. It is Foucault's claim that the formative rules of this system will be determined not by the content of the statements, their reference to nondiscursive objects, or the intentions of believing subjects, but ultimately and fundamentally by the interrelationships that exist between discursive entities. Out of these interrelationships will emerge formation rules, objects of inquiry, and the conditions of possibility for specific discourses and discursive changes. Thus, relations immanent to the discourse will always be the explanation "in the final instance." Consider the following passages from *The Archaeology of Knowledge*:

> What properly belongs to a discursive formation and what makes it possible to delimit the group of concepts, disparate as they may be, that are specific to it, is the way in which these different elements are related to one another. . . . It is this group of relations that constitutes a system of conceptual formation. (59–60)

> Psychiatric discourse is characterized not by privileged objects, but by the way in which it forms objects that are in fact highly dispersed. This formation is made possible by a group of relations between authorities of emergence, delimitation, and specification. One might say, then, that a discursive formation is defined (as far as its objects are concerned, at least) if one can establish such a group. (44)

> By *episteme*, we mean, in fact, the total set of relations that unite, at a given period, the discursive practices that give rise to epistemological figures, sciences, and possibly formalized systems. (191)

These accounts of the discursive formation constitute a key part of my argument that Foucault's view can be called coherentist. Understood in this way, a discursive formation sets out what is statable and what can have a truth-value, and Foucault's description of discursive formations describes them as delimited through a principle of organization that emerges out of immanent groups of relations. It is relations between statements and between statements and other discursive elements (and in some cases nondiscursive elements, though these are always *practices* rather than *things*) that produce justification-conferring structures, rather than the correspondence of the content to an external referent. It is the structural features and strategies discernible at the level of a discursive formation that create the possibility for a particular set of statements to have meaning and to be given a truth-value (79).

This establishes that Foucault's account is immanent rather than transcendental, since immanent relations are the efficacious elements that organize discourses. But what kind of relations are they? Foucault distinguishes his conception of discursive relations from traditional structuralist or functionalist accounts:

> Discursive relations are not, as we can see, internal to a discourse: they do not connect concepts or words with one another; they do not establish a deductive or rhetorical structure between propositions or sentences. Yet they are not relations exterior to discourse, relations that might limit it, or impose certain forms upon it, or force it, in certain circumstances, to state certain things. They are, in a sense, at the limit of discourse. . . . These relations characterize not the language used by discourse, nor the circumstances in which it is deployed, but discourse itself as a practice. (46)

In typical fashion here, Foucault spells out what his notion of discursive relations is not, warning his readers to avoid assuming that he is simply invoking already familiar theories of language. The outlines of his own view are harder to discern: what does it mean to say that discursive relations operate at the limits of discourse? In order to understand more clearly the *kind* of relations Foucault posits as operative in constituting discursive formations, it will be helpful to explore in turn the issues of meaning, justification, and truth.

In one of his early works, *The Birth of the Clinic*, Foucault declares that he will treat the texts of clinical discourse as an entity to themselves, without recourse to an intention or referent "behind" the words. In place of reference or intentionality, Foucault proposes to look for the meaning of a statement in terms of its position within the particular discourse in which it exists, or out of which it emerges. Accordingly, he explains that, after having rejected both intentionality and reference as adequate or necessary explanatory concepts, the only analysis left to him would be one that treats the entities of a discourse "as events and functional segments gradually coming together to form a system. The meaning of a statement would be defined not by the treasure of intentions it might contain . . . but by the *difference* that articulates it upon the other real or possible statements, which are contemporary to it or to which it is opposed in the linear series of time."[19] This claim that meaning is established through the internal relations between statements, where the meaning of any element—word, proposition, or theory—is determined by the discourse in which it subsists,

19. Michel Foucault, *The Birth of the Clinic: An Archaeology of Medical Perception*, trans. A. M. Sheridan Smith (New York: Random House, 1975), p. xvii (my emphasis).

would be called by analytic philosophers a coherence theory of meaning. It is on a coherence theory that "the relations that they have among themselves" determines the meaning of any given discursive elements.[20] Each element is characterized by its difference from other elements, thus creating a circular chain or a grid of distinctions with mutual relations of dependence. Hence, a statement that has no discernible connection or relation to any other statement is without meaning.[21]

Using Foucault's terms, a statement can be defined as meaningful if it is statable within a discourse. The rules of discursive formation do not mandate specific truth-values for specific statements, but open up a delimited space in which some statements can be meaningfully expressed and understood. For example, it is likely that in the dominant discourse of Greek citizens in the fourth century B.C., a statement condemning homosexuality as a sexual malfunction would result in puzzlement rather than rejection. The concepts necessary to generate the statement, for example, "homosexuality" as a sexual identity, as well as the discursive rules necessary to determine its truth-value, did not exist in that discourse. Therefore, the statement would have been meaningless. The absence of a conceptual category of "homosexual identity" might not be apparent if we were to look only at the practices of Greek citizens (from the perspective, that is, of our own dominant discursive formation), but the absence would become apparent through an archaeological analysis at the level of the discursive formation. As Foucault says,

> The conditions necessary for the appearance of an object of discourse, the historical conditions required if one is to "say anything" about it, and if several people are to say different things about it, the conditions necessary if it is to exist in relation to other objects . . . these conditions are many and imposing. Which means that one cannot speak of anything at any time. . . . The object

20. Ibid., p. 94.
21. On the basis of this type of mapping procedure, more than one, and perhaps indefinitely many, corresponding systems could be established. In other words, if only internal relations can be identified, then more than one substantive *content* could be given with the necessarily relationally isomorphic *structure*. This problem could be substantially diminished if one claimed that only actual, historically existent discursive systems, or systems of belief that real believers actually believe, are under analysis. Donald Davidson makes a related point in arguing that beliefs are not in general voluntary, and therefore that the objection to coherentism on the grounds that it will lead believers into accepting fairy tales is groundless. Given Foucault's preference for "case-studies" of real historical discourses over more abstract theoretical claims about knowledge, we might see him as making a Davidsonian kind of move here. But then it might be argued that this leaves his analysis at the level of historical description rather than epistemology. This latter issue shall be discussed in Chapter 5. See Donald Davidson, "Empirical Content," in *Truth and Interpretation: Perspectives on the Philosophy of Donald Davidson*, ed. Ernest LePore (Oxford: Basil Blackwell, 1986), pp. 331, 327.

[of discourse] does not await in limbo the order that will free it and enable it to become embodied in a visible and prolix objectivity; it does not preexist itself, held back by some obstacle at the first edges of light. It exists under the positive conditions of a complex group of relations.[22]

This passage anticipates a discussion we shall begin shortly, concerning the internal relationship between ontology and meaning, or the immanence of ontological configurations within discursive formations.

Foucault sometimes refers to the kind of formation rules that determine meaning as a grammar or flexible set of guidelines for the generation of statements. Such a grammar would demarcate three categories of statements: meaningful and true ("Mars is the fourth planet"), meaningful and false ("Mars is the fifth planet"), and meaningless ("Mars is angry"). Like the American pragmatists, Foucault takes meaningfulness to require having a possible truth-value; to be statable a statement must be situated within a discursive formation such that we can know under what conditions (that is, relations) it can be affirmed or denied. There is a sense in which I can *understand* the statement "Mars is angry": it is not meaningless in the way that gibberish is meaningless. But there is another sense in which unless one can determine the truth-value of a statement, and thus unless a statement has connections to other discursive elements, it has no meaning. The statement "Mars is angry" once resonated within a particular discourse as it no longer does in ours.[23] There once were agreed upon procedures for determining its truth-value, such as consulting the Oracle at Delphi, whereas today such procedures for confirming or disconfirming the claim no longer exist. The possibility of having a truth-value and identifiable procedures for determining truth-value refers once again to the necessity of having relations of a specified sort with other elements of a discourse.

In order to understand not only how statements become meaningful but also how they come to be epistemically justified, more needs to be clarified about this account. What are the elements that must "resonate" for a statement to be meaningful, and in what specific way must they do so? Foucault's coherentism is not the familiar version involving logical relations of consistence or mutual support between propositions, which is why he says that they are not merely internal to a discourse. For Foucault, statements cannot be adequately analyzed merely as the bearers of propositional content; they are also bearers of an "enunciative function" which

22. Foucault, *Archaeology of Knowledge*, p. 45.
23. See Foucault, "Two Lectures," p. 112.

is identified neither with grammatical "acceptability" nor logical correctness, and which requires if it is to operate: a referential (which is not exactly a fact, a state of things, or even an object, but a principle of differentiation); a subject (not the speaking consciousness, not the author of the formulation, but a position that may be filled in certain conditions by various individuals); an associated field (which is not the real context of the formulation, the situation in which it was articulated, but a domain of coexistence for other statements); a materiality (which is not only the substance or support of the articulation but a status, rules of transcription, possibilities of use and re-use).[24]

It is immediately evident from this passage that for Foucault more and different kinds of elements will be involved in the determination of a web of beliefs than is usually thought to be the case: mere logical relations between propositions will not determine justification or meaning. The concept of the associated field is the closest we come to the traditional account of coherence as a domain of interconnections between statements. But logical relations are only part of what is involved in determining the functional capacity of a statement. The above passage claims that if a statement is to "operate"—which in this context means if it is to function within a discourse—grammatical and logical correctness are insufficient and perhaps even unnecessary. There are a number of other elements involved. A justified belief will require the proper kind of connection between the statement and a referential, a subject, an associated field, and a materiality. This web of interconnecting elements cannot be reduced to a correspondence relation between the statement and an external or extradiscursive realm. Though the terms "referential" and "materiality" might imply such an extradiscursive realm, the passage above makes such an inference impossible by giving decidedly discursive characterizations of these terms. A referential is a principle of differentiation by which the object world comes to be constituted; a materiality is a set of rules of transcription that affect possibilities of use for specific statements. Thus, there are no elements posited here that would qualify as constituent of a world-in-itself.

Especially important to note is the way in which forms of subjectivity are connected to a discourse. Foucault argues that a discursive practice sets out the "legitimate perspective for the agent of knowledge"[25] and involves rituals that determine "the individual properties and agreed roles of the speakers."[26] In other words, who may speak about what to whom is deter-

24. Foucault, *Archaeology of Knowledge*, p. 115.
25. Michel Foucault, "History of Systems of Thought," in *Language, Counter-Memory, Practice*, ed. Donald Bouchard (Ithaca: Cornell University Press, 1977), p. 199.
26. Foucault, "The Discourse on Language," in *The Archaeology of Knowledge and The Discourse on Language*, p. 225.

mined at the level of the discursive formation. Foucault's primary examples are drawn from the religious confessional-turned-therapeutic rituals in which the roles for speakers and hearers are severely circumscribed and arranged according to their perceived relationship to the production of truth, which it is the main business of the confessional to extract. The penitent/patient must speak of his experience, as a sort of raw transmission, but the truth is given by the priest/therapist who must interpret the experience to sift out its essential deep truth, and in regard to this truth the penitent/patient can only play the role of respectful, appreciative hearer.[27] Foucault makes his point more general, and argues that discourses always include such a division and arrangement of speaking and hearing practices.

Habermas makes a similar claim in his essay "What Is Universal Pragmatics?" when he argues that a pragmatic dimension is inherent to linguistic utterances, a dimension that involves the discursive arrangement of participants in the linguistic event.[28] It is precisely within this pragmatic dimension that Habermas believes we can discern the implicit linguistic norms to which we can appeal for an ethics that aspires to the universal. Foucault's account does not posit the existence of such universal norms but focuses instead on the effect that the arrangements and determinations of the participants and their roles in discursive events have upon the way notions of the self are constituted (for example, the self as a mechanism for taking in perceptions in a specifically prescribed manner, or as a locus of innate ideas or deep truths). It is in this sense that subjectivity, understood here as the internal experiences of consciousness as well as behavior, is discursively constituted. Discursive formations involve not only concepts of the self, but the practices and experiences such concepts make possible. A statement within a discursive formation, involving an associated field, a referential, and a materiality, will constitute the available subject-positions its hearers may assume, with experiential effects. This analysis could be usefully applied to account for systemic oppressions in which, for example, linguistic practices make no space for women with epistemic authority, bodies without racial hierarchy, or workers without need of management. Rage is often the result of such inarticulable exclusions.

We need to return to the type of interconnection Foucault believes to exist between these discursive elements. Is the relationship between materiality, referential, subject, and associated field a relationship of coherence or logical consistency? Foucault denies that the connection between statements can be characterized as simply grammatical or logical, where the lat-

27. I have analyzed Foucault's account of the confessional in more detail with Laura Gray in "Survivor Discourse: Transgression or Recuperation?" *SIGNS* 18 (1993): 260–90.
28. Jürgen Habermas, "What Is Universal Pragmatics?" in *Communication and the Evolution of Society* (Boston: Beacon Press, 1979), pp. 1–68.

ter is explicated as "formal coherence or conceptual connection."[29] He also rejects the view that the link between statements in a discourse originates at the psychological level, or that they all enjoy an origin in a form of consciousness that is constant or identical (115). Thus he rejects the main orientation to belief-formation adopted by analytic epistemology and phenomenology. Instead of relating statements within a discourse through their psychological causality or their grammatical or logical connections, Foucault claims they "are linked at the *statement* level" (115).

> What has been called "discursive formation" divides up the general plane of things said at the specific level of statements. The four directions in which it is analyzed (formation of objects, formations of the subjective positions, formation of concepts, formation of strategic choices) correspond to the four domains in which the enunciative function operates. And if the discursive formations are free in relation to the great rhetorical unities of the text or book, if they are not governed by the rigor of a deductive architecture, if they are not identified with the *oeuvre* of an author, it is because they bring into play the enunciative level, together with the regularities that characterize it, and not the grammatical level of sentences, or the logical level of propositions, or the psychological level of formation. (116)

Here the character of the connection is simply expressed as a regularity, that is, a uniform conformity to a common set of rules (which is precisely the way in which Foucault has said that discourses can be delimited). Regularities between statements reveal the formative structure that conditions the possibility of specific objects, subjects, concepts, and strategic choices. Regularities also reveal the system by which the succession, dispersion, repetition, and coexistence of statements is governed. The result is not only a system of exclusion but a productive economy regulating both generation and distribution.

Foucault's account shifts the epistemic evaluation of statements away from an evaluation of their propositional content or the intentional features of believing subjects. In a sense we have yet to define, meaning and truth are constituted at the discursive level. An evaluation at this level will involve as a central consideration the relations between statements, objects, subject positions, and strategic choices. Foucault's concept of the enunciative function thus brings into play the whole context of the discursive event.

Foucault's coherentism is thus a richer version than traditional accounts in two ways. The kinds of elements he considers involve more than simple

29. Foucault, *Archaeology of Knowledge*, p. 115.

statements and include objects, concepts, subject-positions (that is, the position of subjects with respect to the statement, whether speaking, spoken to, spoken about, or ignored), and practices of a nearly infinite variety. The principle by which such a large and diverse grouping of elements is linked centers on their internal relations. But these relations are heterogeneous and not restricted to logical consistency: the relations Foucault mentions include ones of consistency as well as succession, dispersion, unity, derivation, exclusion, mutual alteration, intersection, and displacement. Given this multitude of relational types, it may seem odd to characterize Foucault as a coherentist. Coherence need not, however, refer only to consistency, but can also mean mutual support. Relations that allow for and guide the proliferations of derivation, mutual alteration, intersection, and even displacement and exclusion offer mutual support in the sense that these disparate operations are grounded in specific forms of connection between elements, or a common frame. In other words, these operations are not random. Moreover, as I have already argued, coherentist epistemology has played an important role in representing a nonfoundational, immanent account of knowledge, and Foucault's account is clearly an exemplar of this.

### Conditions of Justification

Let us now turn to the issue of Foucault's notion of justification, which is best captured in Foucault's account of "discursive practice." The first thing to note is that it cannot be an internalist account. Foucault says that the concept of discursive practice "must not be confused with the expressive operation by which an individual formulates an idea, a desire, an image; nor with the rational activity that may operate in a system of inference," nor indeed with any subject-generated action at all.[30] A discursive practice is guided by a "body of anonymous, historical rules, always determined in the time and space that have defined a given period, and for a given social, economic, geographical, or linguistic area, the conditions of operation of the enunciative function" (117). Only an externalist theory of justification could be extrapolated from this. Foucault seems to care little about the doxastic states of individual believers, except insofar as these exhibit features of subjectivity made possible by a discursive formation. Knowledge is defined as a subcategory of a discursive practice—which means that not everything possible within a discursive practice will count as knowledge—and as more general than a science or the set of all sciences at a given historical point. Sets of statements become characterized as

30. Ibid., p. 117.

knowledge when they exist in a certain configuration of elements which are "formed in a regular manner by a discursive practice, and which are indispensable to the constitution of a science, although they are not necessarily destined to give rise to one" (182). This definition does not reveal much, except that to count as knowledge a statement must be able to function within a science or a potential science, which returns us to the notion that the criterion of knowledge is its functional relationship to other discursive elements. Within the available categories of Anglo-American epistemology, such a view would constitute an account of justification that could only be understood as both externalist and coherentist.

Strategies or procedures of justification, such as scientific practices, are historical, contingent, and discursively constituted. One of Foucault's central aims in *The Birth of the Clinic* is to refute the dominant narrative of empirical progress in eighteenth-century medicine as a "discovery" of the method of observation. On Foucault's view, the priority given to "direct" observation as a justificatory strategy for medical theories and diagnoses was based, not on a discovery, but on a shift at the discursive level. Foucault points out that the gaze, though hailed as pure and preconceptual, can only function successfully when connected to a system of understanding that dictates its use and interprets its results. "What defines the act of medical knowledge in its concrete form is not . . . the encounter between doctor and patient, nor is it the confrontation between a body of knowledge and a perception; it is the systematic intersection of two series of information . . . whose intersection reveals, in its isolable dependence, the *individual* fact."[31] Thus Foucault shares the view now commonly held by philosophers of science that a "pure" observation is not an observation at all, in the sense that to count as an observation it must support a theory or diagnosis. It will not become an observation until and unless it can be deployed within a relevant theoretical context. "The smallest possible observable segment . . . is the singular impression one receives of a patient, or, rather, of a symptom of that patient; it signifies nothing in itself, but assumes meaning and value and begins to speak if it blends with other elements."[32] It was not, therefore, greater proximity between preexisting knower and known that produced the current configuration of justificatory practices in medicine. Against the empiricist account, Foucault holds that "a more precise historical analysis" (which we can infer is his own) reveals that the shift to modern medicine involved a transformation of "the type of objects to be known" and "the elements relevant to a possible epistemic knowledge (*savoir*)."

31. Foucault, *Birth of the Clinic*, p. 30.
32. Ibid., p. 118.

What is modified in giving place to anatomo-clinical medicine [or the privileging of the gaze] is not, therefore, the mere surface of contact between knowing subject and the known object; *it is the more general arrangement of knowledge that determines the reciprocal positions and the connection between the one who must know and that which is to be known.* The access of the medical gaze into the sick body was not the continuation of a movement of approach that had been developing in more or less regular fashion . . . ; it was the result of a recasting at the level of epistemic knowledge (*savoir*) itself, and not at the level of accumulated, refined, deepened, adjusted knowledge (*connaissances*).[33]

Discursive changes thus affect not only the discursively constituted objects and subjects of knowledge, but also the epistemically preferred relationship between the two. It is this relationship that bears most directly on the issue of justification, but it is configured and reconfigured at the discursive level. A change in the justificatory hierarchy from authoritative texts to the medical gaze was a change constituted by and only meaningful within a given discursive formation. Thus, procedures for justification, and theoretically sanctioned data or facts that can confer justification, change between discourses because the relations internal to discursive formations are reconfigured.

We might summarize Foucault's views on justification as follows. For any given particular belief to be justified there are at least three conditions that must be met, and all of these conditions involve the configuration of relations within a discursive formation. First, a statement must have a potentially identifiable truth-value. Given Foucault's theory of meaning, this first condition could be characterized as the requirement that a statement be meaningful before it can be justified. In *Discipline and Punish* Foucault provides interesting examples of this first condition. What might be called the problematic of criminality, or the set of questions asked about those accused of a crime, have significantly changed in France and generally in the West since the seventeenth century. At that time, the questions boiled down to whether or not the accused actually committed the crime and whether the law actually covered the deed in question. Now, however, an entirely new set of questions are routinely asked that were never considered before. Even if the accused committed the act, to what extent is the accused guilty? Was it an act of temporary insanity, an act caused by social conditioning, drug influence or hormonal imbalances, or an act determined by inherited characteristics? As Foucault puts it, "It is no longer simply: 'Who committed it?' But: 'how can we assign the causal process that produced it? Where did it originate in the author himself? Instinct, unconscious, environment,

33. Ibid., p. 137 (my emphasis).

heredity?' "[34] Thus, in seventeenth-century France the statement "The accused committed the deed but is not guilty" would not have had a truth-value, whereas today it does.

The truth-functional status of any given statement will most likely involve the categories of analysis possible within the discourse, or the "fixing of norms for the elaboration of concepts and theories."[35] For example, in one given discourse on criminality only two categories pertaining to murder may be operative—the category of murderer and the category of non-murderer—whereas in another discourse multiple categories might exist which involve insanity, premeditation, intentionality, chemical dependence, and physiological state. Foucault's suggestion is that this change does not represent simply a discovery of the psychological and physiological features of criminals, but a shift of focus from the crime itself to the prior state of the accused (a shift which of course constructs "the accused" as a form of subjective identity). It is only after that shift has been made that the multiple categories of criminal subjectivity will be constituted.

This brings us to a second condition of justification. In order to have a truth-value, a statement must be about an object whose existence is recognized within the discourse. Discourses are not merely "groups of signs" but "practices that systematically form the objects of which they speak."[36] The most notable example of such an "object" is human subjectivity, conceived (and experienced) since modernity as rational, potentially self-transparent, autonomous, and the authoritative origin of all our sensations and beliefs.[37] Much of the inquiry within the human sciences presupposes this subjectivity as its object of study. Foucault resists the notion that we can separate the process of justifying beliefs from the way in which those beliefs constitute the objects which they are about or which they presuppose. The usual notion of epistemic justification contributes to or participates in this act of ontological demarcation. For example, Descartes's reference to his clear and distinct ideas as justifying evidence in favor of the real referent of those ideas presents a claim about the nature and demarcation of his mind and self. One of the implications of Foucault's account of knowledge, then, would be that we need to look at how the framing of epistemic problems such as justification work against the visibility of epistemology's constitutive effects on its objects.

34. Michel Foucault, *Discipline and Punish*, trans. Alan Sheridan (New York: Random House, 1977), p. 19.
35. Foucault, "History of Systems of Thought," p. 199.
36. Foucault, *Archaeology of Knowledge*, p. 49.
37. See Michel Foucault, "Afterword: The Subject and Power," in Hubert L. Dreyfus and Paul Rabinow, *Michel Foucault: Beyond Structuralism and Hermeneutics*, 2d ed. (Chicago: University of Chicago Press, 1983), pp. 208–26.

A third condition of justification involves the "definition of a legitimate perspective for the agent of knowledge."[38] Discourses set out acceptable procedures and perspectives through which to appropriate knowledge. For example, Foucault argues that beginning with the sixteenth and seventeenth centuries the will to knowledge "imposed upon the knowing subject—in some ways taking precedence over all experience—a certain position, a certain viewpoint, and a certain function (look rather than read, verify rather than comment), [and] prescribed . . . the technological level at which knowledge could be employed in order to be verifiable and useful."[39] This particular shift marked the rise of perception as the central justification-conferring operation, as against previous practices such as consistency with received dogma or confirmation by authority. Epistemic practices are ranked by discursive formations according to their truth-conduciveness. Conceptions about legitimate knowing practices and what constitutes reliable evidence are internal to a discourse, including procedures of justification or acceptable methods of appropriating knowledge. Propositions confirmed via currently acceptable procedures of justification will be epistemically privileged over propositions confirmed by procedures less valorized or perhaps even invisible within the current discursive formation.

Thus far, Foucault's account of justification seems to remain at the descriptive level. In the passages we have explored he is not discussing the epistemic validity of accounts of justification, but describing how theories and practices of justification are constituted within discursive formations. If we require of a theory of justification that it explain under what conditions a belief can be called justified, Foucault provides us with such a theory in his descriptive account of the generation of discourses. This sort of account is arguably not an epistemology, however, to the extent that it does not offer any epistemically based evaluation of the described practices of justifying beliefs and does not advance an argument about whether the current practices of determining justification are in fact truth-conducive either in an absolute sense or compared to other possible practices. Therefore, the preceding discussion of Foucault's views on justification may appear to confirm the claim that Foucault's project is not epistemological.

Such a conclusion would be premature. It assumes that Foucault's account remains at the descriptive level because it does not entertain or engage with a transcendental concept of truth, nor establish the relationship between justification-conferring practices and an extradiscursive truth. As I have suggested, Foucault's account of justification has all the signs of an

38. Foucault, "History of Systems of Thought," p. 199.
39. Foucault, "Discourse on Language," p. 218.

externalist account precisely because Foucault relates justified beliefs not to the intentions of believing subjects but to the ways in which statements come to be labeled "true." The latter process he explicates as entirely immanent to a discursive formation, but to decide that for this reason his account cannot be epistemological is to refuse seriously to consider the tenability of an immanent concept of truth. The critical question determining the status of Foucault's account should be, not whether he develops an immanent or transcendent concept of truth, but whether there is any *epistemically normative* content to Foucault's analysis of knowledge.

In his writings after 1970 Foucault developed an account of "subjugated knowledges" and argued for an epistemic criterion of truth that would be based on determining where a given statement is situated with respect to the subjugated and dominant knowledge(s) of its historical context. This work moves beyond the purely descriptive account of knowledge more characteristic of his structuralist period and away from a sociology of knowledge or an epistemically neutral account of knowledge. His later work also combines in an interesting way political and epistemic elements in its defense of subjugated knowledges.[40] Since it has a decisive bearing on whether or not Foucault's account of knowledge can be called an epistemology, I will discuss this issue and his arguments with respect to it more fully in the following chapter. For now, we must complete the discussion of Foucault's coherentism by turning to the most opaque epistemological issue in his work: his characterization of truth.

The issue of Foucault's views on truth is complicated and difficult to assess for a variety of reasons. For one thing, he changes his view drastically in midstream when he introduces the concept of power/knowledge in his post-1970 writings. Nor does Foucault ever pay sufficient attention to the issue of the ontology of truth that his own view must be associated with, usually dismissing this issue as lacking interest for him or as capable of being set aside. I believe, however, that Foucault developed the beginnings of a powerful new account of truth, and one that is more than merely provocative. In the remainder of this chapter I will sketch this new account very briefly to establish that it is a coherentist account. I will wait until the following chapter to take up the epistemological problems and questions to which this new account must give rise.

For Foucault, truth is internal to a discourse, an emergent property of a certain configuration of discursive and nondiscursive elements and prac-

40. On the periods in Foucault's writings, see Arnold Davidson, "Archaeology, Genealogy, Ethics," in *Foucault Reader*, ed. Hoy; see also Dreyfus and Rabinow's defense of their assertion that Foucault's early work can be called structuralist despite his claims to the contrary, in their *Foucault: Beyond Structuralism and Hermeneutics*, xi–xxvii. Gutting discusses the appropriateness of this label in *Michel Foucault's Archaeology of Scientific Reason*, pp. 266–70.

tices. Truth is produced by large social apparatuses and is thus implicated in the distribution of power relations. It is never "outside power," but is always "a thing of this world."[41] Such an analysis makes clear that politics and metaphysics are inseparable. To say that "truth is a thing of this world" relates to Foucault's claim that it is internal to a discourse: it does not represent a correspondence relation *between* a discourse and a transcendent realm, but is a part of *this* world, that is, our world.[42] Ontologically this could be interpreted either as a form of idealist antirealism which holds that reality just is the discursive realm, or alternatively it could be interpreted as a weak version of realism which holds that our only access to reality is through discursive interpretations. Given either of these positions, it is relatively easy to see how politics enters in. If truth is underdetermined by a "brute reality," and if the realm of discourse is itself highly diffuse and indeterminate, it becomes easy to argue that power structures and power relations contribute significantly to the final determination of what gets to count as true. Foucault's case studies in the human sciences all provide specific examples of this very point.

Foucault's account of the ontology of truth is thus a coherentist account. As we have already seen, he takes the object of inquiry to be in some important sense constituted rather than discovered by a discourse. An object of inquiry

> exists under the positive conditions of a complex group of relations. These relations are established between institutions, economic and social processes, behavioural patterns, systems of norms, techniques, types of classification, modes of characterization; and these relations are not present in the object; . . . They do not define its internal constitution, but what enables it to appear, to juxtapose itself with other objects, to situate itself in relation to them, to define its difference, its irreducibility, and even its heterogeneity, in short, to be placed in a field of exteriority.[43]

The ontological status of objects referred to in truth-claims is dependent on the above listed heteromorphous relations. This dependence is not merely linguistic or conceptual, but ontological: "Problematization doesn't mean representation of a pre-existing object, nor the creation by discourse of an

41. Foucault, "Truth and Power," p. 131.
42. This notion of the world was conceptually described in the Husserlian tradition as referring to the realm of "lived experience," but Foucault does not want to tie it to the realm of human consciousness. For Foucault, to say that truth is a thing of this world is to say that it is a product of discursive formations rather than transcendent reality, which is not to imply that it is created by humans or that it refers to their experiential consciousness, but that truth is the "anonymous" development of discourses.
43. Foucault, *Archaeology of Knowledge*, p. 45.

object that doesn't exist. It is the *totality* of discursive or non-discursive practices that introduces something into the play of true and false and constitutes it as an object for thought (whether in the form of moral reflection, scientific knowledge, political analysis, etc.)."[44] Foucault's claim that discourses create the objects of which they speak is a theme he has reiterated in his work at least since the mid-1960s; the only innovation in these passages is his inclusion of nondiscursive practices. The relevant point here is that objects of knowledge emerge from a totality of practices, and thus from the whole set of diverse relations that is the focus of his account of discourses. This view represents a coherentist ontology of truth in that the criterion and the definition of truth refer us ultimately to the configuration of relations between elements, be they discursive only or discursive and nondiscursive.

Before moving on let me note that such a view of truth is not necessarily in absolute contradiction with all features of a commonsense realism. Foucault never discusses simple perceptual or analytical statements such as $2 + 2 = 4$ or "I see a pencil before me." He does, however, indicate that his conception of discursive formation does not require calling all such beliefs into question, as in this passage on discursive changes: "To say that one discursive formation is substituted for another is not to say that a whole world of absolutely new objects, enunciations, concepts, and theoretical choices emerges fully armed and fully organized in a text that will replace that world once and for all; it is to say that a general transformation of relations has occurred, but that it does not necessarily alter all the elements."[45] This leaves open the possibility that most commonsense and simple perceptual beliefs may remain constant through discursive changes. Even though everything relevant to knowledge is linked in some significant way to a discourse, discourses are commensurable with one another. Now, there are different explanations we might give about why certain beliefs remain constant, one of which would be their causal connection to a mind-independent reality. Foucault does not venture a hypothesis, but his concern to highlight the governing role of discourses does not entail a rejection of any and all such hypotheses or versions of realism. I have argued that Foucault's account of meaning, justification, and truth can be usefully understood as a coherentist account. More than this, Foucault's version of coherentism can advance the development of coherentist epistemologies beyond the state of its current impasse. In the remainder of this chapter I will summarize the coherentist interpretation of Foucault and present an argument for its advantages.

44. Foucault, "Concern for Truth," p. 257 (my emphasis).
45. Foucault, *Archaeology of Knowledge*, p. 173.

## Foucault the Coherentist

Coherentism is an immanent account of knowledge that takes beliefs to be justified via their relationship to a system of mutually supporting elements. Foucault's account of knowledge is consistently immanent in its rejection of reference, intentionality, and any transcendent notion of truth as explanatory concepts for the generation of knowledge. It is coherentist in that Foucault identifies discourses, which are the operative loci of knowledge, as constituted by complex relationships between its diverse elements. Despite the diversity of the elements Foucault introduces and the multiple forms of relations he describes, discourses constitute a unity formed by the regularities between statements. There was a period in which Foucault was read as the "philosopher of discontinuity": as only positing ruptures, breaks, disunities, and the like. It is true that in his approach to both history and discourse Foucault fought against closed dialectics, historical teleologies focused on sameness and identity, and conceptions of discourse as a bounded domain with clearly marked or impenetrable borders. He insisted on introducing chance as a key player in history and he maintained Gaston Bachelard's focus on epistemological breaks against the smooth flow of a progressivist narrative of science. For these reasons an attribution of coherentism to Foucault may seem odd, but as Foucault himself somewhat peevishly complained in response to his label as the "philosopher of discontinuity," his argument had not been with the existence of unities but with (1) their representation as objective rather than the result of provisional formulations, and (2) the notion that there is always a single overall "principle" or form of a discourse or a society that exerts absolute hegemony in every discursive microcosm.[46] Foucault's social landscape is an extremely uneven one, in which all dominant paradigms are continuously under barrage. This picture does not, however, militate against his analysis of the regularities and exclusions inherent to discursive formations. That is, throughout his various works Foucault has described, not an endlessly dispersed, diffuse concoction of elements that admit of no characterization because of their fundamental intrinsic heterogeneity, but provisional accounts of identifiable discursive formations which reveal significant connections and relations of mutual support between diverse elements, thus making possible the development of his concepts of the episteme, the positivity, and even discourse itself.

Manfred Frank has critiqued Foucault's concept of the discourse on just these grounds. There exists an unresolvable contradiction, writes Frank, between Foucault's claim that discourses are ungovernable and nonuni-

---

46. Foucault, "Truth and Power," pp. 111–12.

form and his claim that discourses can be described and analyzed scientifically and are constituted by discernible principles of formation.[47] I think that Frank perceives a contradiction because he downplays the extent to which Foucault insists on the contingency and instability of all discursive formations. This emphasis allows Foucault to describe the structure of discourses as they crystallize at specific moments, but it also lets him claim that all such structures are open to break and rupture and therefore incapable of being controlled or even securely predicted. Foucault's conceptualization of discourses, epistemes, and even positivities portrays them as open rather than closed, and internally always involved in various degrees of contestation and struggle rather than seamless consistency, but to characterize them thus is not to differ from most modern descriptions of the coherent web of beliefs actually existing within science itself. Who would not agree that the paradigm of quantum mechanics is both dominant and highly contested? To posit coherence as the mode by which discourses authorize certain claims as "knowledge" does not commit one to a closed clocklike mechanism where only harmony exists, or even to the view that knowledge is actually produced only via coherence. Breaks and ruptures obviously make the creation of new knowledges possible. The status of knowledge will only be conferred, however, via some coherentist process that can "verify" new claims by connecting them, in Foucault's terminology, to a materiality, a referential, a mode of subjectivity, and an associated field.

Foucault's version of coherentism contributes constructively to the development of coherence epistemologies and to epistemology in general in at least three important ways. (1) His account makes possible a strategy whereby the truth-conduciveness of coherence as a criterion of knowledge can be established. (2) Foucault points a way out of the impasse of conceptualizing knowledge as either science or ideology and begins to formulate a new and better articulation of the relationship between politics and knowledge. (3) Foucault provides a much richer and more diversified concept of belief systems and coherence relations, which strengthens the usefulness and plausibility of coherentist accounts of knowledge. I will briefly develop each of these points.

Coherentist accounts of justification have typically foundered on the difficulty of establishing that coherence by itself has any necessary connection to truth. One way around this is to claim that reality is itself coherent and therefore that systems of belief which maximize coherence will by that act maximize their likelihood to be true. But it is difficult to justify the claim

---

47. Manfred Frank, "On Foucault's Concept of Discourse," in *Michel Foucault: Philosopher*, pp. 112–13.

that reality is simply coherent, and especially difficult to justify this claim without a circular regress that relies on a coherence criterion in order to be established (for example, if one were to argue that a coherent reality is the best explanation of the evidence, meaning that it is the most intelligible explanation or the one that best coheres with the evidence).[48] Foucault's account has the virtue of linking a coherentist ontology of truth with a coherence account of justification, which results in making coherence a truth-conducive criterion. Like Gadamer's account, Foucault's claim for a coherentist ontology of truth is more than a mere assertion. In his view, discourses constitute the objects of which they speak; he gives detailed analyses of the human sciences to support this claim in the case of objects such as madness and sexual and criminal identities. Given this, the establishment of a regularity between a new belief and a preexisting discourse is sufficient to establish its epistemic justification because that is just what justification and truth consist in: they are emergent properties of discursive entities related in specific configurations. If Foucault's account has weaknesses, one of these is certainly the vagueness with which he explicates the nature of the relationships that produce truth. This vagueness, however, does not exist in his specific examples of particular discourses, but only in the general account he tries to develop in *The Archaeology of Knowledge*.

It is Foucault's coherentism that spurs him to argue against the usual distinction drawn between science and ideology.[49] On Foucault's view, such a distinction is mistaken because the traditional way in which ideologies are identified in fact holds for all knowledge. That is, if ideology is defined as knowledge that has an intrinsic relationship to power or that has strategic relations to specific political and economic practices in a given society, then all knowledges can be categorized in this way. If so, the usefulness of the category of ideology is obviously diminished and can no longer serve as the pejorative alternative to a science conceived as enjoying some greater epistemic legitimacy. Foucault also challenges critiques of science *as* ideology because these critiques assume that there is a purposeful manipulation of science by conscious interests. This gives much more efficacy to the knower, in this case en masse, than Foucault will allow. Foucault calls into question the direction of the causal arrow from given subjects to dominant knowledges and suggests that causation actually runs the other way.

Foucault's conception of knowledge by the early 1970s was that it always has ties to and is in fact formed via its relationship with social, economic, and political practices. It is through knowledge in its relationship with these practices that forms of human subjectivity are both produced

---

48. This is the error Laurence Bonjour makes in his argument for coherence, *The Structure of Empirical Knowledge* (Cambridge: Harvard University Press, 1985).
49. Foucault, *Archaeology of Knowledge*, pp. 184–86.

and constrained. But Foucault resists the conclusion that all knowledge is ideological. Why? Surely there were multiple reasons: his desire to distance himself from Marxism even in its structuralist Althusserian variations, his sense that ideology is still tied to the positing of a "false consciousness" fundamentally at odds with his own account of the discursive construction of subjectivity, and probably his realization that the notion of ideology would put too negative a spin on his concept of power/knowledge. For, unlike Althusser, Foucault posits no "science" that can offer an epistemically privileged relief from ideological knowledge. Within the tradition of "ideology," a knowledge's connection to politics means that it is never "really" knowledge but some type of irrational subjectivism or political demagoguery, or at least a partial and distorted perspective. The latter conclusion follows from two assumptions Foucault does not share: (1) that ties between knowledge and politics produce a "distortion" of the truth, and (2) that when politics or power enters the scene the possibility of reconfiguration can only be enacted by force. The concept of distortion relies on the possibility of a pure truth, free of power relations, which can offer up simple, accurate representations of the Real. Without that possibility, the charge of distortion loses its meaningfulness: what is it that becomes distorted?

Foucault is not, however, committed to the view that truth is determined by power and that therefore we can reduce all epistemological considerations to political analyses and power struggles. It is for this reason he insists on the dyadic concept, power/knowledge, in which neither term is reduced or subordinated to the other. To analyze knowledge in its relationships to the strategies and effects of power and to insist that a fully adequate account of existing knowledge systems can never simply leave aside these relationships is not to reduce knowledge to the conspiratorial machinations of power. It is simply to complicate the analysis of knowledge and, in my view, to place it on a more plausible grounding. Foucault's case studies of knowledge systems in the human sciences should, again, dissuade us from the view that Foucault sees the production of knowledge as hopelessly deceptive: these studies are very much informed by an Enlightenment belief that we can improve (in both epistemic and political senses) the process of knowledge production by coming to a better understanding of how it occurs in all of its murky and complicated relationships, and that we might even come to master the "games of truth."[50]

50. Foucault, *The Use of Pleasure: History of Sexuality*, vol. 2, trans. Robert Hurley (New York: Pantheon, 1985), p. 7.

This brings me to my final point with respect to the contributions of Foucault's analysis: his enriched concept of coherence. For some readers, no doubt, his introduction of elements such as power and politics as well as nondiscursive practices, subject-positions, and the like, into an account of knowledge only muddies the waters and complicates the possibility of a "clean" account beyond repair. It is certainly true that his account is messier than perhaps any to date because it brings in a larger and more various number of elements and conceptualizes their interrelationships in more and diverse ways. Perhaps this is because he does not take common sense or simple perceptual beliefs as his starting examples of knowledge, or even the relatively clutter-free arena of the natural sciences, as most other epistemologists have done. Instead, he focuses on the very messiest of sciences and from these analyses produces a new conceptualization of knowledge.

This approach can be seen as a strength of his epistemology rather than its fatal flaw. There is no good reason why common sense or simple perceptual beliefs should be privileged as keys to the understanding of knowledge (by common sense I am referring to beliefs such as the belief that the world has existed for longer than five minutes and that this room will continue to exist after I leave it). In fact, it is more persuasive to argue just the reverse. Rarely is it these sorts of beliefs whose justification or truth is called into question and therefore as examples they can provide only a shallow and even simplistic picture of knowledge-acquisition. One argument used in their defense is that these beliefs allow us to "pare away" the inessentials of the knowing process and see only the essential elements. This sort of reason is used sometimes to explain why physics has been able to make such significant advances: because it works with fewer variables than do the biological or the social sciences, it can generate conclusive results much more easily. But is this something that epistemology should want or need to emulate? Certainly not on Foucault's view. Paring away such variables mystifies the actual process of knowing and distorts our conclusions. The claim that such variables as power are only extrinsically relevant is itself an epistemological (and metaphysical) claim. Foucault's entire corpus is dedicated to establishing that all knowledge is connected to a discourse in all of the latter's heterogeneous manifestations (though the connection between discourses and some common-sense and simple perceptual beliefs may be inconsequential), and that therefore all knowledge is connected to such messy variables as subjectivities, power, and even desire. Moreover, given the relatively uncontroversial nature of simple perceptual and common-sense beliefs, it seems more important to spend our time analyzing the more difficult and complicated cases, such as the ones Foucault himself studied. As Wittgenstein knew, it is the philosopher's insistence on complicating straightforward beliefs that leads to our greatest muddles;

perhaps then we should begin with those beliefs already in need of analysis rather than producing complications on our own.

If this is the right tack, then Foucault's more rich and diversified conception of knowledge systems and coherence relations will contribute to a project of epistemology that takes as its starting point and as its focus not the simple, uncontroversial beliefs but the most complicated, controversial, yet powerful ones of our era. His account has the advantage of being closer to actual practices of knowledge production, and he contributes toward our inchoate understanding of the complex relationships which in fact exist between knowledge, power, and subjectivity. I have tried to establish thus far that Foucault's account of knowledge can be usefully characterized as a coherentist one, skirting over the issue of whether the account he develops can be fairly called an epistemology in the first place. In the following chapter I want to turn to this latter issue.

# CHAPTER FIVE

# "A new politics of truth . . .":
# Power/Knowledge as Strategic Epistemology

Epistemology as a historical practice has had four principal aims: (1) to achieve a general understanding of knowledge, belief, justification, truth, and other epistemic terms, either through conceptual analysis or through reflection on how they are used in practice; (2) to understand what it is to know something, that is, to define the difference between knowing and having a true belief; (3) to determine the limits of human knowledge; and (4) to provide a legitimating explanation for our claims to know, and thus refute epistemological skepticism. Michel Foucault's work contributes to the first three of these projects while rejecting the viability and necessity of the fourth. In this lack of attention to the problem of skepticism, he is certainly not alone in the history of epistemology.

The main person who might argue otherwise is Richard Rorty, who reads the history of epistemology as organized almost exclusively around the problem of skepticism and who characterizes pragmatism as an alternative to epistemology on these grounds.[1] Rorty's conception of epistemology and philosophy is excessively narrow, however, collapsing epistemology to foundationalism and metaphysics to a commitment to a Kantian ontology, and thus excluding much of even analytic philosophy from his definition. I will argue against Rorty's position by example rather than by taking on his specific points. In my view, it is vital to include Foucault and other continental philosophers within the tradition of epistemology. One could argue for this on pragmatic grounds, claiming that only from a position inside will their

1. See Richard Rorty, "Pragmatism and Philosophy," in *Consequences of Pragmatism* (Minneapolis: University of Minnesota Press, 1982), pp. 113–14, 139–40, pp. xiii–xlvii. See also Richard Rorty, *Philosophy and the Mirror of Nature* (Princeton: Princeton University Press, 1979).

views be taken up as relevant and worthy of serious consideration. But one could also argue that the absolute incommensurability that Rorty seems to posit between epistemological inquiry and contemporary continental philosophy is historically implausible. This is not, of course, to deny that there are major differences, and that some of those differences concern the very understanding of what knowledge is and how it might be analyzed, but this again represents an area of difference that also exists within analytic epistemology itself.[2]

In this chapter I will try to show how Foucault can be understood as contributing to the first three projects listed above and why he rejects the fourth. The critical question that will determine whether or not Foucault's account of knowledge can be included within the domain of epistemology concerns whether or not his account has a normative dimension, that is, whether he offers not only a description of knowing practices but also an evaluation based on some sort of epistemic criteria. His critics have argued that Foucault's account of knowledge has no epistemic dimension either because (1) he offers only an empirical description of knowledge such as the sociologists of knowledge following Karl Mannheim offer, in which the question of the validity of truth-claims is effaced and both true beliefs and false beliefs are subjected to the same method of analysis; or (2) because his account of power/knowledge in the end collapses to power, in that power is the only operative determining element and truth has no independent effective status over the realm of knowledge. Both of these charges raise the issue of relativism, since an account that remains at the descriptive level or that ultimately reduces to power cannot establish a nonrelativist epistemic evaluation of alternative claims. I will consider these charges as they are developed by Peter Dews, Jürgen Habermas, and Charles Taylor. On the basis of this discussion I will then explore how Foucault's work challenges some common assumptions in the tradition of epistemology and what sort of impact he might have on our inquiry into the nature of knowledge.

## Foucault's Account of Epistemic Terms

In relation to the first project, Foucault provides more than ample accounts of epistemic terms. His accounts do not describe how these terms are most commonly used or understood, and in fact he contradicts almost every common assumption about knowledge and truth. Neither does Foucault

---

2. For a characterization of continental epistemology since Hegel and its general differences from Anglo-American epistemology, see my entry in *A Companion to Epistemology*, ed. Jonathan Dancy and Ernest Sosa (Oxford: Basil Blackwell, 1992), s.v. "Continental Epistemology."

provide analytical definitions or conceptual analyses of these terms based on their logical implications or Latinate roots. As paradoxical as it sounds, the account Foucault offers is as an account of what, in his view, knowledge and truth "really" are, that is, the way in which they actually operate and are produced within discursive formations. He provides such an account for our familiar epistemic terms and also introduces new terms such as episteme and positivity. Let us look at the characterizations he offers.

> Knowledge is that of which one can speak in a discursive practice. . . . Knowledge is also the space in which the subject may take up a position and speak of the objects with which he deals in his discourse. . . . Knowledge is also the field of coordination and subordination of statements in which concepts appear, and are defined, applied and transformed (at this level, the knowledge of Natural History, in the eighteenth century, is not the sum of what was said, but the whole set of modes and sites in accordance with which one can integrate each new statement in the already said). . . . Lastly, knowledge is defined by the possibilities of use and appropriation offered by discourse.[3]

For Foucault, knowledge is not just the sum of justified true beliefs. It encompasses this set ("that of which one can speak in a discursive practice") but it also encompasses the "space" in which a subject may take up a position as a knower and the "field" in which statements are arranged and concepts defined. The term "knowledge" as Foucault uses it does not refer to an idealized abstraction that measures currently held justified beliefs against a potential absolute understanding of the Real, but to a concrete, material domain consisting of statements (*énoncés*) which have a positive truth-value and effects on subjectivities and practices. In so far as Foucault defines knowledge within the actual rather than the possible, his definition is more descriptive than normative. Foucault defines his neologism "episteme" as follows.

> The analysis of discursive formations . . . is what has been called . . . the analysis of the *episteme*. This episteme may be suspected of being something like a world-view, a slice of history common to all branches of knowledge, which imposes on each one the same norms and postulates, a general stage of reason, a certain structure of thought that the men of a particular period cannot escape. . . . By *episteme*, we mean, in fact, the total set of relations that unite at a given period, the discursive practices that give rise to epistemological figures, sciences and possibly formalized systems. . . . The episteme is not a form of

3. Michel Foucault, *The Archaeology of Knowledge*, in *The Archaeology of Knowledge and The Discourse on Language*, trans. A. M. Sheridan Smith (New York: Pantheon Books, 1982), pp. 182–83.

knowledge or type of rationality which . . . manifests the sovereign unity of a subject, a spirit or a period; it is the totality of relations that can be discovered, for a given period, between the sciences when one analyzes them at the level of discursive regularities.[4]

The episteme, then, might be thought of as a structure of rationality that guides and constrains the production of knowledge in a given era. It should not, however, be conceptualized as a paradigm or a set of rules or precepts that exists ontologically apart from and perhaps prior to systems of knowledge. It is something whose contours only appear in their specificity after a process of historical reconstruction from a different historical vantage point, à la the owl of Minerva. It is not perceptible from within, but only from the outside. It should therefore most properly be understood as an entity that emerges from a network of infinitesimal relations between a mass of actual, particular entities—beliefs, practices, texts, methods, and subject-positions.

The above passages reveal why it is sometimes difficult sharply to differentiate Foucault's concept of knowledge from episteme, and even from some of his other epistemic concepts. They are not spatially separate, but represent different features of what may be the same set of phenomena. Epistemes are prior to knowledges in the sense that they constitute at least part of what Foucault calls the preconditions of specific knowledges. On the basis of this concept of the episteme and the way in which it figures in Foucault's conceptual history, *The Order of Things*, we can characterize Foucault's approach to epistemology as a search for and study of epistemes, that is, as a historical analysis of the formations and transformations of historically specific and particular discursive systems. I shall say more about this in a moment when we look at Foucault's contributions to the second component of epistemology.

Foucault has also written quite extensively on the nature of truth, explaining that "all those who say that, for me, truth doesn't exist are being simplistic."[5] Certainly Foucault's entire project, which he often defined as

4. Ibid., p. 191. We may note with interest that Foucault describes the episteme as that which the men of a particular period cannot escape and may wonder what this means for his own work. Unlike many of his commentators, I do not believe that Foucault meant to exempt himself from this constraint or position himself as working from an anterior plane unencumbered by such limitations. In the interview entitled "Truth and Power," he speaks at some length about the changing intellectual climate in which he worked and which allowed him to formulate the ideas he did. Michel Foucault, "Truth and Power," in *Power/Knowledge: Selected Interviews and Other Writings 1972–1977*, ed. Colin Gordon (New York: Pantheon Books, 1980), pp. 109–33, esp. 109–11 and 115.
5. Michel Foucault, "The Concern for Truth," in *Michel Foucault: Politics, Philosophy, Culture*, ed. Lawrence D. Kritzman (New York: Routledge, 1988), p. 257.

concerned with the "history of the relations between thought and truth," was centrally concerned with the nature, preconditions, and effects of truth. His account of truth, however—not just of currently dominant knowledges but of truth-claims themselves, including his own—is notoriously elusive. Here are his most well-known passages explaining truth, parts of which we have already seen:

> Truth is a thing of this world: it is produced only by virtue of multiple forms of constraint. And it induces regular effects of power. Each society has its regimes of truth, its "general politics" of truth: that is, the types of discourse which it accepts and makes function as true; the mechanisms and instances which enable one to distinguish true and false statements, the means by which each is sanctioned; the techniques and procedures accorded value in the acquisition of truth; the status of those who are charged with saying what counts as true.[6]

> "Truth" is to be understood as a system of ordered propositions for the production, regulation, distribution, circulation and operation of statements. "Truth" is linked in a circular relation with systems of power which produce and sustain it, and to effects of power which it induces and which extend it.[7]

Here Foucault, sounding almost like an anthropologist, seems to be describing how the concept of truth operates in linguistic communities. But he is also advancing his own understanding of what, in "reality," this thing we call truth actually *is*. It is internal to our world, rather than a relation between it and a transcendental realm or a world-in-itself. Its defining criterion is historically variable and relative to different societies. And, in all of its differing manifestations, it is intrinsically political, in the sense that it not only induces political effects but is vitally connected to and interdependent with systems of power.

Foucault's explanations of epistemic terms might seem to offer no epistemically based evaluations of better and worse processes of belief-formation. His fulfillment of the first task of epistemology—the explanation of epistemic terms—will not contribute to the second and third tasks—the differentiation between knowing and true belief and the demarcation of the limits of knowledge—if his account remains a neutral, empirical description without an evaluative dimension that is in some sense epistemic and not merely political. Let me turn now to address the charges raised by many of Foucault's commentators that Foucault's account remains at the sociological level or that it collapses to a consideration of power.

6. Foucault, "Truth and Power," p. 131.
7. Ibid., p. 133.

## Power/Knowledge: Epistemology or Sociology?

Foucault's account might be said to resemble a sociology of knowledge more than an epistemology if Dews is right that Foucault's views on truth are ultimately Nietzschean because they posit that all truth-claims are relative to the constitutive historical and discursive conditions which produce them.[8] If this is indeed true of *all* truth-claims, then there is no outside means of evaluation or independent epistemic criterion. (The problem of self-reference to which such a universal claim is subject can be sidestepped once we see that it is an epistemological problem but not a metaphysical one: that is, we may not be able to justify such a universal claim from within an account that relativizes all truth-claims, and yet we can entertain the possibility that in fact it is true across regimes of truth.) In Foucault's early work, it is true that he attempts to bracket out the question of substantive truth and explore knowledge as a species of a discursive object-domain that can be analyzed using a positivist methodology. In response to criticisms that such an analysis could not sustain either political critique or an account of the context that conditions discourse, Foucault introduced power. As Dews and Habermas have argued, this does not necessarily solve the problem of his inability to make critiques on epistemic grounds, but for the moment let us focus on the charge that Foucault's account is merely sociological or empirical.

The same sort of charge has been made against Willard Quine's project of "naturalized epistemology," which characterizes knowledge by how we actually determine it rather than by idealized notions of what it should be. Critics of naturalized epistemology argue that it cannot advance a normative theory of justification that would make epistemic evaluations of candidates for truth. It is this requirement that perhaps more than any other demarcates epistemology from sociology of knowledge because epistemology seeks not only to *describe* how knowledge is produced but to *justify* it, and specifically to justify certain justificatory practices over others, ideal or actual. Whether Foucault's account of knowledge is epistemological will depend on whether he can be shown to offer such a metajustification.

There are two ways in which Foucault contributes to a normative epistemological project. He offers philosophical arguments against subject-centered procedures of justification which take the individual knower as the locus of the justifying process. And he argues against ahistorical accounts of particular justificatory strategies and criteria. In a review of two books by Gilles Deleuze, Foucault offered a revealing account of "knowing" and

8. Peter Dews, *Logics of Disintegration* (New York: Verso, 1987), p. 182.

"judging" and of his disagreements with traditional philosophy.[9] Knowing, he says, is "determining an event on the basis of a concept" while judging is "measuring the phantasm against reality, by going in search of its origin." He criticizes philosophy on the grounds that "philosophy tried to do both, it dreamed of itself as a science." Following Deleuze, Foucault's argument is that "thought" cannot be captured in this way: it does not work through a method that compares elements completely outside of thought to elements within it. Events and (what we call) reality are always constituted by thought. Furthermore, Foucault says that "thought must consider the process that forms it and form itself from these considerations." What these remarks suggest is that Foucault, like Rorty, tends to reduce philosophy and "knowing and judging" to specific formulations and traditions within the history of philosophy, and considers his own work as separate and qualitatively different. But notice that within the space of the project that Foucault does endorse, the possibility of normative work is maintained. If thought is to "form itself from these considerations," then thought can improve itself through the process of identifying its own historical a priori, a process Foucault initiates. This is at least a version of what Dews calls for—"the capacity of the human subject to reflect critically on the categories through which it grasps itself"[10]—though with a bare "thought" standing in for the subject. It would seem to be a mistake for Dews to think that Foucault cannot countenance anything beyond a simple description in regard to knowledge. Of course, we will need to say much more to make the case that Foucault's project works to avoid a self-defeating relativism and the perpetual oscillation between the political aspirations and epistemological nihilism that Dews attributes to him. We have shown, however, that Foucault's account is not merely an exercise in sociology of knowledge, which seeks mere description, but a project whose aim is the improved epistemic status of thought itself. In what sense, however, is Foucault concerned with the epistemic or epistemically relevant status of thought?

Foucault offers a normative account of the history of knowledge. When he describes for us the connection between power and knowledge, it is not his aim that we become abstractly better informed or that we increase and strengthen the hegemonic power of dominant discourses. Foucault sides openly with the "subjugated knowledges" which have been delegitimated by dominant forms of knowledge that have aspired for hegemony over the entire discursive field. He clearly hopes that his explanatory accounts will contribute, not to the destruction of power or the end of its relationship to

9. Michel Foucault, "Theatrum Philosophicum," in *Language, Counter-Memory, Practice*, ed. Donald Bouchard (Ithaca: Cornell University Press, 1977), pp. 177–78.
10. Dews, *Logics of Disintegration*, p. 184.

knowledge (since such goals are hopeless), but to the intervention and negotiation of new limits on the dominating effects of power/knowledge. The
dominant regime of truth in contemporary Western discourse is, in Foucault's view, built upon claims to universal generality and upon transcendental metajustifications that are chimeras. Thus Foucault seeks to expose
the mystifying self-understanding of present discourse just as the heroes and
heroines of the Enlightenment sought to expose the oppressive authoritarianism and dogmatism of the Scholastics. For this reason Foucault is sometimes categorized as more of a "high modernist" that a postmodernist.

The basis of Foucault's critique, however, is fundamentally different
from that of all other modernist projects, which are predicated on concepts
like autonomy, freedom, the separation of power and knowledge, and the
liberation of subjectivity. Because of the differences, Foucault's approach to
epistemological questions is difficult to articulate. Not until the Cartesian
inauguration of a critique of Scholastic dogmatism was epistemology indi-
viduated as a subfield within Western philosophy. Only from within such a
critical project did the issue of knowledge become a problem requiring
analysis. Both empiricists and rationalists argued against the Scholastics'
privileging of authority and argued for a shift to the scientific method on
the basis of transcendental arguments, a priori claims, and the invocation
of ahistorical truths about human beings, God, reality, and our sensory apparatus. Such forms of argument became canonized in the tradition of epistemology.

In contrast, Foucault's evaluation of the current regime of truth explicitly rejects any claims that are transcendental, a priori, ahistorical, or politically neutral. He asserts that the only criteria to which we can appeal
will be historically situated and contingent, that both knowledge's object
and its subject are constituted by it, and that the domain of truth is irreducibly plural and heterogeneous. The only evaluative criterion that Foucault endorses is one based on whether a knowledge claim supports or
disrupts the dominant discourse's drive for hegemony. "It's not a matter of
emancipating truth from every system of power (which would be a
chimera, for truth is already power) but of detaching the power of truth
from the forms of hegemony, social, economic, and cultural, within which
it operates at the present time."[11] This is not offered as a cross-cultural,
transhistorical criterion of adjudication, but as a strategic intervention into
current discursive power relations.

> The role for theory today seems to me to be just this: not to formulate the
> global systematic theory which holds everything in place, but to analyze the

11. Foucault, "Truth and Power," p. 133.

specificity of mechanisms of power, to locate the connections and extensions, to build little by little a strategic knowledge. . . . The notion of theory as a toolkit means: (1) The theory to be constructed is not a system but an instrument, a *logic* of the specificity of power relations and the struggles around them; (2) That this investigation can only be carried out step by step on the basis of reflection (which will necessarily be historical in some of its aspects) on given situations.[12]

Whether or not such a position is an adequate epistemology, it at least establishes that Foucault is interested in more than mere description, or description for its own sake. He advocates subjugated knowledges not as "a matter of a battle 'on behalf' of the truth, but of a battle about the status of truth and the economic and political role it plays" or in other words, "of constituting a new politics of truth."[13] The fact that he will not claim to be on the side of a universal truth superior to all others does not entail that he has no evaluation to offer. To take Foucault on his own terms, we must allow for the conceptual possibility of localized norms of evaluation. Further, he avoids problems of self-reference by applying this prescription toward the local and the particular to his own position, or in other words, he ascribes the same limitations to his own position that he ascribes to others. A Foucauldian analysis of Foucault, then, would reflect on the instrumentality of his own discursive interventions in specific situations. This is what I propose to consider, in relation to the situation of dominant Western epistemological discourses.

This apparent privileging of strategic considerations immediately raises the charge that such an analysis would have no epistemological content: that it would be concerned only with the struggles around power relations and the role of knowledges in relation to these struggles, without any concern for truth. Habermas has raised just this criticism of Foucault: "Not only are truth claims confined to the discourses within which they arise; they exhaust their entire significance in the functional contribution they make to the self-maintenance of a given totality of discourse. That is to say, the meaning of validity consists in the power effects they have."[14] Taylor has similarly argued that Foucault "refuses" truth: "There is no order of human life, or way we are, or human nature, that one can appeal to in order to judge or evaluate between ways of life. There are only different orders imposed by men on primal chaos, [and] these different forms involve the imposition of power. The idea of 'regimes of truth,' and of their close

12. Foucault, "Power and Strategies," in *Power/Knowledge*, p. 145.
13. Foucault, "Truth and Power," pp. 132–33.
14. Jürgen Habermas, *The Philosophical Discourse of Modernity*, trans. Frederick Lawrence (Cambridge: MIT Press, 1987), p. 279.

intrication with systems of dominance, is profoundly Nietzschean. In this relationship Foucault sees truth as subordinated to power."[15] For both Taylor and Habermas, the principal problem that follows from Foucault's reduction of truth to power is that he is, as a result, incapable of sustaining political critique: if his own genealogies have no more epistemic authority than the claims he rejects, then he cannot provide an effective rejoinder. Dews argues similarly that Foucault's critique of power cannot work because it "lacks an epistemological dimension," meaning that he offers no "assessment of the truth of the discourse studied."[16] Like Habermas, Dews follows Theodor Adorno and Max Horkheimer in their claim, contra Mannheim, that a critical standpoint on society must be able to claim truth.

My main concern is not with Foucault's ability to sustain effective political critique, but with the charge that in his account of knowledge only power is operative as a determinate force or evaluative criterion. Both Dews and Habermas recognize that Foucault offers more than a neutral or relativist position with respect to knowledges: his work post-1970 champions subjugated knowledges against dominant knowledges and thus offers a nonrelative judgment that goes beyond the descriptive orientation characteristic of *The Order of Things*. Foucault characterizes subjugated knowledges as "naive knowledges, located low down on the hierarchy, beneath the required level of cognition or scientificity. I also believe that it is through the re-emergence of these low-ranking knowledges, these unqualified, even directly disqualified knowledges (such as that of the psychiatric patient, of the ill person, of the nurse, of the doctor—parallel and marginal as they are to the knowledge of medicine—that of the delinquent, etc.) . . . that criticism performs its work."[17] Thus, his answer to the Frankfurt School's concern with having epistemic grounds for political critique appears to be a form of perspectivism, in which the perspective of what might be called oppressed knowledges can work to dislodge the supremacy of the dominant discourse.

This move is not without its problems, however. For one thing, Foucault offers no criterion of evaluation other than a knowledge's positioning vis-à-vis dominance, and thus suggests no way to distinguish between the plethora of subjugated knowledges in existence. If the doctor is a surprising presence in the passage quoted above, the other examples of disqualified knowledge could be seen as convenient choices: within the category of subjugated knowledges we would surely have to include fundamentalist cults in Texas, pedophilic networks, and contemporary Nazi groups that deny the Holocaust. Each of these represent a knowledge, complete with a

15. Charles Taylor, "Foucault on Freedom and Truth," in *Foucault: A Critical Reader*, ed. David Couzens Hoy (Oxford: Basil Blackwell, 1986), p. 93.
16. Dews, *Logics of Disintegration*, pp. 191–92.
17. Michel Foucault, "Two Lectures," in *Power/Knowledge*, p. 82.

body of texts, alternative worldviews, and shared practices, and on Foucault's criterion it would seem they should be championed as sites of critical intervention.

A second problem arises because Foucault's evaluative criterion involves solely the question of power. This critique, according to Dews, leads only to simple reversals of knowledges in the dominant position rather than to transformations.[18] If subjugated knowledges are privileged only in respect to their position vis-à-vis the dominant discourse, then their "success" will mean that there is a change in content at the top without the newly dominant knowledge having any claim to better epistemic status—for example, being recognized as a better representation or more accurate account.

Yet a third problem is noted by Habermas. Foucault's perspectivist solution to the problem of relativism parallels Marx's move to avoid the relativism of a materialist account of knowledge by epistemically valorizing the perspective of the working class.[19] But this only works to the extent that the working class can be shown to instantiate the interests of the universal, a claim that even Georg Lukács's efforts could not render plausible. Foucault, however, offers no such pretenses for the privilege of subjugated knowledges, and therefore even on his own view they can have no more epistemic credibility than dominant knowledges. Habermas concludes that, once again, the criterion of evaluation Foucault is using to support subjugated knowledges turns out to rely only on considerations of power.

Thus, each of these objections follows from the claim that Foucault replaces epistemic criteria with political ones in his formulation of the intrinsic connection between truth and power. Unlike members of the Frankfurt School—who argue that power or structures of domination produce certain forms of rationality (for example, instrumental reasoning or empirical-analytic knowledge) but that a critical conceptual thought can be developed with its own autonomous dynamic—Foucault seems to totalize the cognitive field, viewing it as saturated by an association with power that is essentially the same everywhere, albeit distinguishable by reference to categories of domination and resistance. Thus Foucault could be seen as arguing for the dissolution of epistemology and its replacement with politics, given that epistemological considerations have no separate weight in his analyses of knowledges.

It is striking, however, that Foucault explicitly rejects the concept of ideology, the main concept associated with a reduction of knowledge to power, and that he insists on maintaining the dyadic relationship invoked in his term power/knowledge, in which neither term gets the upper hand.

18. Dews, *Logics of Disintegration*, p. 217.
19. Habermas, *The Philosophical Discourse of Modernity*, pp. 280–81.

We should admit . . . that power and knowledge directly imply one another; that there is no power relation without the correlative constitution of a field of knowledge, nor any knowledge that does not presuppose and constitute at the same time power relations. These "power-knowledge relations" are to be analysed, therefore, not on the basis of a subject of knowledge who is or is not free in relation to the power system, but, on the contrary, the subject who knows, the objects to be known and the modalities of knowledge must be regarded as so many effects of these fundamental implications of power-knowledge and their historical transformations. In short, it is not the activity of the subject of knowledge that produces a corpus of knowledge, useful or resistant to power, but power-knowledge, the processes and struggles that traverse it and of which it is made up, that determines the forms and possible domains of knowledge.[20]

This analysis does not collapse knowledge to power: power and knowledge operate as two halves of a system that creates the conditions for the production and authorization of new knowledges, modes of knowing, and objects of inquiry. Neither knowledge nor power can be reduced to or replaced with the other in discursive analysis. It is not the case that in exploring the deep structure of truth we will come to see that, at bottom, it is really just power; rather, there is a dyadic, reciprocal, and interdependent relation between the two phenomena. Epistemic criteria are not superfluous, but they always work alongside political criteria, which means that we can no longer pursue epistemological inquiry separate from political analysis. The force of this critique is not to show that power is the only determining criterion operable in constructing fields of knowledge, but that knowledge has no autonomous existence apart from power.

It is precisely this claim that causes Dews, Habermas, Taylor, and other commentators to believe that Foucault cannot have an epistemology. Their shared implicit assumption is that epistemic considerations must involve a truth concept that is fundamentally autonomous, separable from power, uncoerced. Although, for Habermas, specifiable interests are always involved in knowledge, within intersubjective communicative action there is an implicit rationality, the form of which is free from power. Because Foucault denies this, and because he denies that there is any knowledge, form of reasoning, or even truth free from an intrinsic, constitutive relationship with power, he is said to be unable to sustain a normative epistemic dimension. This is where his critics are mistaken. They conflate the claims that knowledge is never free of power and that truth is immanent to the

20. Michel Foucault, *Discipline and Punish*, trans. Alan Sheridan (New York: Vintage Books, 1979), pp. 27–28.

discursive domain with a claim that power is all that is operative in the constitution of knowledge. But the immanent status of Foucault's concept of truth is decisive for understanding Foucault's concept of power/knowledge. When truth is conceived as ultimately transcendent, as referring to something above and beyond the human realm, then only an autonomous conception of knowledge can provide an epistemic dimension. Foucault denies truth's transcendent status, and so he is read as playing not epistemology but another language game, and offering simply a new version of an ancient position on knowledge: skepticism.

Thus, I believe that critics of Foucault's epistemological views have essentially begged the question. Instead of addressing his immanent account of truth and his insistence that power and knowledge cannot be separated, they have denied that his claims about knowledge have any epistemic content. In other words, they have defined his account as outside epistemology by a prior, uninterrogated assumption. On Foucault's view, however, knowledge *cannot* be disassociated from power, so there can be no criterion of belief that has only to do with knowledge and nothing to do with power. This is not the same as a position that would collapse all cognitive considerations to power.

Still, if we concede Foucault's point for the moment that power and knowledge cannot be disassociated and that truth cannot be conceptualized outside of power/knowledge fields, it may seem as if only the power side of the dyad is at play in his proposal to promote subjugated knowledges. He often appears to privilege political considerations over epistemic ones, as in the following passage: "It's not a matter of a battle 'on behalf' of the truth, but of a battle about the status of truth and the economic and political role it plays."[21] Here Foucault certainly sounds as if he is only interested in reconfiguring the politics of truth and is not interested in any other epistemic considerations.

The fact is, however, that Foucault's preference for local, subjugated knowledges over global ones is based on considerations that involve both power and knowledge. It is not merely because they have the potential to subvert hegemonic discourse that Foucault champions low-ranking knowledges, but also because Foucault believes that hegemonic knowledges always have to exert a violence (in both an epistemic and a political sense) on local and particular knowledges in order to subsume them within their universal structures. Something at the local level is always distorted or omitted in order to enable the reductionist move of containment. This, he says, is

the inhibiting effect of global, *totalitarian theories*. It is not that these global theories have not provided nor continue to provide in a fairly consistent fash-

---

21. Foucault, "Truth and Power," p. 132.

ion useful tools for local research. . . . But I believe these tools have only been provided on the condition that the theoretical unity of these [non-global] discourses was in some sense put in abeyance, or at least curtailed, divided, overthrown, caricatured, theatricalised, or what you will. In each case, the attempt to think in terms of a totality has in fact proved a hindrance to research.[22]

Here, Foucault provides epistemic reasons to reject hegemonic discourses, but reasons that do not imply a correspondence theory of truth or an apolitical account of knowledge. Subjugated knowledges are valorized not because they present a more accurate representation of the Real as it exists in itself, or because they have a less important connection to power, but because they do not require the amount of violence, distortion, and omission that global knowledges require, and their recalcitrance to total subsumption helps to block a hegemony that would claim dominion over each and every infinitesimal social and discursive event. Thus, they have a *different* relationship to power, and given power's role in the "constitution of a field of knowledge," this different relationship will constitute a different field. Dews takes Foucault's claim that power is the precondition of knowledge to mean merely that power sets the stage for knowledge to dance upon, a fairly mild formulation of their relationship which would be consistent with the belief that knowledge has its own immanent dynamic. But I think Foucault means for the concept of precondition to imply more than this: the Panopticon, for example, which is Foucault's paradigm concept of disciplinary power, exerts determinate effects on the structure knowledge will take, on its objects, its modalities, its authorized methods of justification. The Panopticon was a spatial arrangement originally designed for prisons with a guard tower in the center of surrounding cells, each with a transparent wall facing the central tower. It allowed for absolute domination through absolute observation by ensuring permanent visibility. This spatial model, which was also adapted for hospitals, schools, factories, military camps, and insane asylums, simultaneously provides a distributive structure of power and a focus and modality of knowledge. Knowledge became directed toward the micropractices of individuals, breaking down groups and time sequences into small units of analysis. Mass production techniques, Taylorism, and the type of knowledge pursued by "efficiency experts" were further forms of power/knowledge made possible by the Panopticon.

The relationship Foucault envisions between knowledge and power is more thoroughly intrinsic than Dews is willing to entertain. Genealogy incorporates this dyadic formulation in its attentiveness to the multiple dimensionality of knowledge.

---

22. Foucault, "Two Lectures," p. 81.

> By comparison, then, and in contrast to the various projects which aim to in-
> scribe knowledges in the hierarchical order of power associated with science,
> a genealogy should be seen as a kind of attempt to emancipate historical
> knowledges from that subjection, to render them, that is, capable of opposi-
> tion and of struggle against the coercion of a theoretical, unitary, formal and
> scientific discourse. It is based on a reactivation of local knowledges . . . in op-
> position to the scientific hierarchisation of knowledges and the effects intrin-
> sic to their power.[23]

The oppositional status of local knowledges is at once political and epistemic, in ways that cannot be clearly disentangled. Their disauthorization
in terms of standard epistemic rules and their resistance to hegemony-
seeking discourses is based on their differential position vis-à-vis dominant power systems, but given Foucault's views about the nature of the
relationship between power and knowledge, this characterization of local
knowledges also implies that the structure of these knowledges will take
a different form. What makes these knowledges local is not simply that
they have not yet achieved dominance, but that they do not aspire to
dominance. They do not construct competing unitary, formal, totalizing
theoretical systems that seek to subsume all local elements beneath a single umbrella, but are formulated as local not just in terms of the range of
their content but also in terms of their structure. For example, this difference might be observed in the contrast between the claim that homosexuality has determinate characteristics, effects, and physiological
manifestations in all its instances and the claim that homosexual practices have a certain set of effects in one particular context. The difference
between these two claims is that the latter does not seek hegemony over
the discursive field in which "homosexuality" is an object, whereas the
former claim does.

This returns us to the three objections I listed earlier against Foucault's
valorization of subjugated knowledges: that he offers no means to distinguish among the plethora of such knowledges, that his valorization, since
it is based purely on a political criterion, can end up only in a reversal without transformation, and that he cannot privilege the perspective of local
knowledges except on political grounds. Each of these objections can be
met once we see that, as the above passage indicates, the distinction Foucault draws is not between dominant and subordinate knowledges but between local knowledges and hegemony-seeking knowledges. The latter set
up hierarchies between knowledges based on the presumption of a total-
ized perspective that would subsume the entire cognitive field under one
epistemic analysis. Such knowledges never actually achieve hegemony on

23. Ibid., p. 85.

Foucault's view, given the irreducibly open, heteromorphous, and contested nature of the discursive terrain, but they aspire to it.

How does this account meet the objections listed above? In the first case, because it suggests that we can differentiate between those currently subjugated discourses which are hegemony-seeking and those which are not. Fundamentalist cults, for example, are generally hegemony-seeking, not in the sense that they want to convert the entire world, but in the sense that they believe themselves to have a truth that ranges over the entire world, over its entire history including every event and individual. This distinction may not provide us with sufficient means to reject all of the subordinate knowledges we may want to reject, but such considerations cannot be set out fully in advance or outside of local contexts (such as constructions of the specific "we" doing the excluding). Second, drawing the distinction between hegemony-seeking and local knowledges makes it clear that a simple reversal will not result from the valorization of subjugated knowledge: a reversal would only occur if the subjugated knowledge were a hegemony-seeking knowledge that gained dominance. Foucault's project, by contrast, aims at "detaching the power of truth from the forms of hegemony, social, economic and cultural, within which it operates at the present time."[24] Local knowledges are important because they can participate in just such a subversion of dominance. Third, Foucault offers an epistemic reason to privilege subjugated knowledges, based not on their instantiation of universal interests but on their very resistance to a universal pretension which would forcibly subsume particulars under a generalized rubric.

An obvious question here is whether, despite Foucault's protestations to the contrary, his account amounts to another unity, a new global theory. After all, he appears to be making epistemic and political pronouncements that cover the whole field of knowledge. When it is applied to the question whether Foucault has an epistemology, this critique raises a paradox: epistemologies are general theories of knowledge, and thus if Foucault has an epistemology he must contradict his preference for the local.

Foucault considers this charge in the same lecture in which he defines genealogy. He says that the genealogical project he has developed has not yet achieved dominance, and thus "the moment at which we risk colonization has not yet arrived."[25] Therefore his project does not yet incur the dangers and problems of global theory. Those who would be dissatisfied with this response, on the grounds that Foucault does not give us sufficient reason to believe that such problems will not occur in the future, should take note of the self-imposed historicist limitations of Foucault's strategic account. His own theory, as a strategic intervention in a specific spatio-temporal loca-

24. Foucault, "Truth and Power," p. 133.
25. Foucault, "Two Lectures," p. 86.

tion, can have no more temporal reach than any other, but its validity will not be based on the question of its immunity from eventual recuperation but on the issue of its current effectiveness. Theory conceived as a toolkit is throwaway theory, not to be judged by its timeless viability but by its currency within a specified domain. This is not to reduce all theory-choice to questions of strategic effectiveness, but to recognize the historical locatedness of theoretical justifications.

## The Limits of Knowledge

This brings us to the consideration of Foucault's contribution to the third project of epistemology that I listed at the outset of this chapter; determining the limits to human knowledge. Perhaps Foucault's contributions to this project are the clearest and least controversial, given the fact that he is so often accused of claiming that no "real" knowledge is possible at all. But there is controversy over the scope of Foucault's attack. Gary Gutting, for example, in his excellent book on Foucault's archaeological analysis of the human sciences, contends that Foucault's critique is in fact restricted to very specific lines of inquiry and to the self-understandings of institutions like psychiatry rather than the whole edifice of knowledge. In advancing this view, Gutting differs sharply with Rorty, among others, who takes Foucault to be calling into question any formulation of reason and knowledge one could advance.

Both sides in this controversy are mistaken in my view. Gutting's analysis, while carefully argued, is based on Foucault's pre-1970 writings. He does not address Foucault's more general comments on knowledge, such as the passages discussed in this chapter. Rorty's error is once again his conflation of epistemology with foundationalism and mirroring ontologies of truth: Foucault is defined as outside the fold because he does not share these theoretical proclivities. But this controversy over the scope of Foucault's critique of epistemology bears only indirectly on the issue of whether Foucault contributes to the epistemological project of understanding the limits of knowledge.[26] What remains clear on all interpretations of his critique is that Foucault's articulation of the "positive unconscious" of knowledge, his elaboration of the relationship between power and knowledge, and his methods of archaeology and genealogy, are all centrally concerned with revealing the determinations and the limits of human knowledge. Those limits are certainly defined most drastically in Foucault's claim that there is no knowledge free or devoid of power.

26. My views on Gutting's position are included in my review of his book, *Michel Foucault's Archaeology of Scientific Reason*, in *Philosophy and Phenomenological Research* 51 (1991).

## Skepticism and Local Epistemology

The fourth and final project of epistemology is the attempt to find a legitimating justification of our claims to know, and thus to answer epistemological skepticism. Foucault offers no contribution to this project, because he rejects its viability. "In the enigma of scientific discourse, what the analysis of the episteme questions is not its right to be a science, but the fact that it exists. And the point at which it separates itself off from all the philosophies of knowledge (connaissance) is that it relates this fact not to the authority of an original act of giving, which establishes in a transcendental subject the fact and the right, but to the processes of a historical practice."[27] This passage reveals Foucault's own formulation of the difference between his work and traditional epistemology. His concern is not to discover the legitimating foundation of our knowledge, nor to combat skepticism, which he takes to be based on transcendental arguments about the "original act of giving," such as Descartes' view that God gave us a sensory apparatus which would ensure our generally correct beliefs about the world. Foucault apparently takes it to be the case that *all* philosophies of knowledge, or all epistemologies, believe in such transcendental metajustifications, divine or otherwise, and likewise reject the possibility of historically understood conceptions of knowledge. I think this bespeaks his ignorance of the currents in contemporary epistemology. In any case, he rejects the project of answering skepticism because he assumes that it calls for and would require a transcendental argument, which he does not believe is available.

The fact that Foucault does not want to take up the skeptic's challenge does not place him outside the tradition of epistemology, even though this contradicts his own self-presentation. Foucault's concern is not to provide a transcendental, ahistorical grounding for knowledge, but to understand and evaluate the production of knowledges in their historical specificity and the ways in which methods of knowledge acquisition that are considered acceptable come into existence and pass out of it. If we conceive of epistemology as the project of understanding our claims to know and providing an evaluation of their claim to validity, then Foucault has an epistemology.

But what, again, of truth? A consideration of validity has no epistemic content if it is not related to the issue of truth, however indirectly. I have said that Foucault's account of truth is immanent to the discursive domain rather than ontologically transcendent—does not this entail its relativism and therefore its ultimate irrelevance? A more accurate term for Foucault's account of

27. Foucault, *Archaeology of Knowledge*, p. 192.

truth is "pluralist."[28] There is no overarching schema or framework to which all the multiple discursively constituted truths might be reduced; thus truth is *irreducibly* plural. This is the reason behind Foucault's tenacious insistence on the local. The Western imperialist discursive tendency is always toward the global, the macro, the big picture. Foucault's intervention points in the other direction: toward the specific, the local, the particular. Thus his case studies of knowledges, his historically specific discussions of subjectivity, his inhibition against universal-sounding prescriptions.

But without a universal truth, there can be no universal normative epistemic criteria ranging across the pluralities of truths. This is what Foucault's epistemologically attentive readers have been searching for in vain, and they have concluded from their failure that Foucault is without normative content. The absence of a universalist norm does not, however, preclude the possibility of any norms whatever. Foucault can thus be said to comply with the nonnegotiable requirement of epistemology, but not on the terms usually understood.

Though I have argued that Foucault's work should be understood as commensurable rather than incommensurable with the theoretical tradition of epistemology, there is no doubt that his work suggests a different take on the enterprise itself. If the division of true/false is a contingent and "historically constituted division"[29] and "the relationship between power, right and truth is organized in a highly specific fashion"[30] in every society, then it follows that epistemology itself needs to be indexed to a location. That is, epistemology is also a "thing of this world," an immanent rather than transcendent activity. We need, therefore, to speak not of epistemology per se, but of specific epistemologies. Schemas of categorization can be developed in different ways, linking epistemology to cultures, economic systems, philosophical trends, or gender formations, and Foucault does not suggest a preference for any particular schema. That choice will be determined in specific contexts by both epistemic and political considerations. The specificity and locatedness of epistemology on Foucault's view, is perhaps the most important distinction to be made between his conception of epistemology and traditional accounts. But to locate epistemology, to tie it to particular historical, political contexts, does not require its eradication: it only requires a new, and wiser, self-understanding.

28. See Thomas R. Flynn's excellent account of Foucault's pluralist conception of truth in "Foucault as Parrhesiast: His Last Course at the Collège de France," in *The Final Foucault*, ed. James Bernauer and David Rasmussen (Cambridge: MIT Press, 1988).
29. Michel Foucault, "The Discourse on Language," in *The Archaeology of Knowledge and The Discourse on Language*, p. 218.
30. Foucault, "Two Lectures," p. 93.

# CHAPTER SIX

# "A human kind of realism . . .":
# Putnam's Immanent Ontology

> The current views of truth are alienated views; they cause one to lose one
> part or another of one's self and the world. . . . My purpose . . . is to
> sketch the leading ideas of a non-alienated view.
> —Hilary Putnam, *Reason, Truth, and History*

The principal problems facing a coherentist epistemology are not epistemological; they are ontological. Knowledge is extensional by definition,
which means that it alludes to more than self-reference, textual consistency,
or even language. Fundamentally, knowledge is considered to be *about
something*, though what either of these words means can be conceptualized
in radically different ways. To be considered knowledge, a claim must refer
to our shared world in some sense, whether it is the "noumenal realm," the
"phenomenal realm," a Ding an sich, or the mind of God, and must not
be reducible to—though it may be mediated by and inclusive of—wishes,
dreams, exclamations, affective states, or language.

So to count as an adequate epistemology, coherentism must be able to
offer a plausible explication of reference (not as a semantic theory so much
as a metaphysics) or what I would prefer to call, more generally, "aboutness": the relationship between knowledge and world. Phenomenologically,
this aboutness captures the otherness inherent in knowledge, its outward
projection, or its relation to being. In analytic terms, we might say that
knowledge is supervenient on otherness or, more familiarly, on externality.
But in neither tradition can knowledge be contained within itself without
losing all intelligibility. Here I would agree with Hilary Putnam when he
says, contra Richard Rorty and Jacques Derrida, that the crisis of representation is a "collapse of a certain picture of the world, and of the conceptions
of truth and representation that went with that picture of the world" but
not "a collapse of the notions of representation and truth" *simpliciter*.[1] In

---

1. Hilary Putnam, *Renewing Philosophy* (Cambridge: Harvard University Press, 1992), p. 124.

other words, concepts such as "knowledge," "reality," and "truth" retain their intelligibility, indeed their indispensability, although they require a radically new philosophical elucidation.

For an explication of this aboutness within a coherentist epistemology, the work of Putnam has the most to offer, in his effort to develop an "internal" realism that can combine basic realist intuitions with conceptual relativism. He has recently called this a "pragmatic" realism or a realism with a small 'r', but I think they represent essentially the same view. More than any other post-crisis philosopher, Putnam has insisted that the bankruptcy of classical realism, with its idea that knowledge must correspond to a world completely independent of human interest or interpretation, does not absolve us of the tasks of metaphysics and epistemology. It does require a rejection of Epistemology with a capital 'E' ("the project of a Universal Method for telling who has 'reason on his side' no matter *what* the dispute") and a rejection of Ontology with a capital 'O' (the project "of a description of things as they are 'apart from our conceptual systems' "). These projects do not, however, by any means exhaust all of the interesting and important questions about knowledge, language, science, values, or our interaction with reality.[2] In particular, there remains the task of developing an account of reason and of the metaphysical relationship between knowledge and the world that can make sense of the ongoing evolution of rationality, the embeddedness of knowledge within value-laden, interest-driven human practices, and the dependence of identifiable facts on conceptual systems. Putnam argues that developing a theory of knowledge and a form of realism within these parameters will require us to transcend the outdated binaries of subjective/objective, fact/value, constructed/real, and ahistorical rationality/cultural relativism.[3] Simply put, we need a new ontology of truth.

This is unquestionably a forbidding task, and most Anglo-American philosophers apparently do not believe Putnam has succeeded at it. It is argued that his internal realism must collapse either toward transcendental idealism or toward a more robust classical realism, and that his arguments against classical realism either work against realism per se or they do not work at all. I believe this reception to be largely based on an unwillingness or incapacity to consider seriously any account of truth other than that associated with correspondence and classical realism; instead of sound critique we have simply a failure of imagination. Such failure is forthrightly defended as "proving" the unintelligibility of what the philosopher cannot imagine.[4] Perhaps this is at root a problem of alien-

2. Hilary Putnam, *The Many Faces of Realism* (La Salle, Ill.: Open Court, 1987), p. 86.
3. This neat list comes from Simon Blackburn, "Enchanting Views," in *Reading Putnam*, ed. Peter Clark and Bob Hale (Cambridge, Mass.: Basil Blackwell, 1994), p. 13.
4. See, for example, ibid., p. 25.

ation, as Putnam himself suggests in the epigraph that begins this chapter,[5] or perhaps it is the natural resistance produced by any such paradigm shift as Putnam is trying to effect.

I will begin this chapter with an explanation of Putnam's account of internal realism, its relationship to coherentism and the immanent form of epistemology I have been exploring, and then I will bring it to bear on the issues and problems of the accounts discussed previously, in particular the truth-conducive status of coherence and the problem of relativism. Putnam presents his views on realism and truth as an alternative to the new skepticism put forth by both Rorty and some deconstructionists, who in their consternation over the demise of classical realism have retreated to the view that language can only refer to language and that concepts like reference and truth no longer have any credibility. Putnam also sees his view as an alternative to the widely influential redundancy theory of truth, or to deflationist accounts, which try to hold onto correspondence despite its difficulties of explication by dispensing with metaphysics, so that correspondence is reduced to a trivial, metaphysically empty concept. Putnam characterizes the redundancy or disquotational theory of truth as an unacknowledged form of positivism because it strips truth-claims down to the making of marks and noises in appropriate situations and denies the necessity of positing anything like intentionality or reference. Thus, in another ironic similarity, both analytic redundancy proponents and continental deconstructionists are trying to find a way to talk about language and meaning without doing metaphysics, a move Putnam regards as hopeless and in the end as self-refuting as the parallel project of the Vienna Circle.

Putnam diagnoses the influence of these philosophical movements—deflationism and deconstruction, two of the most widely accepted positions on truth among theorists today—as caused by an excessive disappointment with the impossibility of classical realism. This disappointment is so great that the theorists who feel it react by saying that, if they cannot have classical realism, then they want no metaphysics of truth at all, and moreover, will not let anyone else have a metaphysics of truth either! They then declare truth to be a redundant concept without philosophical import, or a dangerous illusion leading to Fascism, but that in neither case is it metaphysically substantive. Putnam insists that this is not only a poor response to the problems with classical realism, it is an unlivable one, as he suggests in the following example:

> If someone approaches us with a gleam in his eye and says, "Don't you want to know the 'Truth'?", our reaction is generally to be pretty leery of this person.

5. Hilary Putnam, *Reason, Truth, and History* (Cambridge: Cambridge University Press, 1981), pp. xi–xii.

And the reason that we are leery (apart from the gleam in the eye) is precisely because someone's telling us that they want to know the truth tells us really *nothing* as long as we have no idea what standards of rational acceptability the person adheres to: what they consider a rational way to pursue an inquiry, what their standards of objectivity are, when they consider it rational to terminate an inquiry, what grounds they will regard as providing good reason for accepting one verdict or another on whatever sort of question they may be interested in.[6]

Truth is neither epistemically empty nor a redundant concept. Our need to understand the meaning of a truth-claim arises out of practical life and is not simply another pointless philosopher's riddle which can be easily discarded.

Moreover, if we go the relativist route, which might, for example, reduce truth completely to structures of discourse, Putnam believes that we cannot treat others or ourselves as cognitive agents capable of more or less accurately referring to reality. In his view, relativism ends up producing an alienated and distorted notion of human experience in the world. Speakers become mere noise-makers, no different in their representational capacities than ants who may accidentally trace the likeness of Winston Churchill in the sand, but without ever knowing that they have done so. I find it very interesting that the most serious problem Putnam finds with an absolute relativist view is its debilitating effect on intersubjective relations.[7] For all of their stated concern with politics, this is an effect few continental philosophers have addressed.

Although Putnam has firmly rejected the skepticism about metaphysics that has motivated such positions, he has rejected the dominant traditions of metaphysics just as firmly. In his view, language can represent more than language, and the norms of rational acceptability that make such representation possible are objective, in a certain sense, as we shall explore. But Putnam also agrees with Nelson Goodman:

Truth of statements and rightness of descriptions, representations, exemplifications, expressions—of design, drawing, diction, rhythm—is primarily a matter of fit: fit to what is referred to in one way or another, or to other renderings, or to modes and manners of organization. The differences between fitting a version to a world, a world to a version, and a version together or to other versions fade when *the role of versions in making the worlds they fit is recognized*. And knowing or understanding is seen as

6. Putnam, *Reason, Truth, and History*, p. 129.
7. Ibid., p. 124.

ranging beyond the acquiring of true beliefs *to the discovering and devising of fit of all sorts.*[8]

Putnam's attempt to combine this Goodmanesque constructivism with his own commitments to realism and rationality is taken by most philosophers as an unworkable project from the start. But much of Putnam's writing has been dedicated to showing how such a combination can be made viable. Thus he has explored the question of the ontology of truth and the issue of realism with more attention and depth than any of the philosophers discussed in previous chapters and has argued that the metaphysics of truth cannot be set aside as a nonissue. Putnam has stipulated several times that internal realism is the name of "a picture of what truth comes to" rather than a definition of truth based on concepts that do not presuppose it.[9] Thus, the concept of internal realism has more to do with metaphysics than with the philosophy of language, overturning the usual order of priority reigning today in analytic works. Following from this, coherence becomes a thesis with more metaphysical implications than it is usually accorded, since within the context of internal realism coherence becomes for Putnam a claim about the primacy of use in determining reference.

It will become clear in what follows that I am not interested in contributing scholarship toward understanding Putnam's full range of views on epistemology and metaphysics, views which—like Donald Davidson's—have shifted dramatically on precisely the issue of realism.[10] Instead, I will focus specifically on the development of internal realism, a view which Putnam provocatively credits to Kant.

### Internal Realism

One claim about which Putnam has not wavered is that a mind-independent reality impinges on and constrains our beliefs. This, for Putnam, is the heart of any realist account of truth, along with the intuition that the most well-justified beliefs of the majority of people may be untrue (a position that I suspect Putnam holds for political as well as metaphysical reasons). Thus, he sees the core of realism as maintaining two distinctions: a distinction between "justification here and now" and truth, on the one hand, and a distinction between that which human beings make and that which we do not make, on the other. This latter distinction separates Put-

8. Quoted in ibid., p. 123 (emphasis added).
9. See Hilary Putnam, "Comments and Replies," in *Reading Putnam*, p. 242.
10. For some of his recent disclaimers, see Putnam, "Comments and Replies," pp. 242–43, 289, 291.

nam's views from Goodman's "irrealism," which makes no separation between the made and the unmade, and it also distinguishes his view from consensus theories or versions of pragmatism which would collapse truth to agreement or to currently justified beliefs. Against idealism, Putnam holds that realism avoids the paradoxical position of asserting that there are only versions (or models, or schemas) and nothing but versions (or models, or schemas).[11] The concept of a version implies that there exists something it is a version *of*. Putnam has consistently rejected all forms of consensus theory, constructivism, and idealism; hence his self-identification as a realist.

Beyond this basic, or "minimal," realism, however, Putnam has argued that there exist (at least) two divergent and distinct types of realism. The first, "metaphysical realism," what I have been referring to as classical realism, holds that "the world consists of some fixed totality of mind-independent objects. There is exactly one true and complete description of 'the way the world is.' Truth involves some sort of correspondence relations between words or thought-signs and external things and sets of things."[12] This view obviously represents the dominant meaning of realism in Anglo-American philosophy (as well as the form of realism generally rejected by continental philosophy), so much so that it is generally the way in which "realism" is defined. What is principally important about it for Putnam is the degree of determinateness it attributes to reality, such that via correspondence relations only one uniquely true description of the world is possible. The ontology of truth for this view is generally characterized as a relation between a proposition or set of propositions and mind-independent reality, a relation that admits of a determinate and unique description of the world.

The new version of realism that Putnam has proposed—internal realism—differs from metaphysical realism on just these points. Internal realism is still committed to the existence of mind-independent reality and our epistemic access to it: hence it remains a version of realism. But the nature of that access and the contours of reality are reconceptualized. Specifically, Putnam says that internal realism is internalist

> because it is characteristic of this view to hold that *what objects does the world consist of?* is a question that it only makes sense to ask *within* a theory or description. . . . "Truth," in an internalist view, is some sort of (idealized) rational acceptability—some sort of ideal coherence of our beliefs with each other and with our experiences *as those experiences are themselves repre-*

11. Hilary Putnam, *Realism and Reason*, vol. 3 of *Philosophical Papers* (New York: Cambridge University Press, 1983), p. 226.
12. Putnam, *Reason, Truth, and History*, p. 49.

*sented in our belief system*—and not correspondence with mind-independent or discourse-independent "states of affairs." There is no God's Eye point of view that we can know or usefully imagine; there are only various points of view of actual persons reflecting various interests and purposes that their descriptions and theories subserve.[13]

Reality engenders many possible true descriptions, or in other words, it underdetermines our theoretical descriptions and so is compatible with more than one. Thus, internalism conceptualizes reality as thinner (or perhaps richer) than on the metaphysical realist version. The world does not come, as Putnam puts it, "ready made," with a "built-in" structure or form. This is a metaphysical fantasy.[14]

Reality is not so thin as to allow *any* description at all, however, and in this way Putnam distinguishes his internal realism from subjective idealism. "To grant that there is more than one true version of reality is not to deny that some versions are false."[15] How, then, are true descriptions to be understood and arrived at? What is the criterion that determines the epistemic adequacy of a description if reality is indeterminate? And what criterion can justifiably adjudicate between conflicting descriptions, or must we accept an ineliminable pluralism between conflicting "true" claims?

Putnam follows the empiricist tradition in positing experience as that which determines the truth-value of theories about the world, but like Otto Neurath and C. G. Hempel (and Kant) Putnam also holds that our experiences are *"to some extent shaped by our concepts,* by the vocabulary we use to report and describe them" and (unlike Kant) he denies the existence of *"any inputs which admit of only one description, independent of all conceptual choices."*[16] Therefore, even though knowledge is founded in experience, it still cannot provide a unique description of the world. Our experience is constituted by beliefs which are inferentially related and connected to specific and variable interpretive systems; it is these relations and connections that provide for their epistemic justification. There is no direct "magical connection" between observation statements and the world they are intended to describe.[17] Thus, any "foundation" is not beyond refutation or substitution. "Vision does not really give us direct access to a ready made world, but gives us a description of objects which are partly structured and constituted by vision itself."[18] Observation does not

13. Ibid., pp. 49–50.
14. Putnam, *Realism and Reason*, p. xiii.
15. Ibid., p. 19.
16. Putnam, *Reason, Truth, and History*, p. 54.
17. Ibid., p. 5.
18. Ibid., p. 146.

provide an unmediated view of reality: what we call experience or observation reports are more like interpretations, or "small theories."[19]

But Putnam argues that this Kantian view is consistent with a Jamesian "natural" realism. Natural realism does not share the metaphysical realist assumption that we may only know something about the world if the objects of perception in the external world serve as causal starting points for our subjective perceptions and subsequent knowledge. Rather, while accepting that the objects of perception are external things, the natural realist does not infer from this that we perceive the way the world is independent of human knowers or human interests, though we do perceive *aspects* of the world. Experience is not *solely constituted* by belief, but it is *always affected* by belief (which, in my view, need not be articulable in propositional or even linguistic form). The fact that experience is shot through with value and mediated by concepts means that copy theories and correspondence theories of truth are inapplicable, but it does not therefore entail that experience cannot be veridical in some other, more complicated manner.

It is interesting to note that Hempel identified the difference between Moritz Schlick and Neurath on this very issue of the nature of perception, a difference that caused one to choose correspondence and the other to choose coherence. Neurath could not hold a correspondence theory of truth while acknowledging the indirect nature of all our evidence about the world; Schlick's faith in the directness of observation reports made it possible for him to retain a commitment to correspondence, but of course few have agreed with Schlick that his excessively thin reports ("red here now") could actually support the whole of science or sustain a foundationalist epistemology. It is this problem that led Davidson, like Wilfred Sellars, to argue for a coherence theory of justification. As Davidson puts it, if perception is "too fleeting" to provide evidence, then we must admit that ultimately we are always justifying beliefs via other beliefs; hence the criterion of justification is coherence or the relations between a belief and other beliefs, rather than a belief's relations to nonepistemic or nondiscursive entities.

On the basis of this line of reasoning Putnam declares that truth itself is internal to a conceptual system. Truth does not represent a correspondence between a completely intrinsic feature of the world and a descriptive proposition, but represents a coherent "fit" between a theoretical description and an interpretive model of reality. " 'Objects' do not exist independently of conceptual schemes. *We* cut up the world into objects when we introduce one or another scheme of description. . . . The objects *and* the signs are alike *internal* to the scheme of description."[20] Putnam rejects,

---

19. Putnam, *Realism and Reason*, p. 209.
20. Putnam, *Reason, Truth, and History*, p. 52.

however, the cookie-cutter metaphor that could be inferred from what he says above, that is, the notion that concepts form the shape (or cut out the cookies) made from some primeval dough. Putnam's conceptual relativity goes deeper than this:

> What is wrong with the notion of objects existing "independently" of conceptual schemes [referring here to Davidson's famous argument] is that there are no standards for the use of even the logical notions apart from conceptual choices. What the cookie-cutter metaphor tries to preserve is the naive idea that at least one Category—the ancient category of Object or Substance—has an absolute interpretation. The alternative to this idea is not the view that it's all *just* language. We can and should insist that some facts are there to be discovered and not legislated by us. But this is something to be said when one has adopted a way of speaking, a language, a "conceptual scheme."[21]

Putnam's version of conceptual relativity entails a kind of "ontological internalism," since even concepts like "exist" and "object" only have specific meanings within a language. This view is strikingly similar to Michel Foucault's claim that objects are constituted by discourses and Hans-Georg Gadamer's view that a true interpretation is an emergent property of a fusion of horizons rather than a correlation between an interpretation and a meaning intrinsic to the text. Though Gadamer's and Foucault's views on truth are often considered antirealist, their accounts are actually consistent with Putnam's internal realist view that truth is an emergent property of (and therefore internal to) relations between epistemic elements—models, concepts, theories, and statements. Of course it is the case that the theories we adopt will be ones that can be observationally verified, but the observations upon which we depend for confirmation are not derived from unmediated direct reports but are based on a model of reality that is itself theory-dependent and revisable. "Internalism does not deny that there are experiential *inputs* to knowledge" but it does deny that there are "any inputs which admit of only one description."[22] Since the empirical content of our theories does not mandate a determinate, unique description, conceptual relativity is consistent with realism. Putnam explains this by saying that "the universe is not a furnished room."[23] The search for the furniture of the universe—ontology's traditional task—is hopeless not because we can never find out what furniture there is but because none exists. Putnam's explanation also implies that reality is amenable to plural descrip-

---

21. Hilary Putnam, *Representation and Reality* (Cambridge: MIT Press, 1992), p. 114.
22. Putnam, *Reason, Truth, and History*, p. 54.
23. Putnam, *Realism and Reason*, p. 23.

tions though not to arbitrary ones; not any size sofa will fit comfortably in the living room but more than one size can.

Is Putnam making claims here about the noumenal realm, thus repeating the critical mistake that many philosophers since Hegel have believed that Kant made? On the contrary, this is where, Putnam's views notwithstanding, his metaphysics seems to me to differ most sharply from Kant's.[24] Putnam considers any talk about a noumenal realm unintelligible and even repellent, because it posits objects without properties and an irreconcilable dualism between the phenomenal and the noumenal worlds. So his metaphor of an unfurnished universe is not meant to imply a realm beyond human experience, consisting of some kind of fuzzy substances that only come into focus through human perception and interpretation. "Models," he says, referring to the most basic ontological category he will allow, "are not lost noumenal waifs looking for someone to name them; they are constructions within our theory itself, and they have names from birth."[25] He insists that to ask questions about "what really exists," that is, behind or beyond our models of reality, is like trying to think about form without content, or an object with no characteristics: it is nonsensical.

The fact that Putnam often refers to conceptual systems as different descriptions of the same "state of affairs" does not reveal an unacknowledged commitment to a noumenal realm. His use of the phrase "state of affairs" is not a reference to a transcendental ontology but to the very ordinary way in which we would account for different descriptions.[26] Conceptual relativity "does not mean that reality is hidden or noumenal; it simply means that you can't describe the world without describing it."[27] Along with Wittgenstein, Putnam urges philosophers to stop wondering what is "hidden behind" the world (as we know it), or what is intrinsic or completely independent of us. The problem with this kind of thinking is not simply epistemological—that it is a hopeless project because we can never *know* what is "back there"— but metaphysical—because it is a mistake to conceptualize (or try to conceptualize) a realm beyond all conceptualization.

This should not be taken to mean that Putnam is an anti- or irrealist; he maintains that objects are supervenient on reality, for example, and not simply on language. But he argues that

> if you want to understand *why* semantic facts are supervenient on facts in the base totality—accepting, for the moment, this way of talking—you must, so to speak, look from above; you must look at the (allegedly) "non-intentional"

---

24. See, for example, Putnam, *Many Faces of Realism*, lecture 3.
25. Putnam, *Realism and Reason*, p. 25.
26. Putnam, "Comments and Replies," p. 247.
27. Putnam, *Renewing Philosophy*, p. 123.

facts about how we use words (e.g. "We often assert 'There's a rabbit' when a rabbit is present, and not very often when there is no rabbit present, or when we don't see the rabbit") from the standpoint of your intentional notions, rather than trying to explain from below—trying to use physics, or behavior science, or computer science, or whatever.[28]

This is not simply an argument about the limits of human knowledge (what we can know from the "prison" of human embodiment), nor is it an argument that entails idealism. Putnam is arguing that the answers to our metaphysical questions are not to be found "below" the level of description, because such a project is internally incoherent. Thus, conceptual relativity follows not from a rejection of the supervenience of semantic facts on facts in the base totality but from a rejection of the *explanatory relevance* of the base totality for semantic facts. Semantics for Putnam is irreducibly intentional, and he has argued at length against the reducibility of intentional notions to nonintentional notions.[29] If intentional notions are not reducible to nonintentional notions, then Simon Blackburn is mistaken in assuming that Putnam's talk of intentional notions implies correlating ontological commitments to fully described nonintentional entities.

A central part of this argument involves a rejection of the notion of intrinsicality, or properties that an object has "in itself." Putnam claims that all of the properties we attribute to objects are secondary in Locke's sense, identified by their power to affect *us* in a certain way, and thus all properties are relational rather than intrinsic. The concept of intrinsic properties presupposes the ontological dualism that Putnam thinks is symptomatic of our alienated metaphysics; in fact, he calls the belief in intrinsicality the "deep systematic root of the disease."[30] Every property has some contribution from language, mind, or context. Given the plural and variable incarnations of contexts, Putnam concludes that both reference and truth must be plural, though not arbitrary. The constraints on truth come at least in part from reality:

My view is not a view in which the mind *makes up* the world, either (or makes it up subject to constraints imposed by "methodological canons" and mind-independent "sense data"). If one must use metaphorical language, then let the metaphor be this: the mind and the world jointly make up the mind and the world. (Or, to make the metaphor even more Hegelian, the Universe makes up the Universe—with minds—collectively—playing a special role in the making up).[31]

28. Putnam, "Comments and Replies," p. 252.
29. See, for example, Putnam, *Representation and Reality*.
30. Putnam, *Many Faces of Realism*, p. 8.
31. Putnam, *Reason, Truth, and History*, p. xi.

Though he refers to Hegel here, Putnam has all along insisted that his is (at least a version of) a Kantian metaphysics, and thus distinguishable from Goodman's happy espousal of multiple "worlds."[32] Putnam sees himself as forging an alternative "between the swamps" of positivist ontologies and the "quicksands of cultural relativism and historicism,"[33] thus putting some secure distance between his internal realism and the major themes of post-Hegelian continental philosophy.

If Putnam self-consciously invokes Kant as his ontological mentor, a symptomatic reading of his defenses of internal realism can also find some un-Kantian aspects which show Putnam taking more of a Hegelian approach, as his final metaphor above reveals. We have seen that, though he claims to be committed to the existence of a mind-independent world, Putnam consistently refuses to address questions about it, utilizing the traditional pragmatist strategy of deflecting such questions on the grounds that they are nonsensical: "It makes no sense to think of the world as dividing itself up into 'objects' (or 'entities') independently of our use of language. It is *we* who divide up the world."[34] Even words such as "object," "property," "relation," and "exist" have no fixed usage, determinate reference, or human-independent basis. Putnam's ontology is thus less constrained than Kant's, more open to multiplicities. Like Hegel, Putnam puts conceptual categories in motion, and they evolve within history rather than remaining absolute. He takes the method of transcendental argument from Kant, but like Hegel he disinvests it from its associations with infallibility and certainty. Transcendental arguments still work to show us what must be the case given some fact, but facts are themselves relative to revisable schemes. Thus, Putnam argues that our rational ideals are *both* transcendentally justified *and* historically revisable.

Putnam also rejects Kant's absolute analytic-synthetic and fact-value distinctions, and binaries such as subjective/objective and constructed/real have no play in his internal realism. For Kant, although we cannot know what is pure world, we can at least know what is pure mind, and the latter is stable across cultural and historical differences. For Putnam, on the other hand, all is irretrievably enmeshed, even mutually constituting: mind and world make up mind and world. His ontology is thus more holistic than Kant's, less susceptible to neat internal division, and closer to Hegel's all-encompassing and more fluid Universal. Given the mutually constituting character of what we call the "subjective" and the "objective" dimensions of reality, these divisions lose their explanatory value and are seen as a clumsy, inaccurate shorthand. For Putnam as for Hegel, knowledge is not

32. Putnam, *Realism and Reason*, p. 226.
33. Ibid.
34. Putnam, "Comments and Replies," p. 243.

about a world wholly separate from human practice, nor is it wholly about human practice: knowledge is about a lived world and is achieved through interactive practice. Thus, Putnam puts forth a more intrinsically integrated ontology than Kant's neat categorical distinctions could accommodate.

For some readers, such an interpretation will provide support for Putnam's reputation as a closet idealist. But my symptomatic readings are not meant to disprove Putnam's declared commitment to realism. Hegel himself is variously interpreted as idealist or realist, depending on how his concept of Spirit is elucidated. It strikes me as more useful, not to mention more fair to Putnam, to frame the debate as a question not about whether he is a "legitimate" realist but about what kind of realist he is, and specifically, whether his ontology is closer to Kant's or Hegel's. Such a debate could avoid the terminological disputes and get on to the more substantive issues, which for me will be whether and to what extent Putnam can offer a truly immanent epistemology.

In order to explore that question, it will be helpful to look next at Putnam's account of justification. For an internal realist, the criterion of validity for competing beliefs must principally be coherence. "What makes a statement, or a whole system of statements—a theory or conceptual scheme—rationally acceptable is, in large part, its coherence and fit; coherence of 'theoretical' or less experiential beliefs with one another and with more experiential beliefs; and also coherence of experiential beliefs with theoretical beliefs."[35] One of the typical concerns with coherentist accounts of justification is the problem of vagueness: how can we know with certainty when something as ambiguous as a fit has been achieved? Reducing the concept's vagueness depends in large part on addressing the problem of scope: how does one know what elements—that is, what other beliefs and experiences—need to cohere? In interpreting a text, for example, or a theory, what contextual elements must be included to determine coherence, and what can be justifiably excluded? If the scope is excessively narrow, dogmatism will result; if it is too open-ended, judgment could take too long, or give rise to too many interpretations without any means of discriminating between them.

Putnam provides a plausible response to these concerns. The judgment of whether and to what extent coherence constraints have been satisfied follows no logic or algorithm; it is rather a " 'seat of the pants' feel."[36] It is impossible to formalize, or to set out in advance, a priori, the legitimate scope for an application of coherence. Yet coherence can still serve as an

35. Putnam, *Reason, Truth, and History*, pp. 54–55.
36. Ibid., p. 133.

objective guide to rational justification because its scope is determined within a specific context of use. This is what gives us the seat-of-the-pants feel. Does it make sense to refer to Athenian politics in interpreting classical Greek philosophy? Of course. What about the earlier traditions of thought in ancient Egypt? This depends on the strength of the case made for its relevance; using coherence as the criterion of justification provides no prima facie argument for the equal relevance of every conceivable fact unless some connection can be established.[37] But there is no algorithm for this. Thus, the application of coherence will be context-sensitive and theory-laden. "We learn [truth conditions and assertibility conditions] by acquiring a practice. . . . We do learn that in certain circumstances we are supposed to accept 'There is a chair in front of me' (normally). *But we are expected to use our heads.* We can refuse to accept 'There is a chair in front of me' even when it looks exactly as if there is a chair in front of us, if our general intelligence screams '*override.*' "[38]

Like James, Putnam holds that our application of coherence is not value-free but "deeply interwoven with" our psychological nature, cultural environment, and ecological needs.[39] These combine to produce what Putnam believes is an objective way of rationally evaluating knowledge claims. In fact, it is *because* our judgment is dependent on these facts about us that there *is* an objective fact of the matter concerning what is rational to believe and what is not.[40] Denying to coherence an algorithm or logical structure does not eliminate all the possible ways its vagueness can be reduced: thus, by tying coherence to practice Putnam can render its application objective even though it is not a priori.

Within the phenomenological tradition, Putnam's argument about the dependence of coherence on its context is correlated with the claim that we are always already in the world, already entangled in practices and committed to beliefs, and engaged in projects out of which our questions about knowledge arise, as do the means of answering them. This practical context, which is material, positioned, and historically specific, provides ready-made criteria for cognitive judgments—not unchallengable criteria, but workable ones by which we determine what is rational on the basis of an objective environment.

Some commentators, such as William Alston, have argued that ontological internalism does not itself entail a coherentist account of justification.

37. Such as has been established, for example, by Martin Bernal in *Black Athena* (London: Free Association Books, 1987).
38. Putnam, *Realism and Reason*, pp. xvii–xviii.
39. Putnam, *Reason, Truth, and History*, p. 55.
40. Putnam holds this despite the fact that he believes these "facts" about us are interpreted and our understanding of them is constantly evolving.

One could still conceptualize true statements as those that correspond to the facts, where facts are understood as partly determined by conceptual systems. This is certainly possible, but a correspondence theory of truth is drained of its metaphysical content by such an approach. Given the historical associations of correspondence with classical realism, Putnam's unorthodox reading of Kant notwithstanding, such a move would also be misleading. If we agree with Putnam that classical realism is unsustainable, we need to develop a different theory of knowledge to represent more adequately internalism's conceptualization of truth. Coherentism fits perfectly here because it connotes, both historically and conceptually, the development of mutually supporting relations within a system, and unlike correspondence, coherence avoids invoking dualist images. Putnam himself calls his internalism a coherentist rather than correspondence account: " 'Truth,' in an internalist view, is some sort of (idealized) rational acceptability—some sort of ideal coherence of our beliefs with each other and with our experiences *as those experiences are themselves represented in our belief system*—and not correspondence with mind-independent or discourse-independent 'states of affairs.' "[41] The point is not that internalism *entails* coherentism and is logically incompatible with correspondence, but that correspondence has a strong tradition of association with metaphysical realism.[42]

I do not mean to collapse the traditional distinction here between knowledge and truth. But the mere logical compatibility between ontological internalism and correspondence is a weak reason to develop the two ideas into a comprehensive account of human knowing. The correspondence theory of truth does not logically or theoretically require a repudiation of a coherence account of justification, but the history of the correspondence theory of truth, as well as the metaphysics invoked by the metaphor of correspondence itself, involves precisely the kind of dualism Putnam wants to overcome. Because this metaphysical dualism has enjoyed a hegemony within modernist philosophies, so much so that it has become part of the sedimented intuition we call common sense, we need a clean break if we are to transcend it successfully.

The ontology of truth Putnam develops within his account of internal realism is therefore best captured as coherentist. Although there may be a

41. Putnam, *Reason, Truth, and History*, pp. 49–50.
42. Correspondence is also famously associated with the redundancy theory of truth, and this could be used to argue for the plasticity of the concept. There are, however, widespread and famous debates over whether in fact Tarski's semantic theory of truth is compatible with correspondence; see, for example, Susan Haack, *Philosophy of Logics* (Cambridge: Cambridge University Press, 1978). As I have argued, although we can make correspondence formally achieve a fit with internal realism, it is ontologically misleading to do so and has no overwhelming advantages I can discern.

correspondence relation obtaining when true theoretical propositions link up with our model(s) of reality, it is not correspondence to reality pure and simple but rather a relation of coherence between and among elements internal to the processes of inquiry. Yet truth can still be robust on this view because the universe is unfurnished: truths can be faithful to reality at the same time that there exists more than one of them, or more than one version of the same phenomenon. Reference operates through connecting a specific interpretive scheme or model of reality with a specific theory, but reference itself is not so much a relation of correspondence as of coherence, because reference is determined by use and use is holistic.[43] Putnam's construal of reference in terms of coherence does not end up in absolute idealism precisely because it is not simply a coherence between beliefs understood as propositions or even mental dispositions. Coherence involves beliefs and their context of use in human practices; thus coherence incorporates the lived world.

Ultimately, the most important aspect of Putnam's coherentism is its grounding in use. It is this grounding that leads to the "open texture" of reference, meaning, and reason, and that also gives his account an objectivity without intrinsic features being ascribed to reality. Putnam's strongest argument against the charge of idealism is this pragmatist orientation; intuitively, his deep commitment to realism must be acknowledged within an account that finds practical activity and material context so fundamental to philosophical justification.

Putnam's focus on "sensuous" human practice with its correlative metaphysics of lived reality and his rejection of intrinsicality and other modernist dualisms constitute an important convergence between his ontology of truth and Gadamer's and Foucault's. This convergence he might willingly entertain, but Putnam's account of rationality also represents a convergence with some of the continental treatments, more so than I suspect he would acknowledge. Putnam's conception of rationality owes much to American pragmatism. Like Gadamer, Putnam is sharply critical of the "method fetishists" who would separate the method of science from its content and in this way try to formalize rationality. Arguing that "the method of science in fact changes constantly as the content of science changes,"[44] Putnam supports the critique of the Enlightenment project, with its unrevisable principles of reason or human understanding.[45] Furthermore, although Putnam claims to repudiate historicism, he holds that, because experiences and theories are partial constructs influenced by our historically specific situations, coherent fits will change throughout history,

43. Putnam, *Representation and Reality*, p. 119.
44. Putnam, *Reason, Truth, and History*, p. 191.
45. Ibid., p. x.

responding to increases in our empirical knowledge as well as changes in our social environment. Thus his conception of rationality actually includes a historicist component.

Putnam nevertheless considers himself in fundamental disagreement with many continental theorists because he does not conclude from the mutability of rationality that cognition is left in the throes of irrational, unconscious forces. Putnam argues that there is another way to conceptualize reason: it consists in our attempt to render our theories and our experience coherent with each other, an effort to make sense of the world.[46] The fact that there is no formalizable principle that can guide this pursuit does not leave it to arbitrary design. What will not change is our striving to maximize the coherence between theories and experience, and thus the role of coherence as the ultimate criterion of rational judgment; this is the unrevisable procedure that maintains continuity across historical changes.[47]

Putnam thinks this view differentiates him from Foucault, whom he interprets as an irrationalist and total relativist,[48] but Foucault's views are actually not so different from Putnam's own. Foucault's analysis of knowledge and regimes of truth suggests that processes aimed at coherence have produced systems of belief through history: relations between discursive elements as well as institutions and practices produce quite systematic discursive formations. What changes historically are the systems of belief and the specific elements whose relations we try to make coherent. But the development of the discursive formations which determine coherence relations continues through different historical periods. Just as Putnam allows that changes in our historical situation will alter our experiences and theories and therefore affect how a coherent fit can best be made, so Foucault argues that social changes will be reflected in our treatment of knowledge. Because Putnam defines historicism as the attempt "to reduce epistemic notions to non-epistemic ones," he ascribes historicism to Foucault but not to himself.[49] As I argued in the last chapter, however, Foucault does not accept a complete reductionist account that would collapse knowledge to power; his famous power/knowledge dyad precludes this. So neither Putnam nor Foucault is a historicist by Putnam's definition.

Moreover, Foucault's argument in defense of subjugated knowledges can be interpreted as an attempt to reform or improve rationality rather than reveal it as an impossible goal. The argument would be that in the previous era when power was thought to exist in the form of centralized forces of

46. Ibid., p. 55.
47. Putnam argues that this is motivated by our striving for Eudaemonia. Ibid., p. 134. I would prefer to explain it pragmatically.
48. Ibid., pp. 155–62.
49. Putnam, *Realism and Reason*, p. 290.

domination, the valorization of reason and method as principles universally available and applicable was strategically useful in subverting the absolute power of the king. The concept of universal reason effected a
decentralization of epistemic authority, which could then be used to demand a decentralized political authority. But in the twentieth century the
morphology of power has changed, and the pressing issues of domination
are less centralized autocracies than decentralized institutional and disciplinary structures that pervade the social field. A revolution of the barri-
cades, directed at taking a central seat of power like the Kremlin or the
Pentagon, will be ineffective in an age when nation-states are functionaries
for dispersed global monopolies. Thus, to champion universal reason
would be to collude with the modern form of power instead of subverting
it. Universal reason has devolved into the disciplined production of docile,
information-processing knowers, with an instrumental reason extended to
all and a critical reason almost abolished. Critical reason has been characterized in the recent culture wars as inherently elitist; in criticizing society
and social practices academics are said to be criticizing the masses, setting
themselves above society in order to pass judgment. On the other hand, the
elitist character of instrumental reason, in which (supposedly) only tech-
nocrats can make informed decisions about significant political issues, is
passed over as inevitable.

It is arguable, then, that, because he criticizes universalist reason, Foucault is not as much at odds with Putnam's views as the latter believes; Foucault does not so much reject rationality as pluralize it and open it up to
historical change. Foucault's is assuredly a more overtly politicized account
of knowledge, but in his recent work Putnam has been arguing for an intrinsic relationship between political goals like democracy and epistemic
success in the sciences.[50] Still, there is little doubt that Foucault's and Putnam's views differ significantly concerning the role of ontology in developing an account of knowledge; Foucault refuses to engage with such issues,
while Putnam, although he is wary of metaphysics, understands that it is
ultimately unavoidable.

It should be clear at this point why I have included the work of Putnam
in this study. None of the three philosophers discussed earlier have attempted to develop an ontological characterization of truth in as much detail as Putnam; thus their accounts remain vague and unformed in critical
respects. Still, Putnam's internal realism has undergone heavy criticism in
recent years, and in the remainder of this chapter I will discuss some of the
major issues raised, such as relativism. I will also discuss one of the impor-

50. See Hilary Putnam, "Pragmatism and Moral Objectivity," in *Women, Culture, and Development*, ed. Martha Nussbaum and Jonathan Glover (Oxford: Oxford University Press,
1995).

tant differences between Putnam and Davidson: though each follows a coherentist account of justification and rejects both metaphysical realism and antirealism, Davidson refuses to make truth an epistemic concept and criticizes Putnam's account of internal realism as inviting skepticism by doing so. If internal realism is a viable position it needs to be defended against its many critics, who have argued that it collapses to antirealism or idealism, that it cannot avoid a destructive relativism, or, from the other side, that it is too conservative to provide a decisive alternative to metaphysical realism. Before we tackle that debate, let us look more closely at the charge of relativism.

## Relativisms

Obviously, Putnam's account is a relativistic one in so far as he defends conceptual relativity. Beyond this, however, some have argued that relativism also follows from Putnam's conception of truth as idealized rational acceptability, by which he means something like rational warrantability under "sufficiently good epistemic conditions," to distinguish it from the Peircean ideal end of inquiry.[51] But like Peirce's notion, Putnam's still works to distinguish actual from idealized justifications, and thus does not entail the claim that all justified beliefs are true. Truth is elucidated in terms of justification, but is not reduced to or coextensive with the class of currently existing justified beliefs, even those considered "most" justified (a status that Putnam would accord to science).[52] "Truth cannot simply *be* justification, I argue, for any number of reasons: truth is supposed to be a property of a statement that cannot be lost, whereas justification can be lost (in fact, justification is both tensed and relative to a person), justification is a matter of degree whereas truth is not (or not in the same way), etc."[53] Moreover, Putnam argues that truth cannot be reduced to epistemic notions like rational acceptability because rational acceptability is itself dependent on its ability to yield true statements.[54] Thus, truth and rational acceptability are interdependent notions, instead of truth being defined in terms of rationality. Still, Putnam maintains that our understanding of what truth means is derivative upon our conception of justification and cannot wholly transcend this conception, even while it is not completely reducible to it.

With his nonalgorithmic account of rationality, however, as well as his conceptual relativity and his opposition to ontological absolutism, how can

51. See Putnam, "Comments and Replies," nn. 4 and 26.
52. Putnam, *Realism and Reason*, p. 84.
53. Ibid., pp. 84–85. See also Putnam, *Reason, Truth, and History*, p. 130.
54. Putnam, *Representation and Reality*, p. 115.

Putnam maintain his unequivocal repudiation of what he calls "unbridled relativism"? We need to distinguish between the kind of relativism Putnam rejects and the kind he accepts. The following passage describes the kind of relativism Putnam accepts: "Why should there not sometimes be equally coherent but incompatible conceptual schemes which fit our experiential beliefs equally well? If truth is not (unique) correspondence then the possibility of a certain pluralism is opened up."[55] Putnam would reject a relativism that made all theories approximations, that confined them to a given subject's particular standards, that defined rationality by current cultural norms, or that made every claim potentially true relative to some model. Nor does Putnam want to relinquish the goal of eliminating conflicting explanations or maximizing theoretical unity in the sciences.

Borrowing a familiar argument from Goodman, Putnam contends that we can avoid an "unbridled relativism" when we come to understand that there is no neutral position from which to judge competing claims. It could be objected that this is a paradox, and that finding a neutral place is the best way to limit relativism. But the sort of unbridled relativism Putnam rejects is a relativism that would relativize all things, and this requires a neutral position from which to make such a general claim. From the perspective of any other, nonneutral position—that is, any particular conception of the world and of our place within it—all competing claims will not appear relative but will be evaluated in light of the particular worldview to be had from our epistemic location. Putnam distinguishes himself from Goodman's view because "in the final instance" he strongly affirms the claim not that all views are relative but that our versions are superior to others "*by our lights*, not by some inconceivable neutral standard."[56] Whereas Goodman emphasizes the fact that, strictly speaking, relativism follows from the lack of a neutral standard, Putnam highlights the fact that, precisely because no one is neutral, we (for *any* given "we") cannot embrace relativism except of a rather empty metaphilosophical kind.

This response to relativism is based once again on Putnam's pragmatist orientation. For the pragmatists, the kind of absolute relativism philosophers have traditionally worried about is not a legitimate or "real" doubt, that is, it is not based on specific sources of doubt arising out of practice. We have reason to doubt specific claims and to take issue with other cultures' beliefs on specific issues, but because these doubts are based on specific reasons (such as lack of evidence, failure to cohere with our other beliefs on the subject, and so on), they do not lead to the all-encompassing suspension of belief that a total relativism implies. Many philosophers as-

---

55. Putnam, *Reason, Truth, and History*, p. 73. See also Putnam, *Realism and Reason*, p. 10.
56. Putnam, *Realism and Reason*, p. 168.

sume that some bedrock foundation or a priori method is necessary to avoid relativism. Pragmatists such as Peirce, however, long ago showed that our beliefs gain nothing from such metajustifications—that is, philosophical justifications that would seek to go beyond the ordinary reasons we might give for our general perceptual beliefs—and that they therefore lose nothing without them. Putnam clearly follows this tradition in that, although he rejects unbridled relativism, he does not take the problem all that seriously. So, like Peirce and many others, he diagnoses both absolute relativism and positivism as founded on the assumption that classical realism is the only realism.

This is not to say that there are no real instances of apparent relativism accepted with respect to actually held beliefs, or that the problem of relativism arises only among metaphilosophers. Aside from the ubiquitous undergraduate examples, relativism is often invoked to address cross-cultural systems of belief. Theorists like C. G. Jung, Claude Lévi-Strauss, and Joseph Campbell have advanced universalist projects to sift through cultural differences for the sedimented basic unities underneath, but such projects have become less plausible and less influential as Anglo-Europeans grow more knowledgeable about other cultures. The waning influence of these universalist systems of interpretation has in turn given rise to a relativist response, in which cognitive differences are said to be explained by culture or discourse, beyond which there is no appeal. Though this might seem to increase the likelihood of intercultural conflicts, since relativism gives up the hope of resolving differences through rational discussion based on shared beliefs and values, it is often believed to lead actually to more harmony, since the adoption of cultural relativism would undermine the West's superiority complex by rendering any overall comparison impossible. Relativism counsels tolerance, it is believed, whereas nonrelativism engenders accusations of irrationality or willful malice and a dogmatic attachment to one's own cultural prejudices.

Although I have many political disagreements with Putnam, as the following chapter will undoubtedly reveal, in this area our views converge. The problem with the relativist path just outlined is that, in the guise of promoting mutual respect, it renders real respect impossible. Tolerance for another person's or culture's incomprehensible positions does not yield respect but grudging noninterference. If I cannot truly understand another's view, or why he or she supports it, I cannot truly take it seriously; I am left to consider the other a mere noise-maker, as Putnam (via Wittgenstein) maintains, or as a curious species interesting primarily for its entertainment value. Anglo-Europeans often take this *National Geographic* attitude toward other cultures, which may offer interesting customs and attractive costumes for Western enjoyment but are unable to engage in serious dialogue or to share decision-making power over any important issues such as nuclear weapons. Thus beneath the tolerance and curious interest always lies a profound sense of superiority. If I cannot at least grasp the plausibility of another's views, I cannot truly accord them the same status as my own. Such accordance as I might perfunctorily give on the basis of "logic" would be merely metaphilosophical, having no association with my cognitive or affective state and therefore unlikely to affect my practice in any way. My tolerance would be based on an abstract acceptance of cultural relativism, a kind of Kantian duty-following devoid of affect, and not on a genuine understanding of why the other's views deserve my respect. This argument does not entail that I must be able to understand *fully* a different set of views before I can truly respect them, but that there must at least be some "real doubt" about the adequacy of my own different views, some specific reason to think the other's views might just have something to teach me, before my respect can be genuine.

Moreover, the actual situation we increasingly find ourselves in rarely allows for a noncommittal tolerance, and certainly not when the differences concern anything of importance. Societies are so interwoven today that few if any exist separate from others; we are increasingly interdependent and mutually influencing. What usually happens when we encounter difference is that we strive to make sense of it somehow, to understand it within its own terms or by making an analogy with something more familiar. This is a better response than the relativist ideal of disinterested tolerance. It is mistakenly believed by some critics of the Enlightenment that striving to understand difference necessarily entails its assimilation to our own norms of rationality and morality, and thus necessarily exacerbates chauvinism. This effect may be common but it is not inevitable. Absolute relativism produces a tolerance for other cultures, but it also removes the need to revise one's own beliefs and practices in light of the differences one encounters. If one strives truly to be "open to the other" as Gadamer puts it, and if one is willing to revise one's own norms rather than hold them back as nonnegotiable, an understanding can be achieved which does not silence or erase the other's "otherness." (Here I part company with the Levinasian politics developed by Drucilla Cornell.)[57] In this process, one does not pretend to be able to be simply open, or to be a tabula rasa with no interpreting systems or prejudices. Gadamer does not counsel us simply to ape the other, accepting all we come across without reflection or critique. His coherentist hermeneutics brings all the elements into play without privileging either our own or the other's. Again, this is entailed by the very respect we

57. See Drucilla Cornell, *The Philosophy of the Limit* (New York: Routledge, 1992). See also Judith Butler's excellent critique in her review essay "Poststructuralism and Postmarxism," *Diacritics* 23.4 (1993): 3–11.

wish to show the other. The liberal attitude of treating others with such deference and delicacy that one never voices one's own views or criticisms is patronizing and condescending, and reveals a lack of respect.[58]

All of this is by way of defending Putnam against a potential postmodernist critique that his opposition to unbridled relativism would lead to political problems for his account. My argument is that a simplistically absolute cultural relativism provides no route to real transcultural harmony. I suspect that relativism is now widely accepted in the West because of a dawning recognition that in the area of cultural differences, Western formations and traditions are not always demonstrably superior; it is easier on one's self-esteem to resort to relativism than to admit that one can learn something important from a previously despised group.

A rejection of total relativism does not need to be based on an acceptance of total universalism or the view that "at bottom, we are all the same." This is a false dilemma, akin to the choice between foundationalism and skepticism. Our metasciences are probably too immature at this point to disprove decisively the possibility of fundamental sameness, but it is clearly the case that the current theories attributing sameness across cultural differences have all privileged one or another set of cultural norms, usually the West's.

We can, however, avoid an absolute relativist position without solving the problem of underlying sameness. Relativism is better avoided by a piecemeal approach than by a global attempt to devise absolute standards once and for all. That is, it is better avoided by small-scale discussions and joint projects through which differences can be explored and understood by all parties. This process is never likely to lead to the utopia of global harmony precisely because it is small-scale; with every difference that is resolved new ones are discovered and others are created through the changes of history and social practice. Nor does the belief that understanding is possible entail that all differences can be resolved in a way that all parties involved will find equitable. But only in a situation of absolute incommensurability (which exists today nowhere in the world) would the attempt at resolution be hopeless from the start; where some element is shared, however slight, there is room to build greater understanding and agreement. The actual situation is that there is an ongoing, interminable need to seek understanding across difference, a need created by the complexity and interdependence of life, not by the lack of foundations or universal reason. Analytic philosophy displays its ideologies and limitations by framing discussions of relativism within examples involving hypothetical Martians

---

58. See, e.g., Satya P. Mohanty, "Colonial Legacies, Multicultural Futures: Relativism, Objectivity, and the Challenge of Otherness" *Colonialism and the Postcolonial Condition*, Special Issue of *PMLA* (January 1995), 108–18.

and the imagined sensibilities of bats. We will achieve much more philosophical clarity by analyzing the issue of relativism within our everyday
world of racism, sexism, and global economic tyranny.

The striving to understand the other, to make sense of seemingly incomprehensible differences, which is often the motivating force (or at least the
historical occasion) behind both the poststructuralist concern with difference and the analytic philosopher's concern with relativism, is simply another description of the striving for coherence. It does not provide any
"standard" or "method" to resolve disputes; there is no algorithm for
managing difference. Coherentism as I see it simply articulates the impulse
for resolution itself, and defines how a resolution would be identified, as
well as how it would feel.

Thus, although the striving for coherence is universal, it provides little
substantive help. The determination of what must cohere will itself be the
subject of dispute, and can be determined only by a seat-of-the-pants feel-
ing of fit, admittedly a variable notion. The striving for coherence can,
however, help prevent easy assessments of superiority or hasty dismissals of
unfamiliar ideas. Gadamer's description of the back-and-forth movement,
in which all initial positions are revisable toward developing the most coherent interpretation, works against a quick assimilation of the other to the
same. Putnam's insistence on the revisability of rationality also keeps our
own norms of reasoning open to learning something new in any encounter
with different systems. It is the concept of universal reason that has proved
to be most supportive of chauvinisms of all kinds, with its quick, a priori
judgments about meaning and truth. Rationality understood as the striving
for coherence should be less likely to encourage chauvinism, not by promoting a simple relativism, but by holding all elements open to revision
within the goal of understanding, and by recognizing the process not as an
application of a prior method but as an evolving movement which must
necessarily remain open to the incorporation of the new and different.

### Incoherence

Blackburn has offered an interesting and perceptive critique of internal
realism's relativism in his disingenuously entitled essay, "Enchanting
Views." Blackburn takes on Putnam's purported repudiation of forms of
classical realisms which involve "correspondence, independence, bivalence,
and uniqueness." In regard to the first three, Blackburn argues that they
can be given relatively nonthreatening interpretations (that is, nonthreatening to metaphysical realism) which would conform to Putnam's internalism, and thus that none of these can be used effectively either to

demarcate internal from metaphysical realism or to reject metaphysical realism.

Several philosophers have made similar claims about correspondence, that is, that the concept is plastic enough to fit almost any epistemology.[59] Blackburn adds to these familiar arguments about the plasticity of correspondence more original ones about the plasticity of independence and bivalence. Moreover, he points out that Putnam himself endorses independence at least in the sense that truth must be independent of "whether a majority of the members of the culture *believe* it to be true."[60] Thus Blackburn argues that, despite Putnam's repudiations, internal realism is not necessarily incompatible with correspondence, bivalence, or independence, and that in fact Putnam himself postulates a version of the last term.

The criterion of uniqueness, however, is where Blackburn believes a real problem exists for internal realism. He considers uniqueness a necessary component of any realism, however modified, because without it we can no longer talk about beliefs but only about "instrumental acceptances" of some nondoxastic kind. This is because the uniqueness criterion is needed to maintain the regulative ideal of consistency in advancing knowledge. Therefore, without uniqueness Putnam's internal realism must collapse into an incoherent relativism. Here is Blackburn's argument:

> Perspectival realism [of which he takes internal realism to be a form] offers a framework within which to reconcile apparent conflict. But the reconciliation only takes place if inconsistency can be shown to be apparent, and that means obtaining a background, different conception of how things are, whereby the initial conflicting views can be seen as only apparently in conflict. If we lack this we are simply left with conflict, and *unable to think* how the different views can be related at all, or even count as views. (20, emphasis added)

Blackburn's "inability to think" past the need for a universal ontology or base totality leads him to argue that such a commitment is endemic to the nature of belief. But this does not follow. Blackburn assumes without argument that when Putnam or Quine says that reference is always relative to a background language, this background cannot determine reference if it is as contextually relative as reference itself. "It is no good trying to anchor one free-floating term by attaching it to another equally free-floating term" (23). In this case, Blackburn thinks, following Barry Stroud, that relativizing a background removes its ability to have a determining effect (23). The form of Putnam's argument, however, is modus ponens: "*if* A,

59. See, for example, Haack, *Philosophy of Logics*; Richard Rorty, *Consequences of Pragmatism* (Minneapolis: University of Minnesota Press, 1982).
60. Quoted in Blackburn, "Enchanting Views," p. 15.

then B." So A does not need to be true (in some absolute sense) for it to imply B with necessity. The determinate status of B is therefore not compromised by its subsistence within a background language that assumes A, where A lacks transcendental or decontextualized justification. All that is affected is B's status as transcendentally true, and not its determinate relationship to A. Thus, we do not need a determinate base ontology to explain belief.

Blackburn acknowledges that "if it denies the imperative toward unity, 'internal' realism may be a yet more radical doctrine than any that employs the image of different perspectives," because the concept of perspective implies that there is some unified reality about which there exist alternative views or interpretations (20). But he cannot bring himself to imagine the contours of such a "yet more radical doctrine."

The requirement of consistency as a regulative ideal can only operate, however, *within* a particular schema or language game. To require that it work *between* them would necessitate a neutral position, unless one allows that for it to work, only one particular point of view is needed within which it works (that is, within which consistency can be applied). The attainment of such a neutral or more fundamental base position is not necessary to motivate or justify either pursuing consistency as widely and rigorously as possible within any given schema, or attempting to find consistency as far as possible between schemas. But the possibility of finding consistency, or a reconciliation of all the differences, between schemas, need not be guaranteed in order to motivate the pursuit of consistency as a regulative ideal in the first place. Neither Goodman nor Putnam have to give up consistency as a regulative ideal simply because they refuse to share the metaphysical assumption that the world is, as a matter of necessity, susceptible to a unique description. It is enough that the multiple valid descriptions it can engender must themselves be internally consistent, and for this we can rely on pragmatic arguments—our need for predictability, communicability, and so forth.

In fact, it is just such pragmatic considerations that Putnam would have us rely on to provide a justification for our own schema (which explains why in hindsight he says he should have used the term "pragmatic realism" rather than "internal realism"). Where Blackburn, like most philosophers, will only accept a transcendental, metaphilosophical, and essentially esoteric justification, and sees anything short of this as arbitrary and ineffective, Putnam sides with Rorty and Goodman (at least here) in claiming that such a justification is not necessary and not possible, and really makes no sense. When a neighbor claims to have seen a rabbit in your yard, and answers your question "How do you know it wasn't an undetached rabbit part?" with the ordinary answers one might give within our language game

(including putting up a tall fence), it simply makes no sense to ask him repeatedly "But how do you *know* it was a rabbit?" Here is where the use-
based tradition in analytic philosophy (represented by Putnam, Goodman,
Rorty, Wittgenstein, and others) merges in important respects with the phenomenological tradition in continental philosophy, which sees our knowledge and its justification as arising out of concrete, material circumstances,
without need of a more transcendental basis.

The world, in Putnam's conception of it, can provide no transcendental
anchor for determining reference, not because the world does not exist, but
because it is unfurnished. As I remarked earlier, Blackburn notes that
Goodman's work met a similar response to Putnam's on the grounds that
"we cannot intelligibly do the required imagining," but he accepts this
complaint as a legitimate criticism.[61] Blackburn believes that reference cannot be founded on use unless we posit a unique and determinate base ontology, because he assumes that reference—along with extension and
ontology—requires consistency to be intelligible. But we all know by everyday experience that it does not. To be consistent, linguistic concepts would
have to have a singular, fixed reference, rather than "an ever-expanding
open family of uses" as Putnam claims.[62] Of course we usually strive for
consistency because it is necessary for communication, but we are often de-
lighted when a new use for a word comes along, and we quickly adapt.
Consider the ways in which computer jargon has overtaken everyday
speech among professionals in the United States: we talk about "user-
friendly" textbooks, lecturing as "downloading", and "virtual" relationships. Why is it so impossible to imagine a universe of discourse in which
a disposition toward consistency works within a system of constant evolution and aggregation that necessarily creates new and diverse relations?
This is the sense in which reference, extension, and ontology are necessarily open-ended for Putnam and thus best understood as determined by coherence relations within a complex network which includes practices and
material contexts as well as beliefs and propositions. Putnam's opponents
are correct to say that at this point the problem is a failure of imagination,
but they are wrong to infer from the failure a conceptual impossibility.[63]

Putnam himself answers Blackburn's charge—that without a determinate account of reference we must forego the belief that semantics super-
venes on reality—by pointing out that supervenience does not require a

61. Ibid., p. 25.
62. See Putnam's reply to Blackburn in "Comments and Replies," p. 243.
63. I am not claiming here that problems of consistency occur whenever a word has more
than one meaning. But if you use the word "grand" to mean expansive and generous and I use
the word "grand" to mean fat, one of us is likely to run into trouble (probably me). Some differences are more compatible than others.

determinate account of reference. Thus Putnam maintains his ability to be a realist (and therefore to uphold supervenience) without having to commit himself to the possibility of a complete description of the world in a language in which all propositions are determinate.[64] Supervenience can be a feature of diverse ontologies, not simply correspondence or transcendentalist ones. Blackburn resembles many of Putnam's analytic readers, who cannot disentangle ontology from determinate reference and thus assume that because he eschews determinate reference Putnam is either an antirealist or simply incoherent. Blackburn is led into this mistake because once again he cannot conceptualize a reality in the way that Putnam does, as either too rich or too thin to be determinate of reference or extension.

## Is Internal Realism Really Realistic?

Alston, one of the most important defenders of foundationalism and metaphysical realism of this century, has recently offered an extended analysis of Putnam's internal realism.[65] Alston's latest project is to develop and defend a new form of realism that he has named "alethic realism," which is a minimalist account that is neutral on metaphysical issues. Alethic realism is committed to the biconditional—"It is true that $p$ if and only if $p$"—as a conceptually necessary truth (which is one of several differences between this T-schema and Alfred Tarski's), but it does not take a position on alternative ontologies.[66]

In order to provide the strongest case for his alethic realism, Alston has tried to give as sympathetic a reading as possible to its major alternatives and their critiques of classical realism, and has thus dedicated three chapters to a careful analysis of Putnam. Not surprisingly, Alston's conclusion, similar in some respects to Blackburn's, is that some features of the form of realism Putnam attacks—metaphysical realism—are not central or nonnegotiable features of alethic realism, and that Putnam's own internal realism is incoherent and implausible. Trying to steal the thunder usually claimed by foundationalism's opponents, Alston argues that it is coherentism, internal realism, and epistemic accounts of truth which demand more of human knowledge than it can achieve, and that it is therefore alethic realism which is closer to our actual epistemic situation. In other words, Alston argues that alethic realism is more realistic than internal realism. Since

64. See Putnam, "Comments and Replies," pp. 252, 254. Putnam also provides other answers to Blackburn's essay that I have not dealt with here.
65. William P. Alston, *A Realist Conception of Truth* (Ithaca: Cornell University Press, 1996).
66. Tarski takes his T-schema to be a material one, rather than conceptually necessary.

I have taken the position throughout this book that coherentism is less removed from real knowing than are foundationalist accounts, these arguments require a response. Moreover, Alston offers representative arguments
to the effect that Putnam must opt either for antirealism or Realism, and
that his conception of truth is collapsible to an epistemic account. Therefore, an analysis of Alston's critique will draw out much of the major debate
concerning Putnam's internal realism.

Before addressing internal realism, Alston discusses the one aspect of Putnam's account that he considers plausible, though he declines to take a
firmly committed position on it either way. In a surprising move for a foundationalist, Alston argues that Putnam's conceptual relativity thesis is consistent with a variety of moderate forms of metaphysical realism and
therefore does not require the repudiation of a metaphysical realist account
of truth and correspondence, nor the acceptance of an epistemic account of
truth.[67] He argues that what is contradictory to conceptual relativity is not
metaphysical realism but an ontological absolutism which would claim
that there is one, unique, true picture of the world. Alston then disentan-
gles metaphysical realism from ontological absolutism by showing several
ways in which Putnam's conceptual relativity thesis can be construed so as
to be compatible with metaphysical realism in the form of alethic realism.
Thus, one can accept conceptual relativity without then being forced to accept internal realism.
    On the face of it, this argument has intuitive plausibility. After all, Put-
nam simply *defines* metaphysical realism as the commitment to what Alston is calling ontological absolutism, rather than showing why the one
entails the other. It is certainly the case that Putnam's main metaphysical
problem with classical realism is the degree of determinateness it accords
reality, or what Alston helpfully calls ontological absolutism. Alston's argument, however, suffers from a misinterpretation of Putnam's metaphysical explanation of conceptual relativity. Alston sets up a false dilemma
between "relativized Kantianism," which can accommodate conceptual
relativity but is also consistent with some forms of metaphysical realism,
and "idealized Hegelianism," which accommodates conceptual relativity
by eschewing realism in favor of idealism or the mind-dependence of all
facts. By relativized Kantianism I think Alston is referring to a historicized
Kantianism, or a Kantianism where the categories of perception are in
motion. Alston thinks that Putnam's statements on internal realism are ambiguous between these two interpretations, but that if Putnam is interpreted as a relativized Kantian, then his account has some merit.

67. See Alston, *Realist Conception of Truth*, chap. 6.

The only possible way to interpret Putnam's internal realism, however, is not as a relativized Kantianism or a form of idealism. Alston does not consider the possibility that Hegel's epistemology, like Kant's, can be variously interpreted, and that on at least one interpretation Hegel was not an idealist, but rather construed the reality to which true statements refer as a reality that incorporates but does not wholly consist of human interests and interpretations, that is, as a lived reality rather than a Ding an sich. This is not a form of idealism, nor is it a position committed to the dualist ontology Kant proposed. It is neither the view that true statements express what "really exists" nor the view that they just express the content of thought or relationships within language.

These latter positions assume ontological dualism, a sharp separation between "mind" and "world." Alston's commitment to this dualism is revealed in his unease with a metaphysics that would lump them together beyond differentiation. Realism according to Alston seems to require some ability to separate out what is mind-independent and what is not, within the scope of knowledge, and if Putnam's theory cannot do this, it must be idealist. Alston sees correspondence theories as tying truth to a reality outside of thought, and contrasts this approach with a Hegelianism that aims simply at the "perfect completion of thought."[68] This suggests his commitment to the very dualism that Putnam is trying to transcend.

Putnam's metaphysics, as I have tried to show in this chapter, resists the realism/idealism schema in which realism defines truth (not truth-value-bearers here, but truth) as what is mind-independent, and idealism collapses truth to mind. Human beings do not make up the world; it would exist whether we were here or not. But truth is another matter. Truth is a property of sentences, which are not mind-independent. For a metaphysical realist, the true description of the world is waiting out there to be written down; for an internal realist, true descriptions are not

> merely copied off from the "intrinsic nature of reality itself." Yet for all that, some of our sentences state facts, and the truth of a true factual statement is not something we just make up. One might say not that we make up the world, but that we help to *define* the world. The rich and evergrowing collection of truths about the world is the joint product of the world and language users. Or better (since language users are part of the world), it is the product of the world, with language users playing a creative role in the process of production.[69]

68. Ibid., p. 186.
69. Hilary Putnam, "Reply to David Anderson," *Philosophical Topics* 20 (1992): 368.

This should dispel attempts to pigeonhole Putnam into either the metaphysical realist or idealist camp. Any attempt to take his shorthand use of terms like "language users," "world," "states of affairs," and so on as proof that he is still caught within dualism is simply unfair, given his persistent arguments that dualistic ontologies of truth which rely on the notion of things in themselves are simply unintelligible.[70]

The main target of Alston's argument on conceptual relativity is Putnam's claim that a realist form of the correspondence theory of truth (which Alston thinks is neatly captured in his own formulation of Convention T) has to be rejected if we concede the interdependence between truth and the concepts and ontologies we set out to work with. Specifically, Alston takes Putnam to be arguing that conceptual relativity is only compatible with an epistemic conception of truth, an issue I will turn to in a moment.[71] If we want to avoid an epistemic conception of truth while maintaining conceptual relativity, then we must significantly restrict its scope. I will address this argument first.

Putnam's conceptual relativity thesis holds that even our basic notions like "object" have no uniquely "correct" use. As a result of this, he says, "apparently incompatible schemes—for instance, a scheme that quantifies over mereological sums and one that denies that there are any such things—may serve equally well to describe one or another state of affairs."[72] Alston goes a long way toward accepting the possibility that this is a defensible position, but he suggests that in ontologically serious cases of conceptual relativity, cases which make a difference in practice and which are incompatible (unlike the trivially relative cases such as those concerning mereological sums), we cannot be "permissive" about metaphysical disputes. Examples he gives of such untrivial disputes would be substance versus process metaphysics, and theism versus naturalism. It is impossible to make these alternative systemic metaphysical theories compatible with one another, and given the substantive nature of their conflict, we cannot simply accommodate both.

Certainly Alston's point is correct from *within* any given conceptual system or ontology. Alston is also correct to point out the differences between a conceptual relativity interpreted as involving only descriptive relativism and one involving ontological relativism. Putnam frequently refers to descriptive relativism in explaining his claim, with such examples as the Fahrenheit/Centigrade scales. Alston is right, however, that descriptive relativism is much more easily compatible with realism than is ontological relativism. But what if some of the same arguments for descriptive relativism

70. Ibid., p. 366.
71. Alston, *Realist Conception of Truth*, chap. 6.
72. Putnam, "Reply to David Anderson," p. 367.

made sense in relation to ontological relativism, so that the more ontologically significant cases which Alston lists were seen to be in some ways analogous to the more trivial cases? Are not different metaphysical systems sometimes useful in different language games, physics and psychology, for example, or philosophy and everyday language? In deciding between such descriptive systems there is often little recourse to neutral or shared criteria: substance metaphysics has X advantages and Y disadvantages, and process metaphysics has Q advantages and R disadvantages, and often the disagreements among philosophers result from the different decisions they make about the most *advantageous* advantages and *disadvantageous* disadvantages. The limitations of one's own view are often recognized but not considered overriding, and this judgment might be based on one's values, perspective, or general philosophical goals.

I would not generalize this scenario to every case of disagreement, but it suggests that substantive ontological disagreements do not always require resolution of the sort Alston assumes: like the different temperature grades, we can recognize that one metaphysical system is more useful than another in a given context. This does not entail the acceptance of an absolute relativism in the sense that from some "neutral" perspective we would have to accord each position an equal epistemic status. There are no neutral perspectives, and there will always be arguments made for and against particular views toward resolution. We can, however, make sense of the (inevitable) situation of general disagreement without saying that only one of the metaphysical systems being promoted can be "the right one" given that the universe admits of only one description. Conflict is shown to result from alternative interpretations, different emphases put on different elements, a different set of "nonnegotiables" in values or theoretical orientation, and so on.

The acceptance of some range of possible plural truths does not commit us to absolute relativism (where every view is ultimately equal) nor does it discourage argument or eliminate the motivation toward resolution. Resolution can be (and often is) motivated by practical considerations and not just intellectual ones; all Putnam has removed is the metaphysical mandate that there must be a complete and total resolution, or that only one view may come out right in the end. I take Putnam to be suggesting that it is actually a colossal assumption that reality is such as to entail only one possible humanly devised, linguistically expressed description. Why should we assume reality to be limited in this way? From this perspective, it is the metaphysical realists who have to stretch our intuitions to accommodate their form of realism, a claim Putnam has long maintained. On an internal realist view, differences do not (always) create logical incoherence or a problem that must be resolved. Thus there is no *logical* or *metaphysical* need to resolve every ontological dispute; this is just an assumption of metaphysical realism.

Alston also tries to salvage some minimal degree of ontological absolutism by arguing that even Putnam's minimalist realism is committed to some portion of absolutism about reality because on Putnam's view (1) reality will not accommodate any possible conceptual scheme, and (2) truth values are determined within conceptual schemes objectively, that is, determinately. But this does not wash. The conjunction of (1) and (2) does not entail a determinate ontology. Alston is conflating the power of reality to constrain our conceptual systems with its power to determine them uniquely. All Putnam will countenance about mind-independent reality is that it has an impact on us and that our knowledge captures "some aspects" of it, neither of which contentions provides any specific direction for ontology.

Alston's main concern, however, and his main worry, is not about conceptual relativity except in so far as it is thought to require the repudiation of an alethic realist conception of truth. Alston interprets Putnam as rejecting this conception in favor of a wholly epistemic account of truth, and here is where Putnam's views come into real conflict with Alston's alethic realism. In regard to the issue of truth, Alston goes on the offensive. He argues that Putnam's epistemic account of truth is both implausible, that is, far removed from actual knowing, and incoherent. It is incoherent because Putnam is committed to an account of truth as both epistemic and indefeasible. Remember that truth cannot simply be justification, according to Putnam, because (for one thing) justification is a matter of degree and truth is not. Alston takes this as a crucial admission, which commits Putnam to a concept of truth that is not defeasible or changeable. The problem then is how to construe Putnam's corollary belief that truth and justification are interdependent, and specifically, that truth is "idealized rational acceptability." Alston believes the only way to make these two claims compatible is to reconceptualize the content of a truth attribution so that it is an attribution about an epistemic state of affairs. Alston resists this "massive reinterpretation" as "obviously false" and "not even coherently thinkable."[73]

Alston offers two reasons to reject an epistemic conception of truth. First, he takes it as obvious that most of our truth-claims are not attributing an epistemic status to anything; we are, instead, making attributions about things in the world, like the weather, or the properties of salt, and so on. The epistemic definition of truth would thus go against normal usage and common intuitions about what truth means. Against Crispin

---

73. Alston, *Realist Conception of Truth*, chap. 7.

Wright, Alston maintains that the right-hand side of the biconditional " 'P' if and only if *p*" has nothing to do with epistemic states. Second, Alston argues that there is no way to explicate the meaning of an attribution of epistemic states if all we have recourse to are claims about epistemic states. In other words, if the content of my truth-claim is ultimately simply an epistemic attribution, then how can I define what an epistemic attribution is itself? Alston's claim is that the concept of ideal epistemic conditions must be explained in terms of the concept of truth, which therefore must be defined independently.

I will argue in the next chapter that the assumption that truth always refers to things in a human-independent world is, in fact, challengeable and not universally shared. The key to this is the fact that, contrary to Alston's disclaimers about alethic realism, his "minimalist" realism is not in fact neutral on all metaphysical matters. The first argument discussed above, about truth-claims referring to the world *rather than* to epistemic states, reveals that he is assuming that "the world" is separable from belief. In other words, Alston takes it as unchallengeable that what "we" (nonphilosophers as well as philosophers who can remember what it is like to think as nonphilosophers) always mean by truth is the set of propositions which would correspond to the view God has of the world, and thus a view without any intrinsic connection to human perspectives, conceptual models, pragmatic interests, and the like. I shall try to sow some seeds of doubt about how obvious this assumption is in the next chapter.

Alston's second argument is more complicated, because it turns on his reasons for interpreting Putnam as holding an epistemic conception of truth. Alston knows that Putnam has recently clarified his position on truth so that it cannot be interpreted as a reduction of truth to justification; Putnam has said he favors a model of interdependence rather than a reduction. Still, Alston points out, the only explication Putnam offers for truth (other than negative ones, such as denying that it admits of degrees, and so on) is idealized rational acceptability, which is clearly an epistemic concept. Putnam has remained consistent in his belief over the years that "our grasp of the notion of truth depends on our grasp of the notion of warranted assertability."[74]

It is not clear from this, however, that the problem Alston identifies—the inability to maintain both an epistemic account of truth and at least a minimal version of realism—necessarily follows. Alston says that to explicate Putnam's account of truth in terms of the T-schema (which Alston takes as the most minimal formulation of realism), we might say something like the

---

74. Putnam, "Reply to David Anderson," p. 365.

following: "When I say 'The sun is shining,' what I am asserting is that a certain statement coheres with an all-comprehensive and fully articulated whole."[75] But this would reduce the claim that the sun is shining to a claim about justification, whereas on Putnam's view when I say, "The sun is shining," the meaning of that claim is that the sun is shining. Putnam's claim that truth should be explicated in terms of ideal epistemic conditions does not pose a conflict with the T-schema. All he maintains is that our notion of truth, both in our abstract discussions about truth itself and in specific truth-claims and negations of truth-claims, depends on our grasp of warrant. This is because our notion of truth has to be based on "concepts we actually employ."[76] In other words, when I say, "The sun is shining," your grasp of that statement and of its implicit truth-claim will involve some assumption that I have looked outside, watched the weather channel, heard this fact from a reliable acquaintance, or derived it from some other process. Thus, Putnam's conception of truth does not forbid us to say that the statement "The sun is shining" means that the sun is shining; what it forbids is an explication of the metaphysical entailments of this claim, which involves positing things to which human beings have no conceptual access. Of course, Putnam will allow that we do have access to such things as the sun, and its light and warmth.

Alston or another metaphysical realist might respond here by saying that a coherentist/internal realist explication of the T-schema must necessarily change the meaning of the word "sun" to something like "an entity we justifiably posit on the basis of its coherence within a comprehensive belief system." This would make sense of Alston's claim that on Putnam's view all truth attributions are statements about epistemic states; we cannot talk about "real" objects because there are no "real" objects on a coherentist, internal realism. Putnam would likely reply here that the concept of real, which takes it as a necessary requirement that a posited object be completely independent of human practices, is unintelligible, because everything we posit refers in some way to human concepts. There is no fact of the matter about which concepts are the "real" ones, according to reality as it exists separate from human practice. So we get on the merry-go-round once again.

The more viable objection Alston raises to Putnam's account of truth is his argument that tying truth to the notion of ideal justification makes truth less reachable than it would be in a standard correspondence account. This is because the notion of ideal justification itself is unreachable. To explicate it we would need to know answers to the following questions:

75. Alston, *Realist Conception of Truth*, chap. 7.
76. Putnam, "Reply to David Anderson," p. 365.

When have we achieved an ideal justification? What makes it ideal? If the ideal requires comprehensiveness (which on coherence models it must), how can we know how comprehensive our coherent system of beliefs is vis-à-vis reality? How can we know when all the relevant evidence is in? It is impossible to know when an ideal situation has been achieved or even what it would consist in, and therefore this notion of truth makes truth actually unattainable, with the result that all of Putnam's charges against alienated epistemologies apply to his own.

Again, however, I think Alston is operating with background assumptions that he does not make explicit and that Putnam does not share. In advancing the above interrogation of the notion of ideal justification, what Alston seems to want is a metajustification of the ideal based on its ability to deliver transcendental knowledge. This is not language Alston himself uses, but it appears to me to be what his demands amount to. That is, Alston assumes that the definition of the ideal must be able to establish its relation to a transcendental notion of reality *for it to be ideal*, and that without the ability to judge whether it can deliver this reality, we cannot attribute to it an ideal status. But Putnam has said all along that our notion of truth is grounded on practices and concepts we already use and understand. The notion of an ideal justification is then an extrapolation, not from the ontology associated with correspondence, as Alston assumes, but from *justification*. It is ideal in the sense that it is a limit concept based on what we know about justification now, and it serves as a heuristic, a guide rather than a necessary requirement, providing a way to evaluate justificatory claims. Why do we know that idealized warranted assertability would be true? For the same reasons that we believe any justified belief to be true or likely to be true, and there are just no other "meta" reasons to which we can appeal.

Alston argues that if ideal justification has no connection to reality then it is unclear why Putnam's concept of truth is not simply reducible to justification, despite what Putnam maintains. Such a reduction would mean that justification has itself no warrant; it confers little warrant on a justified belief to say that justification is conducive to truth if truth is simply defined in terms of justification. According to Alston's argument, then, Putnam's conception of truth ends in a vicious circle. Truth is not, however, simply conferred on any justified belief; our concept of truth is based on, but exceeds, any actual case of justification. Hence it is idealized justification. This does not entail that every feature of the world is accessible to us. A total reduction of truth to justified belief would not allow for inaccessible truths, and yet clearly these are possible (indeed, all too probable).

What leads to misunderstandings is that Putnam sometimes equivocates on his use of the word "truth." On the one hand, he has repeatedly stated that his view does not "limit truth to what is accessible to human beings."[77] On the other hand, he makes statements like "There would have still been a world [if there were no language users], but there would not have been any *truths*."[78] In the first usage, truth is clearly independent of human practice: it refers to something like reality apart from human interaction. In the second usage, Putnam is not talking about truth but about truths, that is, things which are true and which are (on his account) sentences. Putnam's commitment to both realism and a conception of truth as idealized justification is not incoherent. Everything about the universe is not necessarily accessible to human beings (this is Putnam's realism); but our concept of correct claims about the universe is based on practices that are accessible to us, and necessarily so (this is his account of truth).

How does this distinction shed light on Alston's charge that Putnam collapses truth to justification? What Alston misses is that Putnam is operating with a different ontology of truth, a different metaphysics. On Putnam's view, truth (in the second sense above) is immanent, and not a feature that corresponds to reality completely separate from us. Remember his claim that truth "is the joint product of the world and language users."[79] This means that truth need not be shown to be completely distinct from justification, because truth is *partly* consituted by our justificatory practices and inquiries. Still, Putnam can continue to maintain that truth is not reducible to justification because (1) truth is idealized justification, which is separate by definition from any actual justification, and (2) truth is not simply that which human beings make up. Truth is the product of the world and it is also about the world. Putnam refuses to accept the idea that an epistemology must be able to differentiate between human beliefs which are about the world as completely separate from us and beliefs which are just about us. This is just what Alston is asking him to do, in demanding that he show how truth is ultimately independent of any human practice like justification.

### Realistic Realism

I have tried to show that Putnam's internal realism marks out a genuine alternative both to an idealism that would see reality as constructed by human beings and to a transcendental realism that wants truths about a reality as it is, separate from any human interaction. Despite the fact that Putnam borrows much from Kant, it is a mistake to interpret his realism as

77. Ibid., p. 364.
78. Ibid., p. 368.
79. Ibid.

a negotiation of the dual realms of phenomena and noumena that Kant projected. If we take seriously Putnam's aspirations to transcend dualism, his version of realism is more arguably a "real" realism, rather than a form of idealism. It is a realism, not in the Kantian tradition, but in the Hegelian and phenomenological tradition, one which understands human inquiry to be operating within a lived world from which our presence cannot be excised. Nor does it need to be: since we are not separated from reality by a chasm, we do not have to be able to span that chasm to have the right to claim truth.

Much of Putnam's defense of internal realism against metaphysical realism is based on his claim that it wins on the "plausibility" front, or as James Conant writes, that it "is more faithful to our actual (both everyday and scientific) practices of adjudicating conflicting knowledge-claims and achieving forms of rational consensus."[80] But many philosophers besides Alston believe that Putnam's form of realism is arcane as well as counterintuitive, in requiring us to redefine radically what we mean by truth.

Obviously, in this chapter I have sided with Putnam. Metaphysical realism has become the intuitive theory within epistemology through its longstanding dominance, but it has never held hegemony. Whether many of the most important philosophers of knowledge in the historical canon really held a metaphysically realist view at all is arguably open to interpretation. Moreover, to the extent that metaphysical realism inclines one to accept scientific realism—or the view that science provides the most accurate depiction of reality—it clearly veers from our common understandings of the world. *Epistemically* to privilege theoretical entities like pi-mesons over tables and chairs is obviously counterintuitive, especially given how rapidly and regularly the community of physicists changes its views about questions of base ontology. To privilege *sense data*—a pared-down skeleton of sensory experience in all its complexity, such as "red patch here now"—as that which is most certain calls for great theoretical leaps of argument rather than simple intuition. In describing this kind of view as alienated, Putnam is in line with Heidegger, who saw the reification of an objectivist perspective on reality as the symptom of a culture severely distanced from its surroundings.

Internal realism conceptualizes truth within the terms of familiar experience, which involves being immersed in a world rather than observing one from a distance. Thus it acknowledges the epistemic significance of perspective, language, and point of view, which *is also* acknowledged in everyday practice. In answer to a question people will often say "It depends on

---

80. James Conant, introduction to *Realism with a Human Face*, by Hilary Putnam (Cambridge: Harvard University Press, 1990), p. xix.

how you look at it," or "It depends on where you're coming from." These "truisms" need not be interpreted as leading to an incoherent radical relativism; Putnam's internal realism offers us an alternative. I recognize the danger in appropriating everyday expressions to support philosophical argument—philosophers love to interpret such expressions in a way that supports their own agenda, but it is often unclear that this provides anything other than current ideology. Moreover, common expressions are open to multiple philosophical intepretations because such expressions are not precise: they lack the precision aimed for (though not always achieved) by philosophical discourse. But my point is that there *is* a recognition of the effect of location, context, and speaker on truth in many common expressions, and internal realism is one way to make sense of this, that is, to make this position *sensible* rather than simply a confusion. There is at least a prima facie case to be made that metaphysical realism is not intuitive to all. Therefore, whatever the limitations of the use of common understandings, it is at least not the case that only metaphysical realism gains support from them.

There is, however, a price to be paid for trying to construe truth within everyday terms. "On this view (mine), then, 'truth' (idealized justification) is as vague, interest relative, and context sensitive as *we* are."[81] There will be no neat categories or rational principles we can delineate, and all the concepts will be "fuzzy." Putnam's innovation within analytic philosophy is to take on the Fregean and logic-inspired demands in the twentieth century to reduce all concepts, including rationality, "to a set of precise rules."[82] As important and useful as he believes the development of modern logic has been, Putnam heretically declares that analytic philosophy has overestimated its epistemological and metaphysical significance. Mathematical logic is sometimes useful for rational thought; it is not the whole of rational thought or its criterion of adequacy. (Nietzsche puts this in characteristically strong terms: "Logic is bound to the condition: assume there are identical cases . . . That is: the will to logical truth can be carried through only after a fundamental *falsification* of all events is assumed."[83] So much for logic as the route to truth.)

Philosophical inquiries bedeviled by both skepticism and mathematical logic have been impossible quests for purity, for boundaries that are absolute and categories that are neatly defined. Such a sensibility, I would argue, is at the heart of both classical realism and deconstruction, the one presuming to have achieved it, the other complaining loudly that it can

81. Putnam, *Realism and Reason*, p. xvii.
82. Hilary Putnam, "Reply to Richard Miller," *Philosophical Topics* 20 (1992): 370.
83. Friedrich Nietzsche, *The Will to Power*, trans. Walter Kaufmann and R. J. Hollingdale (New York: Random House, 1968), sec. 512.

never be achieved. Putnam's sensibility returns us to the Hegelian, phenomenological, and pragmatic traditions, which start and end with lived
reality. Neurath, another coherentist, offered a famous image of human
knowledge as forever having to reconstruct a raft while it is out to sea. Putnam offers this happy revision of that image:

> I would put ethics, philosophy, in fact the whole culture, in the boat, and not
> just "science", for I believe the parts of the culture are interdependent. And
> second, my image is not of a single boat but of a *fleet* of boats. . . . People are
> passing supplies and tools from one boat to another and shouting advice and
> encouragement (or discouragement) to each other. Finally, people sometimes
> decide they don't like the boat they're in and move to a different boat alto-
> gether. (And sometimes a boat sinks or is abandoned.) It's all a bit chaotic; but
> since it is a fleet, no one is ever totally out of signalling distance from all the
> other boats.[84]

The collective, heterogeneous process of pursuing knowledge cannot be
contained in precise formulae nor restricted to a single style or method.
This is, for better or worse, a more "*human* kind of realism."[85]

84. Putnam, *Realism and Reason*, p. 204.
85. Ibid., p. xviii.

# CHAPTER SEVEN

# Coherence in Context

Perhaps nobody yet has been truthful enough about what "truthful-ness" is.

—Friedrich Nietzsche, *Beyond Good and Evil*

In English the words "realm" and "real" share a common root, and in premodern times the word "real" meant "regal" or "royal," that is, "pertaining to the king."[1] In Spanish the word *real* still means both "real" and "royal." Such an association implies a connection between what is real and what is in the royal jurisdiction, that is, what the king controls, owns, and has dominion over. In premodern mythic Europe, the royal realm comprised all that the king could see, all the lands and peoples visible from the elevated overlook of the king's castle. This overlay of epistemic structure onto a political dominion had an effect on the ontology of truth; it might even be said to have constituted an ontology of truth whereby the real was that which was visible to the king.

This notion of the real implies a corollary concept of truth that combines both perspectivism and authoritarianism, a concept that accords with the practical history of European epistemic conventions in which epistemic credibility correlated with rank and privilege, and justification was conferred only on the perspective of the authorities.[2] The identity of these authorities was the source of much dispute, and religious leaders contended with their secular competitors for the position of truth's arbiter. Whether it was the prerogative of the Inquisitor or of the king and his court, knowledge was a possession only for elites. If you were a peasant,

1. See Marilyn Frye, *The Politics of Reality: Essays in Feminist Theory* (Trumansburg, N.Y.: Crossing Press, 1983), p. 155. This chapter was inspired by her illuminating discussion of the ways in which philosophy and language can conceal forcible exclusions and thus neatly erase oppression with a metaphysical flourish. See also *Webster's Unabridged Dictionary*, 2d ed.
2. See Steven Shapin, *A Social History of Truth: Civility and Science in Seventeenth Century England* (Chicago: University of Chicago Press, 1994), pp. 86–95.

serf, or tradesman, your judgment in such matters about the Christian character of your neighbor Mary Smyth would be deemed irrelevant when the ranking regional cleric came to the village and pronounced her a witch. If your daughter had been "seduced" by a member of the local gentry and you went to court to accuse the noble of unfair treatment, the magistrate only need hear the noble's denial of the charge to assess his judgment of the case in the noble's favor. Peasants, women, slaves, children, Jews and many other nonelites were "known" to be liars, epistemically unreliable and unable to distinguish justified beliefs from falsehoods. Women were too irrational, peasants too ignorant, children too immature, and Jews too cunning. Slaves, as Aristotle famously argued, were so naturally prone to deceit that they had to be tortured to tell the truth.

Historical progression between epochs never creates absolute breaks; there are no total displacements, only gradations of change.[3] Is it any wonder, then, that the Enlightenment epistemologies that came after Scholasticism, whether rationalist or empiricist, continued to carry this legacy of authoritarian perspectivism? The Enlightenment attributed epistemic justification only to those subjects who could demonstrate the proper epistemic attitude, characterized by the use of reason and the maintenance of an objective stance. Unsurprisingly, these subjects turned out to be the dominant male elite. As sociologist of science Steven Shapin puts it, "Gentility powerfully assisted credibility."[4] Who could attain the new stance of objectivity required by the scientific method? Certainly not women, children, the insane, or anyone driven by impassioned commitments, whether religious or political. Shapin has shown that, in seventeenth-century England, slaves, peasants, and any other workers beholden to others for their livelihood (a group which, notice, included *all* women) were assumed to flatter, cajole, and appear agreeable of necessity, and hence to develop only with difficulty the virtue of truthfulness. Shapin's recent foray into the genealogy of modern epistemology in his book, *The Social History of Truth*, demonstrates that lower-class people who were beholden to others for their livelihood were considered unreliable because they had to acquiesce in order to support themselves; the very rich and powerful were also considered unreliable because a strict adherence to the facts might compromise their ability to protect the interests of the court and to thwart their many enemies.

---

3. Alasdair MacIntyre, "Epistemological Crises, Dramatic Narrative, and the Philosophy of Science," in *Paradigms and Revolutions: Applications and Appraisals of Thomas Kuhn's Philosophy of Science*, ed. Gary Gutting (Notre Dame: University of Notre Dame Press, 1980), pp. 54–74.
4. See Shapin, *Social History of Truth*, p. 124. For an excellent explanation of why cultural studies of science are relevant to epistemology, see Joseph Rouse, "What Are Cultural Studies of Scientific Knowledge?" *Configurations* 1 (1992): 1–22.

It was very widely understood in sixteenth- and seventeenth-century English society that the possession of great power and responsibility might compromise integrity, and that places of power were places where truth could thrive only with the greatest difficulty. . . . By contrast, the middle position might be accounted the place where scope for free action was greatest. Here one might be content with one's portion and be free of the necessity to secure more; here one might have easy communication with those afraid of greater men; and here one might have no need of preferment and no fear of superiors.[5]

Thus it turned out that "simple independent gentlemen," who were of independent means and in a middle-class position between the powerful and the powerless, nearly alone among the population had qualifications sufficient to pursue the truth objectively. Scientists, in particular, became the newly authorized epistemic agents, and during these centuries (recognized) scientists were nearly always Gentile males who had income-generating property. Truth was what this elite said it was.[6]

Who could master reason? Only those with a temperament sufficient for objectivity (that is, detachment), which certainly excluded the same groups listed above (peasants, women, and so forth), and only those with sufficient education in the new doctrines of science. Thus scientists and "men of reason" were accorded the highest epistemic authority through their exclusive ability to wield reason, on the assumption that independent gentlemen had no political, social, or economic vested interest that they might want to protect or that might cloud their perceptiveness to certain areas of lived reality. This epistemic structure proved even more impervious to contestation because the open perspectivism of the monarchists and the papacy was replaced by the cloaked perspectivism of Bacon and Boyle. The Enlightenment is sometimes presented as an era which validated every adult human being's rational capacities: this is an anachronistic misreading. The fact that universal suffrage was not achieved until the twentieth century was not an aberration; it is entirely consistent with the Enlightenment's elitist conception of epistemic abilities.

The lesson to be drawn from this is not that epistemology is reducible to a strategic discourse for the maintenance of elite power. Bacon and Boyle, as well as others such as Locke and Kant, produced a rich legacy of thought about knowledge, as did the Scholastics despite their beliefs in divine authority. Critical rereadings of Enlightenment epistemologies show that they were partly structured around the legitimation of domination,

5. Shapin, *Social History of Truth*, pp. 100–101.
6. Ibid., esp. chap. 3.

but this was not their only organizing principle or theoretical effect.[7] A more attentive and contextualized reading of Western epistemology's history shows that, contrary to the usual assumption, it has never really eschewed perspectivism, as long as the perspectives that were privileged were those of the dominant elites. Nietzsche knew this, but he had no motivation to extend epistemic authority beyond the heroic masculine few who could brave God's demise. Nietzsche's only goal in revealing the inherent perspectivism in philosophy was to criticize the cowardice of universalist systems that refused to acknowledge their own self-regarding motivations.[8] His work does help to show that the subjectivity of the knower is not a new preoccupation in philosophy. Nor has it been eliminated in the modernist epistemologies, despite claims to the contrary. The problem is not simply that epistemologists have recently tried to eliminate subjectivity but failed. Rather, a symptomatic reading of the sort I have been discussing here suggests that, although modernist epistemologists have attempted to eliminate subjectivity as an overt feature of their accounts of knowledge, they have allowed a very particular subjectivity to structure their epistemologies in a more covert manner, with predictably self-validating results. Thus, it is not that we must now come to see that perspectivism is the best epistemological account, but rather that a covert perspectivism has been accepted all along.

Foundationalist epistemologies with universalist aspirations have been imprinted and constrained by what is visible, not to the king, but to the (middle-class male) philosopher, a fact which no doubt can account for, among other things, the valorization of propositional over practical knowledge, and of mental work over manual. What has been generally visible to the philosopher are the types of direct sensory knowledge available to educated males, a rudimentary understanding of science, and the prevailing common sense (read: ideology) of the European dominant classes. The sensory knowledge typically available to women and to men of the lower classes was generally out of range, as was non-European knowledge and the social perspectives of the oppressed. As a result, among philosophers

---

7. There is a growing tradition in the philosophical canon of new readings that juxtapose rhetorical analysis and philosophy. See, for example, Michele LeDoeuff, *The Philosophical Imaginary*, trans. Colin Gordon (Stanford: Stanford University Press, 1989); Susan Bordo, *The Flight to Objectivity: Essays on Cartesianism and Culture* (Albany: SUNY Press, 1987); Andrea Nye, *Words of Power: A Feminist Reading of the History of Logic* (New York: Routledge, 1990); Genevieve Lloyd, *The Man of Reason: "Male" and "Female" in Western Philosophy* (Minneapolis: University of Minnesota Press, 1984); Robert C. Solomon, *The Bully Culture: Enlightenment, Romanticism, and the Transcendental Pretense* (Lanham, Md.: Rowman and Littlefield, 1993).
8. See, e.g., *Beyond Good and Evil*, trans. by Walter Kaufmann (New York: Random House, 1966), sec. 198.

metaphysical conceptions of disembodiedness flourished, a sharp evaluative demarcation was made between science and "magic," and "civilization" was identified as coextensive with European liberal societies. It is no coincidence that foundationalist epistemologies have identified the foundations for all justified belief in some variation of this rather arbitrary collection: European science (the foundation for logical positivism), the sensory experience of philosophers (the foundation for empiricism), and the available "common sense" or intuitions proper to the philosophers' gender and station (the foundation for rationalism). Thus, foundationalism has been built on top of a very particular perspectivism, through which it gained its plausibility within the philosophical milieu.

To repeat, the task in epistemology today is not, by acknowledging this perspectivism, to deconstruct or self-destruct. As many philosophers since Hegel have understood, we must come to grips with the implications of the historical and social locatedness of knowledge. This will force us to acknowledge that the Western canonical tradition (which, of course, is not *simply* Western) includes elitist epistemologies that worked to privilege dominant European males and was therefore both Eurocentric and patriarchal. But this tradition is no monolith structured by a single coherent ideology which can be assessed as a totality; it consists of polychromatic, sometimes contradictory strands which vary not only in content but also in validity and effects. Thus, what is needed is to begin to root out the philosophical underpinnings of epistemological domination, and to develop accounts of knowing that can acknowledge its multiple and heterogeneous sites of production and forms of articulation—a project that will in some respects continue the self-critical tradition of the Enlightenment and make use of its tools.

Attempting to construct a new and more effective transcendental universal will not, however, work to root out authoritarian perspectivism, since this would only replicate the erasure of the historical and social location in which all knowing is grounded. It is not perspectivism per se that is the problem with modernist epistemologies: it is the authoritarianism of their perspective.

In fact, although Hegel inaugurated the project of developing an epistemology with explicit historical and social dimensions, his own contribution toward it retained the desire to establish the absoluteness of knowledge despite its historical limits.[9] For Hegel the ultimate truth was represented by the perfect identity of subject and object, a notion which effects not a mediation of difference but its elimination. A Nietzschean-cum-Foucauldian

9. See Michael S. Roth, *Knowing and History: Appropriations of Hegel in Twentieth-Century France* (Ithaca: Cornell University Press, 1988).

genealogy of this conception of absoluteness, a conception in which representation does not admit of degrees and there is a singular truth about the world, would no doubt reveal that it is rooted at least in part in the desire for mastery over an infinite totality. It begets an epistemology of imperialism, or, in Hegel's terms, a freedom of the few. An epistemic mastery over the total whole is fundamentally incompatible with a recognition of knowledge's intersubjective nature as well as its perspectival roots. Intersubjective relations, unlike relations between a subject and an object, cannot generate that sort of total mastery or total identity; rather, they point toward limitation, a back-and-forth movement, and, where possible, a harmony of difference rather than an erasure of it. Perspective cannot yield totalization. Hegel's epistemological perspectivism ingenuously maintained Europe's supremacy by claiming mastery over the totality—even while it acknowledged its incapacity to transcend its own location—through a historicist dialectic in which European knowledge sublated all other forms, acknowledging their existence but subsuming them within its own higher universal.[10] In this system, all knowledge is perspectival, but all perspectives are not equal, and thus Hegelian epistemology instantiates once again the authoritarian perspectivism characteristic of the Enlightenment. Therefore, although the Hegelian legacy helped to inaugurate within the West a process of historical self-reflection, this legacy is only partially trustworthy. We are still in the process of uncovering the ineliminable unconscious, irrational, and political elements at work in the production of accepted knowledges. Modernism inaugurated this self-reflexive moment, but its ability to transcend Eurocentrism was limited by its own historical context. Today, the illusion of Anglo-European supremacy is much more difficult to maintain.

Although I share a commitment to epistemology and metaphysics with most analytic philosophers, then, the principal justification I would give is different. Hilary Putnam, for example, says that it is just a fact that human beings will always want to discuss knowledge and reality, as if these are "natural" problems arising from human experience. In the same way, Jean-Paul Sartre thought at one time that individual alienation from others was a natural problem outside of history or the particularities of social structures. Hume perhaps started this tradition within epistemology, suggesting that skeptical doubts are the inevitable outcome of any sustained reflection on human knowledge. It may be that these claims are right, or at least partially so. It may be that critical self-reflection is a persistently recurring feature of human practice. While the specific direction or content of that reflection may change (like Michael Williams, I have skeptical doubts

10. See Robert Young, *White Mythologies* (New York: Routledge, 1990), chap. 1.

about the inevitability of epistemological skepticism), perhaps there will always be some such reflective activity. Today, however, we can appeal to more immediate, historically specific reasons to engage in philosophical work on knowledge and reality than timeless human dispositions. As I have argued, we particularly need to do this work today because of its social and political importance. Currently our choices consist of an authoritarian perspectivism or an all-pervasive repudiation of knowledge, both of which are unsatisfactory. I would argue that this debate reaches beyond the confines of our universities and pervades many popular arenas of discourse and practice as well, where it is expressed in the common sense of our era. This dilemma obviously cannot be resolved or redirected simply by esoteric work in the academy, but the university is certainly one of the many sites in which dominant notions of knowledge are being remolded.

The project of contemporary epistemology, as I have described it, should be to reconceptualize epistemic justification and truth in a manner that is normative and epistemological and not merely sociological and political, though it must involve these dimensions of knowing as well. In the remainder of this final chapter I want to build on the works discussed previously to argue that a robust coherentist epistemology is particularly capable of offering such a reconceptualization. The virtue of a robust coherentist epistemology is that it can incorporate an acknowledgment of inherent perspectival constraints in its formulation of knowing without sacrificing the link between knowing and truth. This means that coherentism has explanatory value in its favor; it offers a way to make sense of the political legacy of modernist science and epistemology without completely reducing these to ideology or to a collection of extra-epistemic forces. I realize that one cannot defend coherentism by arguing for its explanatory value without making a circular argument, because explanatory value in the end amounts to coherence. Circularity in this context is not vicious, however: I am not trying to show how coherentism defeats skepticism, but how it can usefully account for our knowing practices and optimally guide them.

I will also argue that we can disentangle coherentism from the authoritarian perspectivism of Eurocentric patriarchies. If the entire web of belief is brought to bear on the justification of new claims, and the meaning of truth is immanent to a lived reality rather than transcendental, then Michel Foucault's long list of discursive and nondiscursive elements—including subject-positions, institutional practices, systems of exclusion, epistemes, and so forth—can be recognized as operative in the production of knowledge. This approach comprises no transcendental foundation, but instead incorporates an inherent partiality to the understanding of epistemic justification. Justification must always be understood as indexed to a context made up of very particular elements which are incapable of conferring absolute justification in the special philosophical sense of an absolute founded on a transcendental.

### Immanent Realism

As I have granted all along, however, the principal obstacle facing such a view is its account of truth. What does it mean to say that truth is immanent? Many critics of coherentism argue that coherence theories of truth lack plausibility because they sacrifice our central intuitions about truth, that is, they abdicate the notion of truth as correspondence to a reality conceived as mind-independent and determinate.[11] But *whose* intuitions are being invoked here in conceptions of reality as "furnished," of its ultimate descriptions as stable, and of truth as a correspondence relation across an ontological abyss? Historian of science Carolyn Merchant suggests that only Western post-Renaissance intuitions demand such a reality in assuming a mechanistic vision devoid of meaning, spirit, or perspective.[12] These intuitions, claimed to be universal, in actuality exemplify the socially produced common sense which I posited earlier to be part of a culturally specific foundation of knowledge. This cold and controlling metaphysics has been criticized by the Frankfurt School, by feminist philosophers, and by new ecology theorists for pursuing a domination over nature that will likely end in the demise of humanity. Poststructuralists see it as assuming epistemic access to an unmediated representation of the real, beyond language, the unconscious, and human practice. Moreover, its determinate characterization of reality is undergoing dissolution from within as Anglo-European cultures can no longer uphold their singular perspective as the only or most privileged truth within a multivocal world.

Still, truth continues to be generally defined as "the way things really are" or "what really happened." I am not disputing the fact that these ordinary language constructions have a large purchase not only on culturally situated common sense but on a host of basic human practices, especially intersubjective practices. When I asked my youngest son Joe his idea of truth, he explained that the truth is "what really happened," which is what the school vice-principal had asked him that very day after a fight on the playground. He had not asked for Joe's interpretation of the events, or his best explanation, but just for the facts, just for the plain truth. Of course,

11. See, for example, Simon Evnine, *Donald Davidson* (Stanford: Stanford University Press), p. 141.
12. Carolyn Merchant, *The Death of Nature: Women, Ecology, and the Scientific Revolution* (San Francisco: Harper and Row, 1980).

the vice-principal's request was for truth-telling, for the children not to lie or omit the truth, but the desire for truthfulness is necessarily related to the idea of truth. By asking the children to tell "what really happened" the vice-principal was trying to get at the truth about the fight, the way it really was.

In idealized terms this account of truth is often thought of as a description that would be given by an omniscient narrator in a realist novel, the Augustinian God's-eye view which has access to simultaneous events all over the world and, indeed, the universe, because it exists outside of time and space. The concept of such an absolute and total narration is incoherent, however. Consider Augustine's characterization:

> It is not with God as it is with us. He does not look ahead to the future, look directly at the present, look back to the past. He sees in some other manner, utterly remote from anything we experience or could imagine. He does not see things by turning his attention from one thing to another. He sees all without any kind of change. Things which happen under the condition of time are in the future, not yet in being, or in the present, already existing, or in the past, no longer in being. But God comprehends all these in a stable and eternal present.[13]

Omniscience cannot coexist with perspective or even with narration, since these imply space and time respectively, and thus in order to imbue God with omniscience Augustine must take Him outside the human realm in every imaginable sense. Such a concept of knowledge, arguably latent in the notion of the thing-in-itself, cannot help guide human practices of knowing even as a heuristic or unreachable but regulative ideal. The combination of perspective and omniscience is unintelligible: there can be no all-knowing perspective because no single perspective could accommodate all others without omission, violence, distortion, and exclusions. Perspectives involve spatially located horizons, and though perspectives can intersect and overlap, no perspective can perfectly capture another without becoming coextensive with it. Even Hegel avoided this mistake: his universal truth sublated only the Real, which was not in fact coextensive with the entirety of events. The popular intuition about omniscient narration is probably based on the novel, a prevalent but culturally and temporally specific aesthetic practice that is no more universal or necessary than nuclear families or abstract expressionism. The identification of truth with an omniscient narration outside time and space would seem to follow from no logical necessity but from specific cultural practices and articulations. This

13. Augustine, *City of God*, trans. Henry Bettenson (New York: Penguin, 1972), p. 452.

notion of truth is neither the only nor the best way to express the idea that truth is "what really happened."

If this is right, then the critical question that coherentist epistemologies need to answer in relation to truth is not how coherence can sustain omniscient narration or an ultimate, complete description or, as Williams puts it, how it can offer an account of our knowledge as a whole. Rather, a coherentist epistemology needs to show how it can be squared with the intuition that truth is, as the vice-principal says, "what really happened." The vice-principal wants to know not what the kids want him to "think" happened, but what "really" happened. He wants truth-telling, rather than lying. He wants to know the facts about the fight, uninfluenced by the children's wishful thinking, even their wishful beliefs or wish-influenced memories of the event on the playground. Donald Davidson expresses this notion as the idea that truth does not depend upon our epistemic powers, clouded as these are by wishes, self-interest, and so on; truth, in other words, is not simply epistemic. Putnam, Hans-Georg Gadamer, and Foucault alike have voiced similar epistemic dispositions: for Putnam, we need to retain the critical separation between truth and what everyone believes, which is why truth should not be equated with the merely ascertained; for Gadamer, truth is *aletheia*, an openness to the other, and thus requires a recognition of our limited control; and even Foucault makes of truth something serious when he says, "It would be pointless to believe that [truth] resides by right in the spontaneous interplay of communication."[14] To reduce truth completely to justified belief is to say that it has no metaphysical content—no referentiality or aboutness—and to make it entirely subject to language or human practice. The point of retaining an ontology of truth is to extend the concept beyond a construction we entirely control. This, then, is the way in which I would articulate the critical hurdle coherence must overcome: how can coherent relations, even when we include both nondiscursive and discursive ones, yield a truth greater than the apparent sum of their parts?

It is worth repeating that coherentism does not need to answer the skeptic's charge that the criterion of coherence must be able to demonstrate a connection between human beliefs and the (transcendental) world. There is no ontological abyss coherentism must span. There is, however, a possible disjuncture between some justified beliefs and truth. We do need to hold onto the understanding that truth represents more than what we happen to believe to be the case, or what we want to believe, or what the majority have believed. Truth is about the world; it is about "the way things really are."

14. Michel Foucault, "The Concern of Truth," in *Michel Foucault: Politics, Philosophy, Culture*, ed. Lawrence D. Kritzman (New York: Routledge, 1988), p. 267.

On the basis of the coherentist epistemologies we have explored in this volume, truth is best understood as indexed to a set of specifics, which include not only what we can see from a given time and place, but where our thinking is at any given moment, as well as the relevant features of reality. This makes truth both plural and changeable, since it is relative to a context richly conceived. But it does not make truth arbitrary or subjective: given sufficiently specifiable contextual ingredients the determination of truth can be objective, in some cases perhaps even conforming to a deductive-nomological method. The so-called subjective elements—the interpretive schema of knowers, their horizons of understanding, the historically specific episteme—are never sufficient to establish truth. Truth becomes apparent when beliefs and practices cohere within a lived reality.

This may suffice for the intension of the term "truth," but what about its extension or reference? In other words, when we use the term "true" to describe a claim, such as a scientific hypothesis, we may mean that the claim is true as indexed to a set of specific contextual elements. But what does this conception have to say about the denotation of the term truth, or the set of objects or events to which it refers? This ontological question must be answered unless we are content to reduce truth to an epistemic concept. Unless immanent epistemology is content to make truth equivalent to justified belief, or to define truth entirely in terms of assertability conditions, it needs to explain the ontological reference of claims to truth.

Truth talk is not merely talk, or empty talk; it is a form of discursive practice with associated effects. It is embedded within a lived corporeal context, not merely an ethereal linguistic realm separated from bodies, practices, and material reality. Truth-claims are about that whole lived reality: they refer to it, intervene in it, represent it. To eliminate any analysis or articulation of the ontological dimension of truth serves only to conceal from examination these relationships between truth-claims and reality. Truth-claims are claims about the nature of human life, about experience, and about our natural environment: the ontology of truth is the explication of the meaning, contours, and limits of that aboutness. Some postmodernists deny truth's ontological dimension because they believe truth-claims are about a constructed reality. Hence they say that the point is to negotiate the features of this constructed reality, not simply to represent it.[15] This mistakenly implies that we have the ability to negotiate the features of our lived experience, which is of course only partly true. We can affect the meanings of events and the intelligibility of experience, and we can alter practices and even our physical surroundings, but we cannot interpret

15. See, e.g., Mas'ud Zavarzadeh and Donald Morton, *Theory, (Post)Modernity, Opposition: An "Other Introduction to Literary and Cultural Theory* (Washington, D.C.: Maissoneuve Press, 1991), esp. chap. 6.

away death, human suffering, and the hole in the ozone layer, or render such things meaningless. They constrain the reach of our interpretive constructions if only by demanding to be interpreted, to be given a signification and a meaning in some form, to be included in our account of the real. Certainly there are phenomena and events we cannot explain or adequately represent, but these descriptive and explanatory limitations are not existential boundaries and thus cannot dictate the scope of truth. At the age of three I might have no words to express an experience of rape; I may have no conceptual categories to make sense of it or to represent it even to myself; yet it would permeate my lived reality nonetheless. There may be similar events that no human being at any age can describe, but only witness. We cannot allow language to circumscribe ontology nor can we replace ontology with language, without erasing significant parts of lived experience.

Postmodernists are not alone in denying the need to develop ontologies of truth: some feminist epistemologists have also been loathe to explore the ontological aspects of truth-claims. But feminist critiques of science and traditional epistemology have only weakened their overall account by failing to pay attention to truth: this failure leaves obscured the status of their own truth-claims and it skirts the metaphysical issues or extensional elements entailed by honorific epistemic terms (whether or not these are called truths). My goal is not to jettison all of the insights of postmodernism or feminist epistemology but to develop an account of truth which I believe their own projects cannot do without.

Every discourse makes truth-claims, assumes and uses evaluative criteria for plausible and implausible claims, and seeks some reference to elements (however variously conceived) outside itself. These criteria, claims, and attempts at reference need theoretical analysis, clear articulation, and epistemological criticism. Powerful discourses are powerful because they resonate in us and connect with other discourses, practices, or experiences, because they help us to make sense of something we have already experienced, or because they are reinforced by other powerful ideas. In short, discourses derive their power from their coherence relations and their supportive connections with other discourses, experiences, or practices. I find an idea or explanation compelling because it makes sense of other things I already believe I know. Alternatively, I resist an idea or explanation when it is counterintuitive, that is, when it conflicts with too many other things I believe I know. Seen in this way, an acknowledgment of the epistemic importance of coherence relations does not strain our intuitions but makes it possible to incorporate our intuitions within an account of real knowing.

Toward this possibility, what I am calling immanent epistemology is aligned with a similarly immanent formulation of realism, a realism without the transcendental evocations of a realm beyond human cognition or interference. An immanent realism would be one that eschewed the Cartesian bifurcations between "man" and world, culture and nature, mind and reality. Cartesian metaphysics posits these binary terms as ultimately independent and autonomous, ontologically distinguishable, and separated by an abyss. We must remember that such an ontology of binarisms is a social construct and does not conform to the phenomenological experience of living or to the conditions of scientific practice.[16] The concept of a thing-in-itself is, after all, just a concept. The fact that we cannot attain it does not automatically mean we lose out on a piece of reality, but just that a particular concept has been found not to fit reality. What is much more real than a conceptual thing-in-itself is the lived world we share, a world of complexity, ambiguity, and richness that exceeds simple dualism.

Dualistic ontologies of self/world are not consistent with our best theories about the self, which understand human subjectivity as the product, reflection, and conduit for natural and intersubjective elements. Binary ontologies emerged out of specific Western masculine identity issues and nascent capitalist formations; they also provided an explanation for experienced phenomena such as false belief, dreams, and hallucinations (all of which the ancients had difficulty accounting for).[17] Dualism offered a philosophical articulation for the rapidly changing worldview and the alienations associated with capitalist expansion. If Hegel was right to say that "philosophy is its time grasped in thought," bifurcated ontologies represent a philosophical articulation of the widespread and deeply felt alienation experienced in the modern West after its encounter with the "new" world.

My point here is that a coherentist ontology of truth need not be thought of as a consolation prize that we get when we give up the hope of achieving "real" truth. In fact, coherentism has some advantages over transcendental conceptions of truth, and some of these advantages arguably involve an increased metaphysical accuracy of description. It remains the case, however, that dualism provided a powerful explanation for false belief. If reality is separated from the mind, the mind can represent that reality either accurately or inaccurately. Change in justified beliefs can be explained without involving ontological changes in reality. False belief and dreams need no counterpart or reference point in the world if the mind is essentially autonomous.

The issue of how to characterize changed beliefs is one that arises not only within the context of philosophical reflection based on modernist as-

16. See Rouse, *Knowledge and Power: Toward a Political Philosophy of Science* (Ithaca, New York: Cornell University Press, 1987), esp. chap. 2.
17. See Bordo, *Flight to Objectivity*; Merchant, *Death of Nature*.

sumptions, but also within the context of everyday, real knowing. After having learned new, disturbing facts about my ex-husband, do I reassess the "reality" of our marriage entirely? Was my previous happiness simply the product of a false belief? Whom was I married to: the man as I know him to be now or the man I thought him to be then? Or, to use examples that involve fewer complicated personal identity issues, I used to believe that the United States was the home of the brave and the land of the free. I no longer hold this belief. I also used to believe that margarine is better for your health than butter, and that sugar intake is linked to hyperactivity. Recent studies have convinced me otherwise, though I wonder what the next studies will suggest. How would a coherentist account of truth characterize such changes? A nonbifurcated realism seems to require that changes in justified belief imply changes in reality itself. How would an immanent conception of truth account for false belief?

I want to think through these deliberately unconventional examples rather than the stock-in-trade examples regularly used in epistemology and philosophy of science, such as changed beliefs about the shape of the earth, phlogiston, ether, or the makeup of oxygen. After all, these latter examples are really relatively easy to explain. The claims in natural science involve complicated inferences and large-scale theories, far removed from immediate experiences including either direct observation or affect. Even beliefs about the shape of the earth involve inference for most of us, and within my phenomenologically accessible world (given that I am not an astronaut), the world is pretty flat (in fact, where I grew up in Florida we used to say that you could stand on top of a car and see the whole state).

When a claim is especially theory-laden—as in the assertion that electrons and quarks exist—it is intuitively obvious that there is no simple fact of the matter. To insist that electrons must either exist or not exist is to transport the practical rules for everyday discourse about observable items (for example, "Either there is a girl in your room or there is not!") beyond their application. Putnam's internal realism can account for scientific changes quite easily by indexing claims to conceptual paradigms or research programs that have their own set of categories and posited entities. Scientific ontologies are internal to models of reality.

But surely it would be unnecessarily purist to say that such claims within science cannot therefore claim truth. This would be to lapse back to a dualist assumption that electrons must be entirely a human projection if we cannot verify their existence in any simple or direct manner. If we think of the ontology of truth in more complicated ways than simplistic one-on-one correspondences, it is possible to account for the actual sorts of changes that routinely occur in scientific explanation, which rarely take the form of "*p* and then not-*p*" but more often seem to be something like "P-Q-R-S-T-U-V and then P-Q-R-#-S-T-U".

Because of the way in which variables hang together, rarely if ever capable of being pulled apart, changes in scientific belief are not well represented as simple negations. Thus, correspondence theorists need not feel compelled to say that belief A was false and now belief B is true, though with some nervous insecurity about belief B's likely longevity. Nor will it ever be necessary to claim, as some thought coherence theorists might, that belief A was true at time $t_1$ but belief B is now true at time $t_2$. We can account for changes more easily by offering partial, complex reports in which it may make the most sense to say that prior, discarded theories contained some truths. This is just to say, of course, that we can take advantage of the notion of scientific knowledge as a progressive accumulation to account for change in a way that does not entail simple negations. Such theories need not involve the claim that science's accumulation of knowledge about reality represents an increase in the percentage of science that corresponds to a transcendental world. Rather, partial changes that involve accumulations can deliver improved practices, greater explanatory reach, and other advantages that refer to the goals set by the research program rather than to a transcendental concept of reality.

Let me return, then, to the examples I raised earlier, which represent realistic problems one might encounter in the process of living. When one radically changes beliefs about other people, states of affairs, or even one's own history and character, how should this be portrayed? Correspondence accounts would seem to have no trouble. They would simply say that my ex-husband was such as he was all along, that my belief that he was my true soul mate was based on lies and mistakes, and was not true. Either the United States is a free country or it is not. Either sugar and butter are obstacles to physical well-being or they are not.

Coherentism has a decided advantage here. If truth refers to a constellation of elements, then a change in belief occasioned by an increase or alteration in the relevant constellation is not a simple negation, but an *altered truth*. What was the character of my ex-husband and the nature of our marriage? I was happy for several years, we developed a strong level of emotional intimacy and mutual support, and subsequent revelations about him can never completely change that history. But my assessment of him and of our relationship lacked some important elements, and the coherence of that assessment did not survive an enlarged and altered reconstellation of knowledge. It is not simply that he changed, or that I changed, though of course we both did. It is that the truth about my lived reality and even our shared lived reality changed. Thus, the belief I had at time $t_1$ remains true despite the fact that now, at time $t_2$, a different belief referring to the same person is true.

The two beliefs are not simple contradictories. They do not refer to or involve precisely the same set of constellations. Nor are they equal, with no standard of assessment to distinguish between their relative validities. Ordinarily, unless there exist strong reasons to do otherwise, we privilege later beliefs which are based on fuller experience. We also ordinarily forgive earlier beliefs, however, recognizing their temporal situatedness. It is true that I might say, "How could I have been so blind?" in regard to my ex-husband or the political realities of the United States. Radical changes of belief (especially about such important matters) generally prompt some self-examination. I might ask what weakness in my cognitive capacities and character produced such apparent blindness, though instead of using those terms I would more likely ask, "Why was I such an idiot?" But unless self-examination leads me to decide that I willfully deceived myself, avoided clear indications, and created my own dream world of happiness, I am likely to accept the earlier belief as true in part. I will conclude that my husband had some positive qualities, that we had some genuine happiness together, but that there was more to the story than I knew at the time. By the same token, I will likely conclude that, in my own narrow corner of the United States, my earlier beliefs were also true in part. All was not unending oppression. Thus, because they are beliefs *about* different things (including myself), I can accept both earlier and later beliefs as true without creating metaphysical incoherence or accepting an outright contradiction or succumbing to a dysfunctional relativism. We do it all the time.

In regard to the delights of sugar and butter (I can only hope this example has not become outdated by the time this reaches print), part of what has changed over the years is health science's theoretical orientations, for example, toward holism and away from the assumption that diseases have single causes, and toward a fuller recognition of the significance of individual physical and lifestyle differences. Whether butter is dangerous to your health depends in part on the kind of life you lead and your genetic inheritance. It also depends on what ingredients are going into margarine this season. Of course, it is also true that new studies sometimes contradict old studies, even when the presuppositions remain stable. In this case, from a new constellation of elements a new truth emerges, arguably better than the first because it is based on a more extensive constellation. We might even want to say sometimes that a prior claim was simply false, though every changed conclusion need not elicit this explanation, and to make charges of false belief we need not have recourse to a transcendental ontology. In fact, given the complexity of life, of science, and of human belief, the reference to a transcendental ontology might create more conceptual problems than it can solve. One would think that most philosophers of science would be prepared to acknowledge this after struggling for a century to maintain scientific realism in the face of scientific developments.

What I am trying to develop here is a concept of immanent realism. In the discussion that follows I shall largely elaborate this concept by contrasting it with Putnam's internal realism and the contextual realism put forward by Williams, and then I shall return to the set of issues I raised in the Introduction. I realize that I am not following the expected route, which would involve defending this notion of an immanent epistemology against the usual list of possible objections an epistemology must address, and thus that my case may well look underdeveloped and underargued. But I am not really interested in showing how it can defeat skepticism, explain the possibility of human knowledge, or set out a clear and limited set of criteria for justification. I am more concerned with the need to avoid a hyperrationalistic account of knowledge, to correct the statement-dominant tendency in epistemology, and to explain its politics. But I will begin with some more traditional concerns.

On Putnam's account of internal or pragmatic realism, there is no version-free description of the real, and given the fact that there are different versions, more than one (true) description of the real is possible. Putnam denies that this amounts to a subjective idealism or that truth is a matter of arbitrary or conventional construction, since once a language game or version has been chosen, truth can be determined objectively. The success of this denial, however, hinges on how a version is chosen. Putnam's answer to this question is basically pragmatics: versions of reality that become dominant have a utility which is related in some sense to human flourishing (which Putnam defines very broadly).

This theory of the real conflicts with a belief in the existence of intrinsic properties, since intrinsic properties are by definition version-independent and therefore independent of any theoretical language or description. Putnam implies that the search for intrinsic properties which will remain stable across versions is like the search for the Holy Grail, highly motivating, perhaps, but hopeless.

I have suggested that internal realism is quite useful in accounting for the changes in science's ontological attributions, but the concept of immanent realism which I find more broadly useful is distinct from internal realism in the following way. Internal realism refers principally to versions or models of reality while immanent realism refers to contexts. To say there are no properties that are version-independent is different from saying there are no properties that are context-independent. Version-dependence involves being incapable of description outside of a theoretical version of reality with its own ontological categories; thus Putnam's realism is internal, or on *this side* of the man/world Kantian schema. Context-dependence involves a relationship not just to theoretical description but to a more inclusive context, which is defined as including not only theory, version, and language game, but also historical, spatio-temporal, and social location. There are no properties of things that are context-independent, just as mass and extension change according to the nearest planet and the current velocity. The notion of property, no less than the demarcation of "things," involves a host of contextual elements, outside of which the notion will lose its meaning. Thus "context" has an ontological dimension that "version" does not, even though ontologies are dependent on versions. Moreover, contexts are not located only on "this side" of the man/world Kantian schema; they work more effectively than versions to break this schema down and overcome its binary separation. Contexts are not mind-made versions of the world, but portions or locations of the world, historically and socially specific.

The best term to capture this concept is "immanence," a word that suggests opposition to a transcendental conception of reality which is by definition beyond all human practice or intervention. Immanent does not imply internal; the latter term demands the existence of an external whereas immanence, although it is often contrasted with transcendence, requires no opposite. Internal and external are conceptualized in terms of physical space in a way that transcendental and immanent need not be. The word "internal" may also connote subjectivity, an association I want to avoid. The term "contextual" has a possible application here, but "context" by itself does not automatically suggest that more than traditional subjectivity is involved; contexts may be assumed to resemble Putnam's versions or a subjective perspective. Even if context is defined more broadly, I prefer the phrase "immanent realism" to "contextual realism" because of the former's connotations within the historical canon of philosophy. Immanent, unlike either internal or contextual, connotes for philosophers the material world, the profane, the human realm, without a God or an absolute knowledge. Consider Aristotle, Hume, Kierkegaard, Marx and Nietzsche: an unlikely assortment, but each offering a philosophy securely tethered to the realm of immanence. Their grounding in and valorization of immanence does not entail an implicit commitment to the existence of a transcendent realm; certainly Kierkegaard maintained such a commitment, but it was not entailed by his conceptualization of immanence. I'll return to this issue when I discuss Williams's notion of contextual realism.

On this account of immanent realism, false beliefs and changes in beliefs are explained by changes in the constitutive elements of knowledge, such as an enlarged discursive formation to which one has access, or an altered perspective gained from an altered social location. These changes cannot be sequestered on either side of the subject/object distinction; they cannot be split in this way. False belief results from some inadequate constellation of epistemic ingredients. Without the subject/object binary, however, truth is not reducible to an epistemic term—this would once again involve trying to locate truth somewhere on that bifurcated neo-Kantian map. On an immanent realist view, the difference between a true claim and a false claim is not always or simply that one represents and the other does not; the difference is in the nature, quality, and comprehensiveness of the representation.

Immanent realism makes it possible to understand why context must always be introduced as a significant variable in determinations of truth, because for an immanent realist the aboutness of truth is not transcendental. (The term context is of course plastic enough to involve an entire ethos of political, social, historically situated human praxis, that is, thought and action in combination.) Is immanent realism necessarily different from traditional accounts of truth? Every concept of truth, after all, must allow for some indexical truths: truths indexed to specific speakers and locations (for example, "I am not pregnant"). But generally only one truth per index is allowed for, whereas immanent realism, like Putnam's version-dependent realism, must allow for plural truths even in one specific indexed location. Different versions applied to the same indexed location might produce different true claims: if, for example, "pregnancy" were defined more broadly, not as that condition which occurs between conception and birth but as a state involving the very capability of reproduction. Some fundamentalist arguments would seem to imply a notion of pregnancy not far from this, when they proscribe contraceptive devices that block conception and refer to such devices as methods of abortion.

Immanent realism will thus be broader than version-dependent (or internal) realism because it introduces more elements to which truth must be indexed, beyond mere versions or ontologically descriptive theories. It is not only versions that produce particular truths when applied in particular locations, but the larger context, which can include such elements as epistemes, subject-positions, and institutions of power/knowledge. Immanent realism has a further significant advantage over version-dependent realism in displacing the centrality of the knower or subject. In Putnam's internal realism, truth is dependent on theory, which is developed by subjects, and thus truth is dependent on constructions of the subject. This may account for why Putnam's view is often confused with forms of idealism: his view is human-centered. On an immanent realist view, truth is an emergent property of all the elements involved in the context, including but not limited to theory. Immanent realism can therefore acknowledge more readily the formative effects that language, discourse, and power/knowledges have on the production of truths, rather than privileging the knowing subject as the necessary center of the knowing process. Here, then, might lie the route to a nonauthoritarian epistemology, one that incorporates an ineliminable partiality and a context-based account of knowing which is, in effect, a more plausible description of real knowing.

## Contextualism Versus Coherentism

In his book, *Unnatural Doubts*, Williams has recently developed an account of contextual epistemology which on the face of it might look very similar to the sort of view I am groping toward here. But Williams argues that contextualism is superior to coherence theories principally in its ability to withstand (though not refute) the challenge of radical skepticism. Williams locates the source of skepticism in the doctrine he calls epistemological realism, and to the extent that a theory of knowledge accepts epistemological realism he thinks it has given away the store to the skeptic. Williams's use of the term "epistemological realism" is specific and original: it is the belief in knowledge of the world as a whole, wherein one might imaginatively stand back to characterize and assess the whole of human knowledge about the world. (Because this meaning for the term is so idiosyncratic, and thus may easily lead to confusion, I will substitute the term "epistemological globalism" for his "epistemological realism.") Williams argues that both foundationalism and coherentism presuppose epistemological globalism, but that contextualism, although it certainly countenances the possibility of knowledge, rejects the idea of general knowledge and need not try to establish its truth-conduciveness by reference to this imaginary whole.

Contextualism is the view that "characteristic possibilities of certainty and doubt will not detach from a given form of inquiry because they are fixed by that form of inquiry's characteristic direction."[18] Thus knowledge is dependent on context, and because contextualism itself does not presuppose epistemological globalism, it makes no attempt to assess all the contexts or their interrelations. In the case of skeptical doubts, within a form of inquiry that involves epistemological globalism, skepticism cannot be fully defeated. In fact, Williams is willing to go so far as to agree with Hume that skepticism is the natural outcome of philosophical reflection about the ordinary concept of knowledge. Unlike Hume, however, Williams holds that this ordinary concept of knowledge is itself not natural or inevitable. In other words, skepticism is the natural outcome (or

---

18. Michael Williams, *Unnatural Doubts: Epistemological Realism and the Basis of Skepticism* (Cambridge, Mass.: Basil Blackwell, 1991), p. 129.

methodological necessity) of a process of reflection that would take as its object the entirety of human knowledge, thus assuming epistemological globalism, but skepticism is not the natural result of Williams's own contextualism. In fact, Williams argues throughout his book that skepticism is ultimately indefeasible within any context that assumes epistemological globalism, but that it is false, or a nonplayer, in contextualism that does not share this assumption. On a contextualist view, knowledge is entirely possible, and even has an externalist component (that is, Williams rejects the identification of knowledge with justified belief), but contextualism considers a general assessment of all knowledge an impossibility.

Williams's criticisms of coherentism follow from this line of argument. Coherentism necessarily involves, on his view, comprehensiveness and systematicity and thus a global account of knowledge, because each individual belief is justified by reference to the whole. "A coherence theorist must hold that local justifications are *essentially incomplete*: for if it is allowed that local justifications can be perfectly in order without global justifications to back them up, the coherence theory gives way to contextualism" (295). So it is really holism which is the problem, or the view that individual beliefs can never achieve justification on their own but that only the whole is arguably justified. It is true that both Quine and Davidson defend coherentism in this way, though they offer slightly different arguments. Williams concludes from this that, whereas contextualism allows for differences between conflicting contexts, coherentism would always have to strive either to resolve the conflict or dispense with one of the different contexts. Thus, coherentism cannot be separated from the quest for a characterization of knowledge as a whole, or epistemological globalism.

I think Williams's contextualism and the immanent realism I have associated with coherentism are trying to move in the same direction. Williams argues that skepticism arises not from our attempt to reach an objective knowledge but from our attempt to objectify knowledge from a "detached, philosophical perspective" (254). Similarly, I have argued that an advantage of coherentist accounts is their more realistic starting position in which the knower is always already in the world, committed to a large array of beliefs, engaged in ongoing projects and practices. Total disengagement is practically and even conceptually impossible. Still, there are two important claims Williams makes with which I disagree: (1) that coherentism is necessarily committed to epistemological globalism, and (2) that we need not jettison the metaphysical realist view of truth, since it is actually compatible with contextualism; thus, for Williams the crucial issue does not turn on whether one accepts or rejects metaphysical realism. Exploring these differences should help to clarify further the viewpoint of immanent epistemology.

The connection Williams draws between coherentism and epistemological globalism goes as follows. An individual belief is justified to the extent it coheres to the web of belief. Only if the web of belief is itself true or largely true can this be a truth-conducive process. Therefore, coherentism is committed to an epistemological characterization of the whole web of belief. But certainly this line of argument is not characteristic of either Gadamer's or Foucault's versions of coherentism as I have developed them. Neither makes any claim about the truth of the whole. And yet at least Gadamer's version retains an ability to defend the criterion of coherence as truth-conducive, on the grounds that truth is an emergent fusion between elements—horizons of readers and texts—and thus that the pursuit of coherence works as the pursuit of fusion and therefore of truth. Gadamer's concept of fusion is not dependent on an epistemological characterization of the whole of human knowledge for its status as truth.

Foucault is clearly not interested in epistemological globalism, nor do his claims about knowledge presuppose it. Foucault's association with the concept of local knowledge and his critique of totalizing accounts is well known. Although his notion of truth and its ontology remains undeveloped, his account of the importance of coherence in establishing truth does not depend on a claim about the whole of knowledge. For Foucault, truth is what coheres because what coheres provides links between forms of subjectivity, practices, and institutions, as well as systems of statements. Foucault cuts the link that Williams thinks exists between systematicity and global epistemology by understanding systematicity as an open process involving generation and distribution and not merely consistency.

Putnam also represents an exception to Williams's supposed rule, making an explicit stipulation connecting conceptual relativity with internal realism. Putnam's coherentism links models and theories, but without any need for global evaluations. If Williams is right that the tradition of coherence epistemologies has been committed to an account of justification at the global or all-encompassing level, then the coherentism of Putnam, Gadamer, and Foucault breaks with this tradition and justifies coherentism from the local site rather than the global.

Clearly, Williams puts forward such a strong, even necessary connection between coherence theories and epistemological globalism because of his own overwhelming concern with skepticism, a concern not shared by any of the philosophers I have treated in this volume. The entirety of *Unnatural Doubts* is an exploration of skepticism, how it is generated and how it can be avoided. Williams apparently sees his approach to skepticism as different from the usual view within epistemology because he is ultimately not offering a refutation of skepticism but an argument for its restricted scope. Nevertheless, he neglects to consider the possibility that an epistemology might be advanced without any concern for the skeptical challenge what-soever. Thus, it is no mystery that he assumes coherence can only be justified via an argument at the global level, since what he thinks coherence epistemologies must establish is how their view can meet the skeptical challenge. I do not dispute that this goal has in fact structured the historical development of work on coherence, but I would dispute the claim that *any* defense of coherence needs to address skepticism. Like Williams, I do not make the refutation of skepticism a necessary component for any viable epistemology, but only for those epistemologies harboring assumptions that would require such a refutation. The only argument that could be made to place coherence epistemologies within this latter category would be a historical and therefore contingent argument, not a necessary, logical, or conceptual one. I believe I have demonstrated in this study some cases of coherence epistemologies that would fall outside Williams's category of epistemological globalism. Therefore, coherentism is an epistemology that exists on both sides of that categorical divide.

The most likely reason that Williams and I differ on the importance of skepticism is that he has a completely nonideological understanding of philosophical arguments and intuitions. Williams seems to think that the full story of skepticism's claim to validity consists in the commitment to epistemological globalism, and he strongly resists therapeutic responses to skepticism which, while they may accurately describe the alienated psychology that engenders skeptical doubts, do not address skepticism at the theoretical level and therefore are fundamentally irrelevant to the debate. In this, Williams's philosophical orientation toward border control is revealed: following the analytic tradition, he wants to maintain neat boundaries between sociological, psychological, and epistemological considerations, and he never even raises the possibility of political considerations.

Another argument that Williams advances for the association between coherence epistemologies and global accounts of knowledge is his claim that any coherentist account would by definition seek the resolution of conflicting knowledge into a progressively total coherent system. Most coherence theories include a comprehensiveness requirement so that coherence cannot be achieved by some ad hoc elimination of troubling, anomalous elements. Williams puts forward contextualism as unique in its ability to allow for epistemological differences without being required to seek some form of resolution. Because different contexts generate different epistemological agendas, there is no overarching program that would require the elimination of conflict between these different agendas.

But whether coherence epistemologies require a resolution of all conflict again depends on the particularities of a coherentist view rather than on inherent necessity. Certainly it is the case that the drive to maximize comprehensive coherence is a drive toward the resolution of conflict, though this does not require the elimination of difference. Some alternative contexts, however, are not necessarily in conflict or competition with one another: physicalistic and mentalistic explanations of the same phenomena can peacefully coexist, as Davidson has shown, without calling each other into question. From a simplistic view, such explanations do conflict, since they offer contrary concepts and categories and different causal narratives to explain a given phenomena or event. On another level, however, they need not conflict because each is doing something different, just as, in Williams's view, different epistemological contexts pursue different agendas.

Of course, it is certainly true that all of the major conflicts in our broad array of human knowledge-claims are not capable of peaceful coexistence. Marxist and neo-classical economic explanations, for example, are contestatory frames for analyzing market behavior. But the above example concerning physicalistic and mentalistic explanations suggests that the mandate toward resolution is not an a priori dictate flowing from coherence in the abstract. Rather, the need for resolutions is more realistically understood as contextual, arising from specific problems in specific contexts. The scientific community is certainly far from a consensus on the need to achieve a grand unified theory that would somehow incorporate all existing scientific knowledge in a way that resolves any theoretical contradictions. From within specific research programs, a totalizing synthesis is rarely necessary to achieve goals or even to justify conclusions. So once again, if we take as our epistemological starting point the situation of real knowing, the mandate to achieve a total synthesis does not follow even from methodologies that base their procedures of theory-choice on coherence. Williams's approach is overall too abstractly idealizing: it does not match up very well to actual processes of justification. Few believe that we know nothing if we cannot justify our global knowledge, and no one of course has a total coherent set of knowledge (except maybe cult followers, but even there I suspect some necessary fragmentation). Should we conclude from this fact that most people really know nothing, an all-too-prevalent philosophical chauvinism, or that if they know anything they do not know that they know it? My argument has clearly been against such a conclusion, and I have tried to show that at least some versions of coherence epistemologies allow us to avoid it.

At the same time, I want to concede that, precisely in real knowing, we do not generally rest content with conflicts that might cast doubt on significant beliefs we hold, or that produce a felt dissonance between one set of beliefs or practices we hold and another set. Thus if I spout feminism to my students and encourage them to take risks in standing up for themselves

while I remain timid and unassertive myself in dealings with my depart-
ment chairman or my husband, I feel a nagging sense of hypocrisy which I
want to resolve. Intellectual movements of the last two centuries have been
profoundly affected by the felt need on the part of many people to resolve
the conflict perceived to exist between religious cosmologies and the
tremendous development of a science that apparently calls these into question. Because the drive toward coherence is part of our actual knowing
practices, there is a tendency to conserve prior beliefs. New paradigms are
not adopted easily, even when the evidence seems clearly in their favor.
These facts should not be reduced to a matter of psychological weakness or
lack of epistemological justification; the drive to make new beliefs and old
ones cohere is obviously an important part of every successful program of
inquiry.

It is also clear, however, that the maintenance of coherence is not all that
is important or epistemically valuable. Epistemic virtue is generally not accorded those persons or theories that achieve coherence "too easily," by
dismissing contradictory claims without sufficient argument or by simply
ignoring contrary evidence. One way to characterize this phenomenon,
however, is within the dictates of coherentism itself. In other words, facile
achievements of coherence are arguably superficial and inauthentic, and
thus not real achievements. This of course raises the problem of scope, discussed in the previous chapter in relation to Putnam's views; how can we
justify limiting the scope of elements that must cohere? But again, such a
problem cannot be solved a priori or in the abstract. The limits of scope
and the relevance of disparate elements must be argued for within a specific
program of inquiry. If I can make a case that the flapping of a butterflies'
wings in Beijing will have a significant effect on weather patterns in central
New York, then I will have made a case that such events need to be taken
into account when we predict the weather. Or, more likely, if I can show
that some modernist philosophers' reactions to the burgeoning cross-cultural contacts of colonial European societies had a significant effect on
their developing accounts of subjectivity, then I will have made the case
that such reactions should no longer be edited from the canon of Western
philosophy, but included in any theory that claims to be a coherent assessment of this textual legacy. We cannot know in advance what the relevant
scope will be, and the claim to have achieved coherence is itself subject to
contextual, and therefore coherentist, constraints.

But to return to Williams's view that coherence epistemologies necessarily lead to global accounts of knowledge, I would also argue that this claim
should be rejected in part because the drive toward coherence is obviously
not all that is important in the development of knowledge, and at least
some versions of coherentism can accommodate this fact. Contradiction,

negation, opposition, and tension play a positive role in the development of knowledge. These elements inspire original hypotheses, providing a structure or framework for coherent theories in the same way that our mortality serves both to structure and to confer value on life. While I was writing this chapter, National Public Radio announced a new scientific finding that the age of the universe may be only half what has been previously estimated. An astrophysicist interviewed on the program said that such a development was "terribly exciting" even while acknowledging that it must call all existing scientific cosmologies into question!

Coherence is never fixed or stable, and its very instability works to guard against facile or premature declarations of its achievement. As I suggested in the Introduction, the inherent exclusions of presentistic theories, which prompt some postmodernists to declare themselves "antitheory," need not lead us to valorize negativity. Two lessons we can learn from Hegel are relevant here. First, it is not negation per se that moves our understanding forward, but what he calls *determinate negation*. Generalized negation, exemplified by radical or total skepticism, leads nowhere, points toward nothing, and therefore cannot guide the movement of understanding anywhere. Thus, contra Barry Stroud, to entertain radical skeptical doubts cannot improve our knowledge, because such doubts can by definition offer no specific alternative procedures or concepts.[19]

Determinate negation, on the other hand, which is a specific negation, does provide a specific direction. What this shows is that the value of determinate negation is dependent on its relationship to affirmation. The particular direction that a determinate negation suggests is conditioned by the specific affirmation it has denied. Thus we have the dialectic, in which negation and affirmation have an interdependence that is substantive in regard to particular cases but also general and abstract. This is what indeterminate negation lacks, as antiskeptical philosophers have long noted. If radical skeptical doubts are generated without any specific reason, they cannot be addressed and the result is that conversation must come to a complete standstill. For this reason Peirce argued that radical skepticism is not even a genuine doubt, since real doubts are felt, arise within experience, and emerge within the context of specific goals, like my need to know whether the expiration date on this yogurt cup is reliable or a trick of the manufacturer to increase sales.

Thus, I fully admit that negation is a critical ingredient in the development of knowledge, but only if it exists in dialectical interdependence with affirmation. This points to the second and corollary lesson from Hegel: that

---

19. Barry Stroud, *The Significance of Philosophical Skepticism* (Oxford: Oxford University Press, 1984), p. 256.

the value of coherence lies in its dialectical relationship with opposition. There is no question of simply affirming one or the other. Clearly, however, the drive toward coherence is primary in the *active* process of knowing. Negation, doubts, and conflicting evidence inevitably arise in the course of experience. One does not need to mandate the inclusion of conflict; one merely need mandate that we not try to ignore or downplay it as it arises. Knowing does not seek negation, nor does it need to do so. The movement of understanding is a movement toward coherence, which will inevitably meet negation all along the way and achieve coherence only intermittently and temporarily. The value of coherence itself, our motivation to pursue it and felt desire for it, emerges only because it is so elusive and unstable, because we live amidst dissonance and contradition. Thus, the argument for coherence is not an argument that coherence is all one needs, but that the need for coherence arises within a context of incoherence. Positing the choice as one between coherence and negation is therefore misleading.

I will discuss this issue more in a moment, but let me first address the final disagreement I have with Williams's account, which concerns his "loyalty" to metaphysical realism. Williams argues that contextual diversity has no conflict with a metaphysical realist account of truth as stable and context-independent because the contextualist is "under no compulsion to show, in some general way, how satisfying diverse collections of such [epistemic] criteria will tend always to ensure the presence of some nonepistemic relation between our beliefs and the world."[20] The combination of contextualism on justification and an externalist commitment make it possible, so he thinks, to claim an extra-epistemic, nonidealist transcendental account of truth without having to demonstrate that this obtains globally. General knowledge is impossible (at least, impossible to claim or epistemically assess), but knowledge is not.

I remain unconvinced. I think Williams is sneaking in metaphysical realism under cover of a deflationary account of truth and a contextually based account of justification. By showing that his account does not require the repudiation of metaphysical realism, he may believe he can hold onto those philosophers who just cannot give this up (a group that I suspect includes

---

20. Ibid., p. 265. Williams's commitment to metaphysical realism may not be accurately described as a commitment to a metaphysical realist account of *truth*, because he agrees with many other analytic philosophers that truth is a semantic rather than an ontological concept. But that difference between his view and mine on truth is not relevant here. He continues to characterize what I have been calling the *ontology* of truth, or the reference of truth-claims, as if this involves a stable, fixed realm outside human practices. Of course, it is also the case that Williams's own preferred view of truth is a deflationist one in which metaphysical questions are left aside. But I am maintaining that he is a loyalist to metaphysical realism because he refuses to consider seriously any alternative, and if he cannot have a metaphysical realist theory of truth he apparently wants no theory at all.

himself). But what can the content of such a view be, in terms of truth? What difference would a commitment to metaphysical realism make within a contextualist epistemology? If it does not make a difference, how can one justify maintaining it? If it does make a difference, then contextualism must surely be weakened by an account of the real that conflicts with the inevitable relativism between contexts. Putnam's internal realism is by far the better way to go here, since it not only allows for ontological differences but offers an explanation of how this can be so within a view that affirms the existence of human knowledge about the world. Williams's account asserts these very different theses without offering any explanation for how they can actually coexist, and thus it must surely compare poorly in persuasiveness to an account that is able to show how our epistemology and metaphysics can cohere.

Ultimately, however, despite my differences with him on metaphysical realism, I find Williams's contextualism largely compatible with the coherence epistemologies I have explored. Both relate knowledge, and not just justification, to a context. Both eschew the need to *refute* skepticism, although the main argument Williams uses in defense of contextualism is, ironically, that it can *avoid* skepticism. Both seek to include within the relevant elements involved in knowledge more than mere beliefs or statements. Contexts involve situations, empirical conditions, and thus a range of material reality inclusive of but not exclusive to epistemic claims. Of course, I very much like the fact that Williams considers it an *advantage* that contextualism can accommodate difference within the epistemic field. If I am right that coherentism has no necessary commitment to global characterizations of knowledge, then coherentism and contextualism are even more compatible than Williams thinks. Perhaps the difference between the two will prove to be only semantic and trivial. Coherentism as I have developed it understands knowledge within a context. Contextualism, on the other hand, obviously needs more than an assertion of context to explain knowledge; knowledge may occur only within a context, but this contextual limitation must surely underdetermine specific knowledges. For this, I would argue, one needs coherence, properly conceived. I have prefered the use of the terms coherence epistemology and immanent realism for the reasons given, but the naming issue is certainly secondary.

## Coherentism on Balance

I want to turn next to a reassessment of coherentism's promised advantages and the major hurdles it must overcome, issues I raised in the Introduction. I have already dealt at some length in this chapter with the advantage coherentism offers in its notion of an immanent account of realism. Part of this argument is that it provides a more realistic ontology of truth. This can also help with the long-standing difficulty epistemology has had in understanding the historical dimension of truth. A number of European philosophers since Hegel have expressed the belief that, as Max Horkheimer and Theodor Adorno put it, "the core of truth is historical."[21] To many Anglo-American philosophers this claim appears to entail that truth, or what we call truth, is in reality ideological, for ideology can be historical whereas our traditional conception of truth or scientific knowledge cannot be. The result is that European proponents of a historical concept of truth are continuously read in the United States as champions of subjectivism and/or irrationalism, or of the belief that the content of human knowledge has little to do with "real" truth.[22]

On a coherentist ontology of truth, however, the conclusion that historical truth must be irrational can be avoided, because on this account, truth can be historical without necessarily descending into ideology and unreason. If truth is *not* a representation of the intrinsic features of reality, if it is rather the product of an interaction between reality and human beings, then truth, and not merely justified belief, can be thought of as historical. We need not relinquish our intuition that truth is beyond our subjective control, but we must relinquish the idea that truth is something wholly other to us, intrinsic or inherent to a reality where our input has been erased or discarded. Truth is historically relative, on this view, without being irrational, subjectivist, or ideological.

I also asserted in the Introduction that coherentist epistemology is based on a more realistic description of actual knowing, principally because it posits a knower who is always already in the world, replete with a large variety of epistemic commitments. The problem with Descartes' thought experiment, in which he tried to imagine giving up all of his beliefs until he reached an indubitable bedrock, was that this very thought experiment was conducted, and could only have been conducted, by holding a number of important beliefs. Descartes had to hold onto beliefs about what counts as dubitability and indubitability, for example. Positioned as he was in time and place, he also continued to be affected by ideologies of many sorts. It is no miracle that at the end of his thought experiment, most of his former beliefs which he temporarily set aside turned out to retain their justifiability, so that he could readopt them in good conscience. The lesson to draw from this miracle is not that we are all helplessly bound by ideology, but

---

21. Max Horkheimer and Theodor W. Adorno, *Dialectic of Enlightenment*, trans. John Cumming (New York: Continuum, 1944), p. 1.
22. One example of this is Hilary Putnam's reading of Foucault in *Reason, Truth, and History* (Cambridge: Cambridge University Press, 1981), p. 167.

that Descartes' proposed method will not work to ensure the epistemic adequacy of our beliefs because it is based on an inaccurate, illusionary account of human knowing.

Coherentism recognizes the unavoidable fact of our prior commitments, our situatedness in specific contexts, and our general tendency from within a set of cognitively relevant practices to conserve that which we think we already know. Gadamer and Davidson argue that neither knowledge nor the identification of error can be achieved in any other context. But Gadamer also shows that this situation need not create closed, self-justifying systems because the horizon of one's prior judgments is constantly evolving through interaction with new texts and new experiences. The worry that coherentism will work to justify arbitrary sets of coherent beliefs and make them immutable to external critique is as unrealistic as Descartes' thought experiment: coherentism within the context of lived reality is rarely applied in this way and when it is, it usually has disastrous results and few followers. Coherentism sets no a priori boundaries around what must cohere and what can be set aside as irrelevant, but in reality such a priori boundaries are unnecessary. The boundaries needed can only be determined locally, within the context of specific situations.

A third advantage I promised with coherentism was its ability to explain how and why apparently disparate elements can be shown to be cognitively linked without recourse to a strong version of false consciousness. That is, it is not simply the case that scientists have been ideologically determined to welcome master-molecule theories or linear accounts of genetic causes, but that theories even in the sciences are given credibility or lent support from beliefs and practices elsewhere that are coherent with their presuppositions, general orientation, or metaphysical commitments.[23]

Helen Longino has recently developed an account of science to show how background assumptions which contain metaphysical commitments as well as contextual values enter necessarily into the process of theory choice.[24] The influence of these assumptions and values cannot be restricted to the so-called context of discovery because they have an important impact on the formulation of hypotheses, the decision to regard certain hypotheses as plausible, the kinds of analogies and models that get seriously entertained, and the determination of the kind of evidence considered sufficient to justify theories. After all these factors are set in place, the process of theory-choice may indeed be seen to conform to a paradigm of objectivity since, as Longino and others have pointed out, once you de-

---

23. Helen Longino, *Science as Social Knowledge: Values and Objectivity in Scientific Inquiry* (Princeton: Princton University Press, 1990), chap. 7.
24. Longino, *Science as Social Knowledge*, chap. 5. Her analysis, although primarily directed at knowing within science, can be applied to epistemology as well.

termine the scale that will be used to assess temperature, the determination of the temperature is really an objective matter. The realm of objectivity in this traditional sense does not, however, extend very far. The models of justification that are considered plausible and thus are up for debate and consideration, the goals of the inquiry itself, its unexamined assumptions about the locus and contours of its research topic—all these elements are significantly influenced by what Longino calls contextual values, which are themselves a function in part of who the scientist is.

A relevant example can be given about traditional epistemology itself. Epistemology has most often assumed that knowing occurs between an individual and an object or world.[25] This typically Western assumption of individualism (which operates as both an ontological assumption and a value) dictates the kinds of problems and hurdles epistemologists set themselves to overcome. For example, how can *I* (by myself) justify my beliefs? How can the massive number of beliefs *I* hold be justified on the basis of my own narrow observational input? How, for naturalized epistemology, can *I* describe the complex brain states involved in various epistemic functions? Most knowledge, however, is produced through collective endeavor and is largely dependent on the knowledge produced by others. It is not achieved by individuals. If epistemology were to dispense with its individualist assumption and begin with a conception of knowing as collective, a different agenda of issues would suggest itself. For example, we would need a more complicated understanding of the epistemic interrelationships of a knowing community; we would want to understand the relation between modes of social organization and the types of beliefs that appear reasonable; and we would need to explore the influence of the political relationships between individuals on their epistemic relationships.

This analysis indicates that the formative assumptions and values of any group of epistemologists, whether privileged European-American males or a national minority, can have a significant impact on the epistemological theories the group produces. This view need not devolve into a dysfunctional, absolute relativism, especially if we begin to acknowledge such influences so that they can be identified for debate and discussion. To assume that the entanglement of political issues entails a radical relativism is to assume that political debate is doomed to irrationality. But political issues are no less susceptible to rational consideration and discussion than epistemological ones. A coherentist epistemology can accommodate and even prompt such discussions by recognizing the interdependence of our disparate commitments.

25. This example is discussed in Lynn Hankinson Nelson, *Who Knows? From Quine to a Feminist Empiricism* (Philadelphia: Temple University Press, 1990), esp. chap. 6.

I mentioned earlier that coherentism faces a number of hurdles, best described as challenges that continental theory would pose if it were to address coherentism directly. The first of these—the concern that coherentism perpetuates a statement-dominant perception of knowledge—has been, I trust, adequately covered. As we have seen, the work of Foucault and Putnam presents cognition within a context of practice, a context that is constitutive both of knowledge and of the criteria of adequacy it must satisfy. On this view, the measure of coherence does not operate simply within a body of beliefs, but within a system of practices encompassing but not reduced to beliefs.

The second hypothetical objection I raised has not yet been addressed in much detail. This objection was concerned with the political danger of valorizing a coherence that requires similarity and sameness and de-emphasizes difference. For someone like Jean-François Lyotard, the pursuit of coherence would be inherently oppressive, because it values connection over disjunction and thus will always try to subvert fragmentation. On this view, the drive for coherence is a drive for control over the whole field of discourse, wherein the whole can be mapped out and arranged according to a single plan, theme, or motif. It thus conflicts with the freedom to break apart, to create new, dissonant formations, and to promote a difference that cannot be incorporated. The pursuit of coherence would be a kind of epistemological totalitarianism.

In his latest polemic against postmodernism, Christopher Norris takes up the related issue of association made between truth and violence.[26] Arguing against Foucault, Paul de Man, and Richard Rorty as well as Page DuBois, Norris considers the case made by postmodernists that philosophical truth is grounded in domination and the desire for mastery and control.

DuBois' recent book, *Torture and Truth*, is especially useful for a consideration of this issue because she makes the argument more explicit and develops a historical case study of the Greeks to support the association between "the appeal to a unitary Truth" and the attempt to maintain "differentials of wealth, power, and privilege."[27] Contrary to an authoritarian truth, she argues, "the idea of equality has its own dynamic, a pressure towards the consideration of all in view as entitled to the privileges of rule by the people."[28] But in its antidemocratic, Platonic origins, truth has been codified as "privileged epistemic access, as a matter of penetrating to secrets which can only be revealed through various kinds of expert hermeneutical technique, or procedures vouchsafed to those few knowing individuals who possess the requisite degree of authentic understand-

---

26. Christopher Norris, *The Truth about Postmodernism* (Oxford: Basil Blackwell, 1993).
27. Quoted in ibid., p. 265.
28. Ibid.

ing."[29] The result is a doubled association between truth and violence: the metaphorical violence of claims which, by posing as absolutes authorized by a metaphysics of presence, necessarily exclude and erase others; and the material violence of torture used persistently in the West to extract truth from inferiors who, because they lacked the requisite rationality or reliability of credible witnesses, had to be tortured to produce truthful testimony.

Norris takes issue with the epistemological skepticism resulting from such arguments and promotes an open dialogic exchange à la Jürgen Habermas as an alternative route to truth which will eliminate or minimize oppression. "What is wrong with [the postmodernist argument] . . . is that it fails to take account of the crucial difference between truths imposed by arbitrary fiat, through presumptive access to *the Truth* as revealed by some authorized body of priests or commissars, and truth-claims advanced in the public sphere of open argumentative debate" (289). Norris admits that the Platonic dialogic model was never really open, but he contests the claim that this is an inherent problem with any model of dialogue. The kinship between torture and truth holds only for truth-claims that appeal to "presumptive sources of revealed or self-authenticating truth" (292).

Norris thus focuses the political critique of truth on the notion of revealed wisdom, where only an authority of some kind can discern it. But surely any concept of transcendental truth would have the effect of obviating the need for open discussion. An infallible, absolute, and stable truth inevitably closes down dialogue by providing the final word. A truth situated within collective lived experience in history, rather than outside of it, calls for collective, decentered procedures of inquiry. In this regard, Norris' dismissal of Foucault as simply a skeptic is unfortunate. Norris never seriously considers Foucault's notion of local truth, which could provide the beginnings of an alternative epistemology that would justify Norris's valorization of public debate. Local truth defies a priori, outside assessments made without consultation or dialogic exchange.

I agree with Norris that an epistemological skepticism inspired by postmodernism is to be rejected, but he portrays the debate here as too starkly characterized by mutually exclusive positions, even while he accuses postmodernists of taking this approach. For Norris, on the one side stand skepticism and relativism, on the other epistemology and truth. Only "logic, reason, and reflexive autocritique . . . can resist the kinds of dogmatic imposition which derive their authority from a mystified resort to notions of absolute, transcendent truth" (288). But how do logic, reason, and self-criticism gain epistemic value? Why does Norris think that they can com-

29. Ibid., p. 262.

pletely eliminate relativism? The argument against postmodern skepticism cannot be successful without an account of truth and the truth-conduciveness of justificatory processes. To defend the ideal of open public dialogue Norris needs to offer epistemological and not simply political arguments.

Epistemologically, there is no way to get around the fact that claims of truth involve exclusion, control, and the repudiation of opponents. The sphere of truth cannot be made politically correct according to the latest formulations. Norris poses Habermas's dialogic model as a better alternative to postmodernism's relativist abdication of truth on the grounds that the dialogic model is epistemically better and politically just as good, that is, just as inclusive and nonoppressive. The better tack, I think, is to look at how oppression is being defined in these critiques of truth. For Lyotard, any ordering at all leads to exclusion and the inhibition of creativity. This claim assumes, however, a liberal individualist definition of freedom as the absence of restraint on individual action, and thus defines processes that involve exclusion and inhibition as necessarily unfree.

A more complex and realistic account of freedom would understand it as constituted within a social context which is necessarily ordered in a variety of ways. Freedom requires a context, just as resistance, in the postmodernist view, requires (and is the natural by-product of) power. The process of achieving truth must involve open dialogic exchange without *arbitrary* exclusions such as those based on sexism or racism, but it must also involve exclusions based on epistemic status. Truth is not therefore necessarily on the side of oppression in its self-privileging or its assumption of authority.

All authorities are not authoritarian. As Gadamer counsels, we must critique Enlightenment assumptions that the deference for tradition and authority is in every case unjustified and always sustains tyranny. Not only must we make distinctions between different sorts of traditions and authorities rather than characterizing them all monolithically, but we must also understand tradition and authority as open to the new, as within history and therefore never fixed, and as constituted in part by those who give deference and thus interpret and apply the tradition. If every authority is seen as authoritarian, the result is a tyranny of structurelessness in which strong personalities hold sway and dominant ideas are left unaccountable. The point in epistemology, as well as in politics, is not to subvert every authority but to make authorities accountable, to acknowledge their fallibility, and to incorporate an analysis of power within any critique of their knowledge claims.

The same can be said for an epistemology based on coherence. The drive for coherence provides structure and a criterion of adjudication. The attempt to harmonize difference will necessitate some exclusion and control, but let us remember that coherence is a limit concept, or a heuristic; there is no possibility that we will ever achieve a totalizing coherence that will remain stable and thus prove stultifying. Given that, the danger that the structuring of coherence imposes is perhaps not so dangerous. As Foucault well knew, it is uselessly utopian to pursue the complete elimination of all structures of power/knowledge. For both epistemic and political reasons, what is needed is a decentered form of structuring, which can destabilize authorities so that they cannot become authoritarian. Coherence epistemologies posit no self-justifying states, no indubitable bedrock, that would create a foundation beyond challenge. Where the ultimate criterion is coherence within a large constellation of elements in a temporally and spatially specific context, rather than a foundation purportedly linked to a truth outside of history, truth will always be temporary and unstable.

I do not believe this shift can be made without a new ontological paradigm. Thomas Kuhn was right to argue that an old paradigm will not fall, no matter how many anomalies it is unable to explain, until a new one has been developed to take its place. The transcendentalized conception of truth will retain its intuitive stranglehold on philosophical discourses until a new ontological imagery can be developed and made persuasive. Moreover, if we acknowledge that these ideas are not unconnected to social location and history, it is easy to diagnose transcendental versions of realism as the overdetermined product of cultural crisis, social alienation, the economic reification of nature, dominant Western masculine identity distortions, the unselfconscious translation of religion into science, and the list could go on. We are passing into a new era. Anglo-European economic hegemony will be displaced as capital is decentered. Economic exploitation of the earth will be modified as prior methods become infeasible. Social relations between men and women will take new forms, as will racial identifications and ethnic politics. Some of the crises of modernism will take new shapes. These will not necessarily be moves toward "progress" in some absolute or overall sense, but there will definitely be movement. Epistemology needs to catch up.

# Index